FORTY YEARS IN AFRICA

FORTY YEARS IN AFRICA

Lamberto Tofani

Book Guild Publishing
Sussex, England

First published in Great Britain in 2006 by
The Book Guild Ltd
25 High Street
Lewes, East Sussex
BN7 2LU

Copyright © Lamberto Tofani 2006

The right of Lamberto Tofani to be identified as the author of
this work has been asserted by him in accordance with the
Copyright, Designs and Patents Act 1988.

All rights reserved. No part of this publication may be
reproduced, transmitted, or stored in a retrieval system, in any
form or by any means, without permission in writing from the
publisher, nor be otherwise circulated in any form of binding or
cover other than that in which it is published and without a
similar condition being imposed on the subsequent purchaser.

Typesetting in Times by
Keyboard Services, Luton, Bedfordshire

Printed in Great Britain by
Antony Rowe Ltd, Chippenham, Wiltshire

A catalogue record for this book is available from
The British Library

ISBN 1 84624 010 7

Foreword

This retrospective is a result of many long years of persistence from my two daughters, Lucia and Linda, who wished to know more about my early life in my birthplace, Somalia. They also wanted to learn more about their grandparents, who died in that faraway land many years ago. They have asked me many times to tell them the story and background of our family, and since I was convinced that it was a fair request, I decided to do my best and try to satisfy their demands.

Firstly, I wish to declare that I have included the following events because I consider them of exceptional interest and therefore worthy of mention; however, this is simply a story of an ordinary family with an ambitious and resolute father. The factor that makes it exceptional is the locations.

I was initially reluctant to begin this book because of my doubt of being able to satisfactorily complete such an exacting task; it is foreign to my usual everyday activities, which have no relation to story writing, and my principal concern was to not embarrass myself when attempting something that could have proved to be beyond my capabilities. My education only reached the level of Italian secondary school, and I would like to request that everyone remembers this fact when reviewing my work – that I could only rely on my natural common sense and experience. This is experience that has been acquired through difficult, sometimes painful years, and has formed my character today. The end result pleases me upon review, as I believe that it genuinely reveals my true personality and my life. My writing is simple and unadorned – this is the style I believe is most effective for this project. I have done a lot of reading during my long years of solitude in different places, both in Italian and English. This has endowed me with a basic although ample literary perception that allows me to avoid writing rubbish.

The story covers three different periods that collectively provide a general perspective of my life. The first part focuses on my father and is set in Africa. It marks the beginning of our family, before I was born. My father was a proud individual, who chose to defy convention in order to uphold his morals; however, his stubborn character seriously jeopardised his otherwise sincere attempt to become a wealthy man. I attempted to retrace his steps, whilst analysing and criticising the mistakes he made in his time, and I believe it has been beneficial to review the actions of an impulsive young man with the mentality and experience of a mature adult. Of course, I realise that it is easy to criticise after the event, without all the relevant details; maybe I have been too stern in my criticism; but in good faith, I do not think so.

The second period describes the consequences that arose from my father's failures. The third not only recounts my own experiences, but also gives attention to the many friends that our family had the pleasure to possess at that time. This was during the thirty-two years I remained in East Africa, Kenya and Tanganyika (Tanganyika is the former name for Tanzania). I greatly enjoy remembering my old friends and the mixed times I had with them. Although some of my relationships ended in a negative way, I now regard those experiences as useful lessons in life, and only a small number were insignificant. Nonetheless, the people that disturb me most are those who are devoid of loyalty, honesty, gratitude and affection. Sadly, there are too many of this sort around. In contrast, I have talked of many great friends I made during my years in East Africa with whom I am still in contact, although we are all old now.

The descriptions of natural life come mostly from everyday experiences and also from safari hunts in Kenya and Tanzania from 1949 to 1980. You will find also that some records do not follow their actual chronological sequence, as I inserted them later when I decided that their inclusion was necessary. All the narrated episodes describe actual events, although the times when they occurred may not be completely accurate.

I dedicated a long section to my father, Giovanni Tofani, and my mother, Colomba. I found it necessary to try to fully satisfy the curiosity of my daughters by providing them with the story of our family. Sadly, nearly all of the subjects of this story have since passed away. I hope that the descriptions of a world that has now disappeared will satisfy the curiosity of my daughters and grandchildren. I also hope that it is of some interest and entertainment to other eventual readers.

Lamberto Tofani
London, 2006

Acknowledgements

My sincere thanks go to Professor Caterina Linares for her help with my rusty Italian; Piero Mannini, who magnanimously offered to do the translation, without whom the book would never have been written in English; Michael Flegg and last, but by no means least, Elaine Ratchford, David Reynolds and Richard Varian for their patience and understanding with my endless computer problems.

Chapter 1

My father was born in Turin in 1886. He was a typical product of the Risorgimento with very high patriotic feelings common to the majority of Italians in that period, and was gifted with considerable physical strength of which he was very proud.

In those days, a man proved his strength in different ways from today. There was no advanced apparatus as we see in gymnasiums in the present, and therefore power demonstrations were much more primitive, such as crushing a walnut between a thumb and index finger (I urge anyone to attempt this who believes it does not require an ample amount of force). Another example would be lifting a man with your teeth by his trouser belt, whilst keeping him in a horizontal position. In order to complete this demanding task, one must obviously possess absolutely sound teeth, and uncommonly strong neck muscles. All of these feats were within the physical capabilities of my father.

He boasted frequently of killing a mule with a single punch to the head. The Mountain Artillery Regiment, the Alpini, consisted of soldiers selected from the strongest young mountain dwellers. Their duties included transporting pieces of artillery by mule up the mountain tracks; but at times, relations between some of the animals and their masters were problematic: some mules' reluctance to carry weights (particularly up the mountain) often severely tested the patience of the soldier in charge of the beast. In military circles, it was rumoured that the Alpini often reacted rather impulsively to the mule's reluctance to co-operate, and in one case it was reported that a soldier became so exasperated by the animal refusing to move that he released a powerful fist to the top of the beast's head. The mule died on the spot.

My father was a man with a fiery and dominant temperament. His strong personality and his constant restlessness meant that he was always travelling. His excessive vitality – in my opinion –

was dangerous unless tempered by a great dose of good sense (which, unfortunately, he didn't have). These characteristics are especially negative when found in a man who is head of a family, as the impulsive decisions that he makes directly affect everyone. As I mentioned earlier, he possessed considerable physical strength. In my opinion, this was another shortcoming, as he was inclined to try to solve every problem with the use of strong methods. We must remember that at the beginning of last century, the strongman stereotype was very much in vogue: he was admired, and respected. However, the majority of the general public also feared him, and my father was a typical specimen of this epoch. From my point of view, this masculine, macho personality, was the prime cause for the destruction of his family, and had particularly serious consequences for his children.

When he was old enough for military service, he enlisted as a cadet in the officer-training school of the Regio Esercito Italiano (Italian Royal Army). There he learned to use weapons, including fencing with sabre and sword, which he enjoyed greatly. At the end of training, he had the opportunity to prove himself at the start of the Libyan–Turkish War in 1911, when he enlisted as an officer. He was assigned to fight on the front line and mostly rode a horse, as he found that it was the most suitable means of transport for the flat Libyan terrain. At the end of that war, he remained an enthusiast of the Libyan campaign, and often would recount the battles that he had fought to anyone who wanted to listen to him – a battle can be a pleasant experience providing that you win, and do not catch a bullet through the head. When one is young, one is likely to be very keen to recall one's wartime exploits and valorous deeds. However, enemies have no faces and no names; very few ex-warriors think of the consequences of war, and seldom spare a thought for a faraway widowed mother, crying for years to come.

After the war against the Turks, my father decided to try his luck in South America: at the beginning of the twentieth century, Argentina was the choice of large crowds of Italian emigrants. Here he developed the ambition to own a hacienda, or farm. The Argentinian period magnified the hard aspects of his character, and he remained the same for the rest of his life. There, among other things, he learned to ride a horse in the style of the Argentinians, another example of his versatility and his willingness to learn. To my father, anything that was of macho flavour was worth learning or having.

The outbreak of the First World War (1915–1918) re-aroused his latent patriotism and gave him the opportunity to combat a new enemy of Italy: Austria. Perhaps it was also another excuse to satisfy his lust for adventure. However, the fact that my father interrupted his South American occupation is the important issue. He returned to Italy even though he could have easily stayed out of the conflict by remaining in Argentina, or indeed anywhere else on the continent. He enlisted in the Royal Italian Army for the third time, and was assigned firstly to a regiment of the Alpini; however, his strong enthusiasm allowed him to participate in the final mission. This involved liberating the Italian territory still in the hands of the Austrians, and he was re-assigned to the trenches face-to-face with the enemy. Italy declared war on Austria on 24th May 1915.

Sometime in 1916 during an encounter with the enemy on Mount Sieff, my father was attempting to blow up an enemy post with dynamite. He was wounded five times. This engagement left him with a partly disabled arm and a crippled leg that compelled him to walk with a very pronounced limp. As a sign of gratitude for his valour and courage in battle, he won the silver medal. The seven months he spent in hospital were proof of the gravity of the injuries he sustained in combat.

However, a short time before his discharge from hospital in Cestello (Florence), he had a serious confrontation with the Colonel-Surgeon of the hospital. The doctor, during his usual morning visit to the patients, for undisclosed reasons, started a quarrel with Lieutenant Giovanni Tofani (or the other way around). One word led to another, the language became heavier, and both men uttered offensive insults. Of course, the Colonel had the advantage of superior rank, and insubordination was considered a very serious offence (especially during the war) so the punishment was usually very severe indeed. Unfortunately for the Colonel-Surgeon, he made the mistake of calling the Lieutenant a 'vile coward' during the exchange of insults. My father considered the insult even worse than its base meaning. He thought that the Colonel was a man who did not even know the meaning of war, yet he still had the gall to question his bravery. His immediate reaction was to completely lose all control (assuming that he still had some control left, at that stage). Employing full use of his eighty kilos plus, he lowered his head, rammed into the doctor, and in a burst of fury rushed him backward towards the open window, with the obvious intent of barging him out. However, in a desperate attempt to save himself before reaching the window, the doctor managed to grab the headboard of a nearby patient's bed, which was carried towards the window together with the Colonel. Only the timely intervention of some male nurses and patients eventually ended the hullabaloo.

Somehow, the story concerning this quarrel was eventually hushed up. I can only guess this was because of the recent award of the silver medal; it would certainly have been embarrassing for the Army to publicise the affair after this accolade! When he came out of the hospital, he requested to go back to the front immediately. This time, however, in view of his disabilities, the Army Command rejected his request, and designated him to non-combat duties in an office of the Army Command in Rome, with the rank of Lieutenant. It was here that he met a young woman named Colomba. He married her and she eventually became my mother.

My mother was born in 1896, in a small village situated on one of the peaks of the Apennine Mountains, in the Abruzzo region. Here she would never have dreamt that a cruel destiny would have reserved her the fate of finishing her days in the humid marshlands of Uebi Scebeli, Africa. In the beginning, marriage opened the door to a new world, a new life and general prosperity, all in a more sophisticated environment than her previous habitat. The first few years were very happy for her, and her husband's restless personality meant that boredom was virtually eliminated; different events arose in succession, most of which were very interesting and colourful, and provided constant new subjects for conversation.

Before meeting my father, she had won a beauty contest in the Prati quarter of Rome (naturally, in those days the women participating in those contests would appear fully dressed). When walking down a street she usually attracted the attention of passing men, which greatly irritated my jealous father, and for this reason he had become involved in many clamorous brawls. Once, during a military parade, the General was about to receive the salute of his troops, and my father was at the head of the soldiers. They were all in line, awaiting the arrival of the General. At these events, my mother was always present among the crowd of spectators, usually standing directly in front of my father. This time she was dressed in the latest fashion: an elegant hat garnished with plumes of egret, and white gloves The General was by now only a few metres away, and the troops were about to present arms. It was then that my father saw a bold Bersagliere (a soldier belonging to the Bersaglieri regiment, who proudly wear hats garnished with the plumes of a rooster's tail), paying some attention to his wife. The sight was too much for him, and his face became twisted by uncontrollable rage. Regardless of the obvious consequences of breaking rank, he limped rapidly across the road and attacked the wretched soldier, who must have thought some madman was upon him. He first proceeded to cover him with punches, then grabbed him by the throat with his deadly vice-like hands, and started to squeeze. The General watched all this with astonished eyes, and was rendered immobile, temporarily paralysed with shock. The wretched Bersagliere, with his tongue hanging from his mouth, half strangled, was grateful for the timely intervention of colonels and captains, who with much effort managed to stop the uneven struggle.

Life in Rome did not agree with my father's character. His thoughts often went back to the brief period of frontier life he had experienced in Argentina, to the freedom provided by open spaces, and to the wild animals that populate it. Nostalgic thoughts were strong, and in the first few months of the year 1919 he told my mother of his desire to change his life and go to Somalia, then an Italian colony. I can well imagine the consternation of my mother and her family. Until the last moment she had hoped with all her heart that he would change his mind; but he did not. Although his attempt to set up a farm of his own in South America had not been successful, he believed there were positive aspects to this project. It had provided him with the necessary experience and confidence to start a similar enterprise in a new area, with climatic conditions similar to those of Argentina (hopefully this time with greater proficiency). My mother was sceptical of the African adventure and did not want to go. She did not want to leave the secure, comfortable and civilised European life for that of an unknown continent; maybe she had a premonition that obscurity awaited them, a hunch that warned her not to accept that drastic change of her life. Unfortunately, she was devoted to her matrimonial oath, and felt compelled to follow her husband.

After having lost sight of the Italian coast, the ship's passengers fell into days of boredom. The Mediterranean Sea did not have much of a view to offer them. The slow steamers of 1920 (unless you were a first-class passenger) offered little in the way of diversion, until the opposite coast was sighted. Even if there were some forms of entertainment on board, the members of my father's family would not have been very keen to laugh and joke if they had known the surprise that awaited them at their landing ahead! Only the view of the ever-present dolphins that followed every ship with their acrobatic jumps provided an ephemeral relief.

Eventually they were in sight of the Egyptian coast and the Suez Canal, which provided a welcome change, and boosted the low moral of the Tofani family, as well as most other passengers on the ship. The passage through the Suez Canal to Port Said offered the explorers a refreshing sight of animated life. Groups of indigenous Arabs dressed in their colourful robes lined both sides of the canal, and talked loudly in their incomprehensible dialect whilst trading their merchandise. As the ship slowly navigated the canal the spectacle continued to fascinate throughout the passage.

It is impossible to imagine the sight upon the arrival of the steamer at the port of Mogadishu in the year 1920. The image that appeared from the bridge of the ship was a daylight dream. It was a marvellous view: quite unimaginable. Under the luminous light of the limpid sky, and against the contrast of the yellow-beige colour of the sand dunes along the coast, the sharp contours of the white houses in the small capital city came alive. High at the left side of the port, a tower tinted with black and white stripes (which was part of the main building and a group of small houses) jutted dramatically towards the sky. The tower and the buildings belonged to the Missionary Order of the Virgin Mary of Turin. Its purpose was to indicate the position of the coast to passing vessels.

The first surprise came next: the port of Mogadishu had no wharf and no loading dock! The water was very shallow at the coast, and it was therefore impossible – even for small boats – to approach the shore so that their passengers could disembark. The ships and larger vessels had to anchor offshore where the water was deeper; then the assistance of another vessel was required in order for the few passengers and their luggage to leave the steamer. This boat approached the ship that was anchored in deeper water, collected the passengers and their goods, and then hastened to the shore as far as the depth of the water would permit without scraping the bottom.

It was then necessary to employ a peculiar method in order for the passengers to avoid getting wet when completing their journey to the shore. Each person was seated on a specially designed chair, which was then loaded onto the shoulders of a robust native, who would transport his precious load to dry land. It was certainly comical when it was my mother's turn to be carried ashore. She held on for dear life, her gown round her ankles, and a tropical helmet perched on her head (an item considered indispensable by all). As she grabbed the chair's handles, her eyes were wide open, her body rigid, and her face wildly contorted with fear of falling into the water. Everybody else laughed, but she did not seem so amused.

The family was not yet complete. So far it was composed of my mother, her husband and her son Vittorio, who was a little over two years of age. She was expecting another child, and my sister Laura was born in a small port in the north of the country, in 1921. At this stage, I feel I have to briefly introduce the author of this manuscript, who is the third and last son of Giovanni and Colomba: I am named Lamberto, born in 1923.

In the Colony's capital, there was a Catholic church, or the Cathedral as they called it in Mogadishu. As time went by, the square in front of the church assumed the function of a Sunday reunion place. There, after the religious services, the adults of the Italian families would meet to chat, exchange the latest news and meet the latest arrivals. All this happened in a gay and festive atmosphere, whilst the young children noisily played around.

My father took full advantage of these Sunday reunions. After making his first friends, he heard many different opinions. From these diverse views he realised that he must have at least a small initial capital in order to have any chance of success in his many business options, and the only way to accumulate this money was to have the Italian Government liquidate his disabled ex-serviceman's pension into a lump sum. After taking the necessary steps, he managed to raise fourteen thousand liras (in 1920 that was a large sum of money). He then went aimlessly around the Colony with his family, without any precise or solid ideas; it was important to know the country well, and examine the diverse environmental possibilities in the north and south of the territory. He evaluated the characteristics of the terrain, checking the moisture levels, humidity and temperature.

He soon realised that rearing cattle herds to be slaughtered would have been an impossible task, even if there had been a ready market for such a project. Whole areas infested with tzetze fly could infect and decimate the herds; this factor effectively rendered these zones thoroughly unsuitable for breeding. Corn was a crop that my father considered potentially ideal, although its cultivation was also subject to very serious problems. The obstacle this time was the inevitable massive assault on the crop from every species of insect in Africa; perhaps the most obnoxious were the indestructible red ants that attacked and destroyed the roots of every cultivable type of plant. In order to complete their gleeful task, the ants had the birds and antelopes as sidekicks.

To have even a small chance of success when cultivating a field, one must have at one's disposal an abundance of water from lakes, rivers or an artesian well. (One must also pray for a sustained absence of the aforementioned pests.) Naturally, to drill a well was costly, and the likelihood of finding water unpredictable. To avoid this problem, the pioneers often chose to set up their farms near stagnant water, and live in unhealthy surroundings. In the early days, the settlers did not clearly understand the danger of living for a long time in these sorts of areas, and tended to try to overcome the early symptoms of sickness by relying on their physical vigour and sturdiness.

Due to its diversity and deadliness, malaria was by quite a long way the most dangerous and common disease in the whole of Africa (it was even more dangerous for Europeans, who apparently lacked any measure of natural immunity against it). This disease was one of the highest causes of mortality in Africa, although in recent years many antidotes and drugs for its treatment have become available. The anopheles mosquito transmits the infection; it attacks its victims with the intention of sucking their blood. The disease is much more dangerous for first-time victims, especially children. The ill-famed cerebral form often did not respond to the only treatment known in those days, which consisted of massive doses of quinine pills. Parents or relatives would not expect a recovery for quite some time, and the prognosis would only change if the first signs of improvement were shown. Even after recovery, the patient is vulnerable to serious anaemia: a state of languor and exhaustion that removes the will to live.

My father was unable to find anything that would provide a realistic hope of success, and eventually decided to return to the capital, where he could find employment in sectors away from agriculture. His chances were dramatically improved by his surveying diploma, and with a bit of luck he found a job as an assistant on the construction sites of the railway, on the Mogadishu–Afgoi section. He began his African life and his search for a profitable business with hesitancy and uncertainty, and his job with the railways was ideal for exploring individual business prospects and ambitions. He always had the agricultural aspect in mind, and when the railway led him to the heart of the territory, he searched for terrain that was suitable for exploitation; above all, he was keeping an eye on the possibilities that were offered by the market. Some of this research often imposed a very uncomfortable life on the family, as it required much adventuring and wandering from one place to another. My mother, who had two small children to take care of, had to endure a life that she could not bear for long.

At the time we were living in a small hut about three hundred metres away from the Uebi Scebeli River, and my father requested absolute obedience from his family when they were living in that harsh, isolated environment. He absolutely forbade anyone to go near the banks of the Uebi Scebeli River. He also forbade anyone to wander outside a pre-designated perimeter around the house. My mother saw to it that we did obey these rules. For us children, the major danger was the crocodiles that patrolled the banks of the river, waiting for an incautious excursion (as they have since been hunted extensively for their valuable skins, their numbers have now been severely reduced). A second potential hazard represented by the river was water pythons. These dangerous reptiles may reach the length of over six metres (about nineteen feet). I leave it to you to imagine what one can do if it manages to catch a child in its coils! They are very good swimmers and like to lurk in shallow puddles near the river, submerging themselves in mud or water, with the head just above the surface waiting for prey. They also roam around the grass insidiously, waiting for any animal that enters their radius. For anyone that is attacked by this monster (for example a native fisherman), escape is almost impossible.

The leopard is another nasty customer to look out for. This feline was one of the major hazards for the human race in Africa. If we needed to go into the bush near the house, my father would always tell us to look very carefully into the trees above, as this feline is very subtle and extremely astute. The colour and design of its fur has mimetic properties, and it can easily camouflage itself almost perfectly in the surrounding foliage, making its ambushes very difficult to avoid. Although it does not ignore large prey, it prefers animals of small and medium size.

Every now and then, leopards have the habit of visiting nearby native huts. During the night, they roam around the homes to look for an easy meal: perhaps a dog, one of their preferred titbits, or even a child that has escaped from its mother's custody. If a leopard finds a child alone and unguarded, it would not ignore the opportunity to attack and abduct him. During my forty years of residence in East Africa, I have hunted in the bush constantly, but I have only managed to spot this elusive animal for a few seconds on a couple of occasions.

Although this part of the story does not concern my father, I would like to explain the differences between the African carnivore of nowadays and those of the 1920s. The felines and other carnivores that populate the African scrub and forest today have slowly learned to be wary of man; however, they also know when they are in a position of superiority, often when they are hungry and ready to ambush a prey in the dark of night. In these circumstances, an attack is possible.

It is common knowledge that a feline's contact with man is directly proportionate to its fear of man. All wild animals in the presence of man assume a cautious, watchful attitude. This is an instinctive reaction to the foreign behaviour of humans. They do not realise how we can maim or kill from far away, as they do not have any knowledge or conception of weapons. In some cases animals adopt a curious, almost interrogative manner when they observe us. This happens usually in zones where our presence has been rare, and in a zone where hunting is intensive all wild animals usually escape from man before he can shoot at them. In the case of felines, they will attack if they do not have a way to escape, have their cubs to protect, or are hungry.

However, even in the 1920s, carnivorous animals took more care towards man in the territories of East Africa frequented by the nomad herdsmen of the Masai tribes. Lions there learnt years ago that humans are not afraid of them, and if attacked do not always flee. A Masai cow would have been a very easy prey, large enough to satisfy the hunger of a whole pride of lions for a few days. Nevertheless, the felines also learnt (at their expense) to stay away from the quadrupeds of the Masai, and even more so from their guardians The lions that dwell in these zones have long since respected and feared these herdsmen: they know that attacking a Masai cow would immediately have provoked a reaction from these courageous men. They would crowd around the guilty feline with their spears, and like a myriad of vengeful red ants surrounding a dying grasshopper, exact instant revenge through retaliation. In case of an attack from a lion, the usual technique adopted by the Masai is as follows:

After forming a group, the herdsmen would stalk the guilty feline, shouting loudly to arouse him from where he is hiding (and also to build up courage for the battle that lay ahead). Everyone prepares to sustain the inevitable impact by holding his oblong shield in front of himself. After sustaining the brunt of the attack, the warrior would fall backwards, using his shield to protect him from the vicious nails and teeth of the beast. His companions would then come to his aid immediately, attempting to finish the beast off with thrusts from their spears. The spears have sharp flat tips of steel, thirty centimetres long, in the share of an elongated leaf. Other warriors would grab the lion by its tail and jerk it violently, thereby impeding the movements of the animal. The highest honour is reserved for the Masai that manages to hold the tail of the lion until the end of the battle. As a result of these frequent encounters, lions have become more cautious and reluctant to attack humans. For this reason, you could inadvertently pass a lion hidden behind a bush only a couple of metres away, and not receive any ferocity from the King of the Jungle.

The majority of Somaliland was half-deserted terrain, alternating stretches of savannah with patches of undergrowth and scrub. The woods were extremely uniform, and crossing the flat lowlands by road or railway could become highly monotonous. The savannahs of Somalia were not as luxuriant as those of other African regions, where the grass was much more exuberant. Because of the scarcity of regular rainfall, the grass found it difficult to grow on this less fertile terrain. The only exception was the vast swamplands that were created by the slow-running waters of the Uebi Scebeli, which generated a copious amount of grass. Unfortunately, these surroundings were very hostile and unhealthy.

The Uebi Scebeli and the Giuba are the only two permanent and important rivers in Somalia. The Uebi Scebeli springs from the mountains near Mechara, in Ethiopia, and joins the Giuba near the village of Jamaame (Margherita). They both flow into the Indian Ocean at a point a small distance north of Kisimaio.

The typical scrub of Somalia grew in the vast plains of the territory. The trees that formed the undergrowth were typically very low-trunk, and the ground was nearly devoid of grass: what little was there grew in fragmented low patches. Therefore, this terrain was quite suitable for crossing on foot. The trees were shabby as well as being small, and the contorted trunks had a small diameter – the foliage was certainly not as lush as in other parts of Africa. However, these conditions permitted you to see for long distances, thus avoiding any unpleasant encounters. This type of low wood was ideal for hunting, and was also preferred by the diverse African fauna. The wildlife that populated the Somali underbrush in the 1920s was infinitely more numerous than the present, just as the carnivore was far more aggressive towards man. The population of Somalia was less than a million inhabitants, but was in an area more than twice as large as Italy (then with about thirty million inhabitants). These statistics give an idea of the vast distances that one could cover without encountering a living soul.

The hours of sunrise on the boundless, savage lowlands of Africa are simply marvellous. And what is there that is so beautiful, you may ask me? Well, to begin with, there is the silence. In isolated places, silence is the voice of the living earth, uncontaminated from everyday noise. The complete solitude that is only felt in the surrounding silence of vast spaces induces a sense of absolute liberty, and confirms that you are entirely your own master. You are free to do whatever you want, without any interference from the faraway outside world. The sensation of peace and personal immunity that pervades you is difficult to understand or describe to the people in the crowded nations of the civilised world.

I now live on the periphery of London, which is obviously much quieter than the centre. But even here there is constant noise: cars, builders, and machines that cut down trees. In the suburbs you can enjoy happy moments of tranquillity, and tranquillity is certainly a great treasure. However, in savage regions you are surrounded by uninterrupted silence – a much more precious treasure. This is part of the well-known 'nostalgia for Africa', which is a collective term for the general pangs of homesickness that affect the majority that have left this continent. Not only do they miss the almost permanently warm climate, but also the prestige that is granted automatically to Europeans, as they are supposed to have a 'superior' culture to Africans (lately this assumption is subject to review). Those that feel an urge to return to Africa are also drawn by the abundant opportunities; even those with only a vague profession can find a job of high remuneration, and enjoy a comfortable life at home with the assistance of a cheap servant. For many others, the attraction is the magnificent scenery and the abundant fauna to hunt, or simply observe. As the song says: 'Here is always Sunday', and it always is in the land of nostalgia.

The 'Kilometre 24' was a small line-inspector house, so called because of its distance from the village of Afgoi (or maybe from Mogadishu, I cannot remember which). It was a small brickwork building, with a couple of empty rooms, situated along the narrow Mogadishu–Afgoi railway, which was still under construction. There was also a reservoir adjacent to the building for the use of the trains, and a hut in the bush about a hundred metres away. It was constructed native-style, but was used by European staff. Inside there was enough room to accommodate an entire family, with all the required accessories (European-style). The floor of the hut was made of cement instead of the compacted earth that was used for native huts; however, the straw roof was not a serious obstacle for insects, and would let in other undesirable guests like scorpions, spiders and small reptiles. The railway company always kept the house in a state of permanent readiness, and it was used frequently by specialised track or train maintenance personnel.

Afgoi was a small village, and hosted about ten permanent Italian residents. There was the customary police station, with a nucleus of *Zptiè* (Somali policemen), under the command of a non-commissioned officer. There was also a post office, but no doctor; in fact, all of the small Italian communities in Somalia were without a doctor, and this was one of the most serious problems in the Colony. One could occasionally be found in some faraway mission; but usually it was necessary to look elsewhere. It was also very hard to obtain one from Mogadishu. By law, they were obliged to assist any patient who needed their services anywhere in the territory;

however, the pioneers had a hard job to make them abide by this law, as they were always very reluctant to leave. The Colony's only hospital was also located in the capital, and only the white population were allowed to use it. The native population were forced to receive attention from the missionary organisations.

At the beginning of 1925, my father and his family were moved to the zone of Line-Inspector House Kilometre 24 for employment reasons. They took over the hut previously described, which was not exactly a holiday resort! At 'Km 24' the everyday hardness and severity was accepted without complaint, and the Lord was thanked at the end of every day. The hard and primitive conditions did not present any kind of problem to a man with the exceptionally durable temperament of Giovanni; however, my mother did not possess the pioneering spirit, and life was very difficult for her. She was a simple Italian housewife, with gentle and beautiful features: a very feminine woman, who certainly did not have the spirit and the courage of Anita Garibaldi (wife of Giuseppe Garibaldi, 1807–1882, the Italian nationalist revolutionary and leader in the struggle for unification and independence of Italy). Because of the agricultural experiments that my father conducted, my mother lived mostly near the Uebi Scebeli River, or other places with unhealthy conditions. The wear and tear that came from this kind of life was now starting to severely reduce my mother's stamina and will, adding to her longing for the company of brothers and sisters left in Italy. Her head was full of thoughts of her relations when she was alone in her hut, although she also loved her new family very much. Sometimes the desire to see her relatives was unbearably strong, as was the persistent presentiment that she would never see them again. She feared that the farewell in Rome had been the last, and this started to frighten her.

After living for some time at Km 24, she started to feel unwell. She had three very young children to attend to now: two boys and one girl. Their age meant that they could not be left unattended for a minute all day and, often, most of the night. She was also expecting her fourth child, and was so exhausted that she doubted she would be able to carry on much longer. Unfortunately, that was a situation common to most women in those days: her mother had eleven children – a life of pregnancy. She was worried that she would have the same fate.

The house was the best one could expect in that place. It was situated at the beginning of the forest amid bushes. It was also very isolated and there was no security fence. The shade of a large thorny acacia growing nearby fell onto the bedroom side of the house for a few hours a day, and this was often the preferred place for the family to pass some time outside the hut. At sunrise, in the cool morning air, it was nice to wake up to the twittering of the birds that were always crowded in the tree. As the hours went by, their number increased, and so did their chirping melody. They always seemed to be the same ones, and were so punctual every day in announcing the sun's rise, symbolising a happiness to be alive. After a while it became possible to recognise each bird, and give it an affectionate nickname.

At Km 24, the family could also discover who had been the visitors of the preceding night. By inspecting the terrain around the house carefully, they could read the imprints left on the ground by the nocturnal visitors. These imprints could indicate the visit of the usual leopard, or more frequently those of a hyena, and sometimes those of a vagrant lion. The morning rituals were always a source of interest to the adults, and a source of excitement for the children.

Nowadays, in my imagination, I can still hear the cadence of a sad, monotonous tam-tam which, every night, all night long, came from a very small village not so far away from us. The villagers would take nightly turns to keep guard, a few at a time. They would sit on pail-supported platforms that were well out of the reach of lion's paws, beating on drums and sheets of metal, trying to keep the felines at bay. Occasionally, we would hear the tam-tam increase in tempo and volume, which was accompanied by loud screams from all the members of the village. All of the family would be awoken by its frantic beat. This meant that lions were roaming near the village, which was in a state of alarm. The loud banging noises would usually make the beasts withdraw. Feline attacks on villages were normally due to the easiness that lions sometimes found in capturing a sheep or cow inside the *zeriba* (an enclosure for the herd). The next day we would know the news of the previous night's attack, and whether or not there had been any victims. It is impossible to realise the levels of stoicism and perseverance that were required to work in this environment. These were the essential prerequisites of the white settlers, whose determination to continue was perhaps fuelled only by the hope of becoming successful and wealthy.

The heavy seasonal rains – which normally start at the beginning of spring – had begun sooner than expected that year. This had caused a serious problem for the railway works near Km 24, where a part of the line had collapsed. The damaged section was about six kilometres from home, so Giovanni had to travel twelve kilometres a day on a mule through the forest. He was fully aware of the hazards of this journey, particularly on the way back home at sundown. After previous experiences of the bush in Africa and Argentina, he was in the habit of going into the forest adequately armed. Every morning, after saddling the mule, he would diligently choose the weapons to carry with him according to the surroundings. For these trips, he chose to carry a high-calibre, long-barrel Colt, suitable for fighting at close quarters. In addition, he would carry a cavalry sabre and a carbine, which both fitted in accessible places of the saddle, ready for immediate use. Although he knew that animals tended to avoid man, he was also aware that the presence of the mule could be an irresistible temptation for hungry felines.

The most suitable time to start the journey was at sunrise. Giovanni looked forward to the six-kilometre trip, which was always interesting until the end, although it required maximum attention in case of possible surprises. Only the calls of the turtledoves, which ogled at each other from nearby trees, broke the silence of the forest.

At sunrise, the short grass was very often wet from night frost. The cobwebs encountered along the way were often large enough to span two trees on opposite sides of the path, maybe two metres apart. They also captured the frost during the night, and the droplets of the water reflected and decomposed the filtered early sunlight like thousands of little diamonds. At the centre of these enormous cobwebs sat the master weaver: an enormous spider waiting for the prey to get entangled in the net. When this happened, it would be on its prey with fast motions of its legs, which are sometimes up to three inches long. The massive and elongated body of the spider is hairless, and is of a lucent black colour. Its black and yellow legs are a peculiarity of venomous specimens. Their cobwebs are exceptionally strong, even capable of capturing birds, and are a mixture of the beautiful and the macabre.

One evening, Giovanni was anxious to get home; he was thinking about his sick wife, and decided to ride on the mule's back rather than walking slowly behind it. The habits of the wild animals vary throughout the day: in the hotter hours of the late morning and early afternoon they take shelter from the hot sun under the shade of trees; they tend to be rather lethargic and indolent whilst lazily lying down on the grass. However, in the cooler hours of the late afternoon, all species of animal become more active. The non-carnivorous animals start to graze, watchful for the presence of predators, and the latter start to hunt the former. The hours of the day just after sunrise and those near sundown are the more rewarding to the hunters, human and feline.

Giovanni was less than two kilometres from home when he heard the hunting call of a group of striped hyenas (or maybe they were a pack of wild dogs), although they were still a fair distance away. He stopped the mule, and after a brief observation realised that they themselves were the targets of the hyenas. The hyenas, attracted and excited by the smell of the mule, had started the pursuit. In order to avoid terrifying Colomba, Giovanni decided not to use the carbine and face the beasts with the sword.

Even when spurred, the mule was no match for the pace of the hyenas. He soon realised that his pursuers were gaining rapidly, and there was no other alternative but to confront the pack. He dismounted and prepared himself for the impending battle: firstly he attached the reins to a tree to prevent the mule from escaping, leaving it as much slack as possible so that it could defend itself by kicking at the hyenas. He then drew his sword and waited for the pack to attack him. The hyenas approached in their peculiar, undulating motion (this unusual motion is due to their hind legs being shorter than their front ones), snarling and baring their powerful teeth. There were five hyenas in the pack, and Giovanni reckoned this was a couple too many for him to have a reasonable chance of escaping alive. Luckily for him, they were a little uncertain and attacked separately in an open semicircle. That gave him the opportunity to defend himself from the nearest beast with a downward stroke of the sword to the head, killing it instantly. Before the next hyena attacked, he quickly turned and purposely pricked the mule with the point of the sword on its rear, knowing that this might provoke a violent reaction. In fact, the mule started to kick at two of the hyenas that had approached it. Giovanni did not waste any time, and rapidly swung around again to deal with another of the beasts that was about to attack him. He delivered another powerful stroke of his sword, this time cutting through half of the neck and shoulder of the beast, which then rolled onto the ground with a loud ululation and died. Giovanni then turned his attention swiftly to the other hyenas, which in the meantime had engaged the mule; however, it was bravely defending itself by kicking at them whilst braying loudly. The arrival of Giovanni convinced the two remaining hyenas to abandon the attack altogether.

Colomba, at home, had not realised what had happened to her husband. Although she had heard the hyenas' calls, she had not paid much attention to them, as they were heard frequently in the forest. She only learnt of her husband's terrible experience when he returned home. The hyenas' carcasses proved the otherwise incredible story, and Giovanni's battle against five hyenas armed with only a sword became the talk of the Colony.

When the work was finished at Km 24, Giovanni and his family returned to their permanent home near the farm and the Uebi Scebeli River.

It may seem incredible that my earliest recollections of life in Africa are when I was little more than two. However, other sources have supplied the information for the majority of the episodes described so far. This information came principally from Vic, who was five years older than me, and therefore had a better understanding of those early events. The other sources are military records concerning my father, and numerous letters written by my mother to her family in Italy. Some of the recollections of my early childhood are rather hazy, and I am surprised that some of them are still impressed on my memory.

A few days after our return home, my father received an injunction that called him back for temporary military service. (When necessary, the Governor of the Colony had the authority to call on all valid civil nationals.) As far as Giovanni was concerned, he had obeyed a few orders in the past, but this was to be the last. The Colonial Government was fully aware of his military experience, and often took advantage of his expertise by calling him back as an officer in command of a number of soldiers. His knowledge of dense forests (often similar to those in South America) was an indispensable prerequisite for attempting such expeditions. His experience of two wars was also useful, particularly the Libyan campaign (1911), which presented many conditions similar to Somalia: a hot climate, limited water supplies, and a harsh desert terrain.

The call was due to a problem that had arisen along the Ethiopian frontier. The men were required to intercept and engage an armed band of Ethiopian cattle riders operating along the Somalian–Ethiopian border. These riders were famous for their acts of ferocity, and would usually steal entire herds of cattle and then destroy the villages after killing the inhabitants. Women and children were shown no mercy. The defeated males were then emasculated and their genitals placed as trophies outside the Ethiopian huts. The organs of a white man were most sought after, as they are foreign and therefore curious. It is no surprise that the adversaries of these riders were fully aware of their barbaric practices. Death on the field was certainly preferable to capture.

Soon after Giovanni had reported to his recruiting centre in Mogadishu, he departed with an expedition corps towards the Ethiopian frontier. The purpose of these expeditions was mainly to display the presence of the State at the frontier, rather than to help the wretched villagers. They began from the capital and travelled on foot, employing a number of mules to carry victuals, water, light machine-guns, assault mortars and ammunition. By the time the expedition got there, the bands of riders had dispersed to all four points of the compass across the vast territory.

My father did not request leave from the Farming Concession, and he would be absent as long as the Governor required his services. The date of his return was unknown to us, and would be a surprise to all the family. My mother was left alone to take care of us, as well as to manage the farm.

I am sure anyone can imagine how difficult our situation was. My father would be away on a mission a hundred kilometres from home, and would be gone for several months. We were twenty-four kilometres from the nearest village, which contained a post office, a couple of policemen and a few Italian residents; but no doctors. Who would defend the family? Not my mother, surely. She was a twenty-eight-year-old woman, and did not possess the fighting temperament. Luckily in those days the indigenous population was not hostile to the few white residents; on the contrary, the settlers commanded the respect and esteem of the local population, as they got much help from their missionaries and doctors. Nevertheless, considering the place and the environment, I think it was quite dangerous to leave my mother and us alone.

Shortly after the departure of my father, we had an invasion of migratory locusts. It was an unforgettable spectacle that has left a firm impression on my memory. It began slowly, and at first there was only a comparatively small number flying around, which provided a strange and fascinating show for us children. However, as the days went by, their numbers increased to biblical proportions. They came in large clouds that obscured the sunlight and would settle everywhere, including the roof of our hut. My mother had to fumigate the roof to prevent it from collapsing, as she had been doing periodically to get rid of other unwanted 'guests'. Several years afterwards in Italy, when I saw a snowfall for the first time, it immediately triggered a strong memory – it was like a swarm of locusts landing of the roof of the house where I was born, near the banks of the Uebi Scebeli River.

For us children, who did not know any other life (even if we were limited by the dangerous environment), the setting felt like paradise. Our family was organised by our father, whose prime objective was self-sufficiency. My mother's contribution was essential: she was capable of baking, which gave us the luxury of freshly baked oven-crisp bread every day. Sometimes she would mould the bread into the shapes of animals to please us. Like most women of her generation, my mother was a housewife who was capable of making cheese and butter. In those days dairy products were classed as luxuries, and my father had plans to set up a dairy. However, he later decided to abandon this initiative in favour of a better one: the production of bananas in commercial quantities.

It was then the turn of the heavy rains to arrive after the departure of the locusts. They were the second most impressive, unforgettable and terrifying spectacle I had witnessed. The rainy season normally started at the beginning of springtime, but had begun earlier than expected that year. Each day, the first clouds would appear on the horizon; high and white, passing fast overhead one after the other, then disappearing in the distance. As the days went by, they became greyer and denser, whilst the rumbling of thunderstorms could be heard far away, and as the season progressed they changed into intermittent low black clouds. Bursts of strong wind pushed them quickly forward and they then discharged their heavy load of rainwater far away; later they condensed and formed a compact and menacing mass, filling the sky without interruption far beyond the horizon, driven forward by slower winds amid thunderstorms and the roaring of rainfall. In the meantime, the three of us embraced our mother tightly in a bundle in the dark hut. We could see the flashes of the thunderbolts coming through the gaps in the straw roof, and we were all filled with terror. They illuminated the interior of the hut with a brief vivid spectral light that gave our faces a ghostly appearance. A loud crash then ensued as a thunderbolt struck perilously close to the house. The incessant disorderly rhythm of the rain created a strange sensation of solitude, and when accompanied by the wind billowing through the treetops on the nearby riverbank, it united us evermore.

As the season went on, the rains' fierceness began to diminish and so did the frequency of their outbursts. It happened slowly at the beginning, with short pauses between downpours; but they would then start again with a renewed intensity. This was until the sun timidly started to sneak a quick look through the ever more rare clouds. After a silent night, the sun shone on the clear sky, and gradually started to vaporise the water from the rain-impregnated soil. This was another experience I will never forget.

Practically every activity in the territory would come to a standstill during the rainy season. Rivers and lakes would overflow their banks, flooding the surrounding country for kilometres and rendering all motorised transport useless. All the non-asphalt roads became rivers of mud. In the territory there are two different types of soil: one is reddish, like the sands of a desert, and the other is black, which is called cotton soil. Both become viscid when impregnated with water, to the extent that the tyres of vehicles lose their gripping potential and tend to finish hopelessly bogged in the mud: some vehicles remained stuck there for weeks. Naturally, during the rainy season, my father's farm came to a standstill and this could last up to two months. The heavy rains also affected the life of the fauna. Large carnivores were particularly at risk because the muddy soil would impair their attack speed, and for the same reason, herbivores also struggled to escape.

The rainy season is also the mosquito high season: with an abundance of stagnant water they can reproduce by the millions every day. Their presence is much more noticeable after sundown, and if a person went bare-chested near the banks of the Uebi Scebeli at this time they would get their skin completely covered by thousands of mosquitoes. In addition, they would find that every one of them was busily enjoying sucking their blood, and would also be very likely to be injected with a powerful dose of cerebral malaria. Mosquitoes are active all night but hate daylight, or any strong light for that matter. Therefore at sunup their presence is minimal, and you will find most of them hanging immobile on the walls or ceiling of your bedroom, waiting for dark and another night of blood-sucking.

They would wait, ready to set down on a bare part of the human body, and emit a persistent buzzing that made sleeping impossible; inside our hut, with only the light of a paraffin lamp, it was impossible to see them. Our attempts to avoid them could almost be described as comical, if the consequences for failure were not so serious. An old Italian song is also near comical at times: '...staying up all night, hunting the terrible beast...' The hunting method is the same for everybody in these conditions:

Whilst pretending to be asleep and holding the nerves in check, try to encourage the diving insect to land on a deliberately bare part of the body. Wait until you feel it starting to bite, and then, as fast as you can, try to squash it with a hard slap. Unfortunately, most of the time it manages to get away, and your failure will be confirmed by the insect's louder hum of victory as it escapes. Further buzzing will then announce its return to have another go at you. So, again, the '...hunt of the terrible beast...' starts anew, and probably ends with the same result as last time. At this point, the victim must decide whether to surrender and leave his body to the mercy of the insect (whilst trying to sleep in the meantime), or to continue the hunt. As far as I know, it has not yet been proved if mosquitoes possess ultrasonic faculties like bats to avoid obstacles whilst flying; however, one thing is certain: the majority of the time they can anticipate the hand's flailing movement, and escape with an exaggerated mocking drone.

In a modern house with electric light but no insecticide spray gun, you should suitably modify the hunt. After pretending to be asleep and having successfully encouraged the insect to land ... etc., and after the usual slap missing the target, promptly switch the light on. You will find that the flying monster (usually in an attempt to hide itself) will immediately perch on a wall or, more probably, on the ceiling. In this instance it would be difficult to reach; but if it has settled on a wall, your slap should be successful, and the only inconvenience will be the resultant smear of blood. Having said everything I know about hunting mosquitoes I will suggest a more appealing and obvious alternative: buy a mosquito net and sleep peacefully ever after (except for the irate buzzing of the would-be tormentors). In the absence of modern prophylactics, new-born babies and young children should be protected against mosquito bites by putting them under a mosquito net at sundown, before the mosquitoes are active. Of course, this precaution is only temporary, and when not under its protection one can only hope for immunity against malaria through luck.

By the way, this insect does not confine its attention to humans Once during an afternoon siesta, I noticed a large fly attached to the white ceiling of the room in which I was resting. I was about glance away when a mosquito tried to attach itself to the back of the fly with the intent, I guessed, to suck its blood. A minor drama then took place between the fly and the mosquito before my astonished eyes, and I then learnt that a fly could kill a mosquito. It was the fly's turn to be irritated for a change, and it obviously did not like to play the role of guinea pig to the mosquito. In a flash, it detached itself from the ceiling, and somehow moved the mosquito onto its chest, trapping it in that position, whilst squashing it against the roof. It then started to flap its wings extremely quickly, in order to apply more pressure on the wretched insect. My sight was excellent then, but when the carcass of the mosquito dropped from the ceiling to the floor, I still had to get up from the bed to confirm what I had seen. Sure enough, it lay there on the ground, dead as a doornail.

I can safely say without fear of contradiction that malaria was then the most feared disease in the world: it was responsible for the highest number of deaths in Africa, Asia, or any other areas where the mosquito was present. During my forty years in Africa, I have been to places known as 'The White Man's Grave' as a result of malaria, and heard of many more. Dar-es-Salaam (the capital of Tanzania) was one of the places unfortunate enough to possess this title. This was prior to the First World War, at the time of German occupation. Once when passing through wild bush that was entirely off the beaten track, I was surprised to come across the solitary grave of a man. It was nearly completely covered by overgrown plants and I would have missed it, had I not stumbled over a cornerstone. From the barely intelligible engraving on the tombstone, I learnt that he had died some decades before, still a very young man. I was perturbed and fascinated as I tried to imagine him still alive, still full of purpose. I would like to have known how and why the man was buried in this isolated place at the foot of an African hill; but my only information was the dates on the tombstone. It had often disturbed and fascinated me to think of the lives of inhabitants of other African graves – graves that tell the story of the early pioneers of Africa: ivory hunters, gold and diamond prospectors, soldiers adventurers, people who found their final resting-place in forgotten areas, people who were full of hope that had failed to meet their ambitions, like my father. Most were victims of the many deadly forms of malaria.

It was during the rainy season when I was taken seriously ill with malaria for the first time, and my father was away from home. As I mentioned earlier, it is far more dangerous for first-time victims – especially babies and young children. I was two and a half years old when I was first struck down, and I very nearly went to heaven at this age. Although I was still young, the disease left an indelible imprint on my memory: I remember my anxious mother looking over my bed for a glimpse of an improvement in my condition, which was a long time coming. I had days at death's door, always in a state of unconsciousness due to my high body temperature, which even large doses of quinine could not control. I remember the hot air inside the hut, the tiredness and the languor, the acute anaemia, the complete absence of appetite. It was a near-death experience, and one that will remain in my memory for ever. I was constantly exasperated by the suffocating heat, and was bathed in sweat which increased the pulsating pain in my body; the only way to have the illusion of a little fresh breeze was to leave the door open. The outside air was as hot as the inside; but the act was still comforting. All these factors added to a malaise which is impossible to describe, but would be all too familiar should I ever encounter it again.

Unfortunately, the open door added much risk to the scenario. Inquisitive reptiles could easily glide in and hide out of sight in the dark. One of their favourite pastimes is climbing, and a bed is an obvious challenge; after this they could either slide under the covers, or hide between the cushions and the mattress. One morning whilst I was ill, a rat and its pursuing serpent both fell from the roof of the hut onto my bed. The snake quickly recovered from the fall, writhed on my body, and restarted the chase, luckily straight out of the open door. My mother and Laura both watched with terrified eyes.

My father was still absent, and there was no peace for my mother.

After my recovery, on the night of a full moon, she had another bad scare. A few hours after midnight, we awoke to a strange snorting noise, coming from outside. A little later it grew louder; the hut started to tremble, and one of the walls began to crumble into pieces; obviously it was the work of a very large beast. My mother grabbed my sister and me, and dragged both of us into her bed, looking wide-eyed towards the disintegrating wall. In the absence of my father, the duty of defending the family fell on my brother Vic, who at the time must have been seven or eight years old. Luckily, my father had already started to train him when taking him along on the occasional hunting party, and he knew how to use the double-barrelled gun and the carbine. The only drawback was that the stocks of both firearms were still a little too long for his size, and he found it difficult to handle them efficiently. Nevertheless, Vic took on the task with courage and decision: he took the gun (which was always loaded) from the hook on the wall, grabbed the lamp, and went outside. He then fired two shots into the air, and a large hippopotamus immediately ran towards the river. After a short pause, we heard the reassuring noise of the animal plunging into the water.

When my father returned from his expedition, he explained that the hippo had leant against the hut to scratch itself. As I grew older, I realised that it had wanted to graze on the straw on the roof, and to reach it he must have put his front legs on the wall, which had caused the majority of the damage.

A few months after my father had returned home, my mother died in a hospital in Mogadishu. She died from an infection after the stillbirth of her fourth child, aggravated by an attack of pernicious malaria. The simultaneous combination left no hope for survival.

In a characteristic act, with a pistol in his hand my father hunted the doctor who had treated my mother. Friends of the doctor warned him of my father's intentions, so he went into hiding. Eventually the Carabinieri (the Italian Military Police) intervened, and convinced my father to see reason. Our mother left us for ever in the year 1925, leaving behind a gap impossible to fill, and infinite desperation in our family. Her life on earth was interrupted, and would never be completed. She died at the age of twenty-nine, when she was in full bloom. A caring mother and bride who was full of love and affection for her family was no more; she was irreplaceable, and we would no longer experience the sweetness of her manner, or the feminine touch that calmed the ire of our father. The leading spirit of our family was no longer with us, and we would never again hear the subdued melody of the Italian songs that she had learnt in her childhood.

My father was desperate. He was conscious of our despair, and was fully aware that his wife had never approved of the African adventure. His remorse and guilt were gnawing away at him, as he believed that the death of his beloved wife was due entirely to his egotism and folly. He then realised that his life would always be a failure, even if any of his business enterprises did succeed: no amount of money would ever compensate for the loss of the most important member of his family. Now he found himself living in isolation, in a place that was extremely unhealthy, with three children aged from three to eight. With the hope of only an occasional visit from a missionary, the future was not very promising.

As an adult, I often consider the problems that confronted my father at this stage. I ask myself what I would have done under the same circumstances, and always come to the same conclusion: abandon everything, return to Italy, and start again, attempting to bring the family up in a more conventional manner. However, even though this scenario would have been ideal for his children, it was completely foreign to his character. For him, abandoning his deceased wife in a faraway graveyard and returning to an easier way of life in Europe would be an act of cowardice. When taking into account his principles and character, I have to admit that he had no alternative. In the same circumstances (assuming that I had the same principles and character), I would have done the same; I would have continued that life at any cost, and waited for my time to die in the same place as my wife.

Laura and I did not pay much attention to the long absence of mother from home. We knew she had gone to hospital to have a baby, and assumed that it was only temporary. Our father then told us that she had gone for a long trip, and it would be a while before she would be back. Waiting for her return was less painful with this knowledge. My own daughters are now both older than my mother at the time of her death. When I see them with their children, I cannot avoid thinking of my mother, and a sudden pang of grief hits my chest like a dagger. It only lasts a few moments, and although it was a long time ago, tears often fill my eyes.

As you can imagine, my mother's absence brought quite a few changes into our lives. My father had to employ a Somali nanny to take care of us, whose name was Mumina. She was young and very willing to look after us, and tried her best to stand in for our mother. Her task was a rather arduous one, mainly due to the cultural differences between us; one thing she could not understand was the obsession of our father, who insisted that we must not be left alone for even a minute. He also strongly stressed that she must not allow us to walk outside the established perimeter around our house: the possibility of encountering a hidden python was a constant threat that could not be neglected. If these orders were ignored, it was possible that my father could vent his anger through physical punishment. As he was away from home all day working, it was necessary for him to rely on scrupulous execution of his instructions, for his peace of mind.

One day, when busy with the washing, Mumina disobeyed father's orders and told the three of us to go into the bush to collect a small quantity of firewood; she felt that three was a large enough number to warrant security from an attack from a lion or hyena. We had collected all the firewood around the house, so we had to go a little further from the hut to look for it: probably about two hundred metres away. Here the trees were sparse enough to allow us to see for quite a distance into the forest, which was peaceful as usual. The silence and apparent serenity were also ideal conditions for the beasts of the forest to rest.

The three of us began our task energetically and in good humour; up to then we had not seen any animals, and had they been there they would not have escaped our young eyes. However, spotting felines requires special attention. It was early afternoon, and at that time of day the cats were usually lying amongst the grass under the shade of a tree, perfectly camouflaged by the natural colours of their fur. This makes it easy to stumble on them before you have the chance to escape; however, we did not know that much about their habits then. All of a sudden, Vic emitted an alarmed cry: 'The leopard! The leopard!' At a distance of about fifteen or twenty metres, under the shade of a modestly sized *Acacia umbellifer*, there was a crouched leopard. It was staring with malevolent eyes in our direction, moving his weight nervously from one hind leg to the other, ready to spring. It must have climbed a tree when hunting, and from this vantage point seen us arrive. He was convinced from our movements that we were not going to approach the tree, and had come down on the ground, ready to attack. Unfortunately for the leopard, the tree trunk had not been large enough to hide it completely from our sight. Our father had told all three of us, especially Vic, about some of the leopard's habits and tricks, particularly its tree ambushes. Therefore we had been paying special attention to the tops and bottoms of the trees whilst walking and gathering wood. Although we saw the leopard very late, we would have been in real trouble if it hadn't been for Vic's timely alarm.

It has become a habit of mine to think back and re-examine episodes like this one. I must pass some comments on this story, with the benefit of common sense acquired through experience. We were already within range of the leopard's attack by the time Vic saw it. If the leopard had attacked us then instead of hesitating, his ambush without doubt would have been successful, and at least one of us would not have got home that afternoon. However, when Vic gave the alarm, the beast was so close to us that we were all paralysed for a moment. I still remember and shiver at the hypnotic power of those yellow eyes, staring malevolently at me. I do not know where I got the strength to turn around and run, and it is impossible to describe the panic that followed. All three of us were well aware of the leopard's intentions, but both Laura and I were still little more than toddlers, and could not run fast enough on our short legs. We must thank God that the beast did not run after us; otherwise, I would not be here writing this story. In the rush to get away from the animal as quickly as possible, everyone's instinctive reaction was to think of themselves, and I was unavoidably left behind. After about fifty metres, I felt a strong pain in my spleen, the consequence of a recently cured bout of malaria, and I had to slow down to a walk. Only fear kept me from stopping completely. However, I soon had to pause more frequently, until the pain in my side became so unbearable I had to stop altogether. I threw myself on the ground with my left side to the wet soil: I knew from past experience this would help alleviate the pain, and hopefully it would stop after a short time. As I said earlier, the leopard had surprisingly renounced its attack on us. To our great relief, we realised that it had not moved from under the tree, and seemed to have lost interest. Vic and Laura waited for me to recover sufficiently enough to be able to walk again, and we slowly made our way home. As I know that a leopard prefers young prey that is incapable of escaping, I can only assume that this must have been a young, inexperienced creature itself. I think that this is the only reason for our lucky escape that day.

Vic and I suffered serious trauma on that and other occasions during our unhappy residence by the Uebi Scebeli River. That is why from then on we avoided recalling anything that happened during those sad years as much as possible, we even stopped mentioning our parents. I have never asked Vic if he remembered that experience, and he has never asked me; but I can only assume that the event has left an indelible print on his memory, as well as mine.

Sometime after the encounter with the leopard, father took us with him to his place of work near the river. I cannot remember why – perhaps Mumina was absent. Anyway, that day Vic and I managed to escape the attention of our father again. While he was busy with his work with his back to us, Vic and I went down to the river. Vic saw an empty lime drum near the bank and put it into the water, which was not very deep at that point. He then got inside the drum, and invited me to do the same. I was not very keen to do this; but he convinced me that there could be no harm in joining him. After I had climbed in, Vic used a stick to push it away from the riverbank towards the centre of the stream. As the drum was taller than it was wide, it was not very stable in water, and when it reached the deeper part it started to sway noticeably. As the movements became more violent, I started to panic, and kept trying to escape, in spite of Vic's angry requests to keep still. The spot that we had reached was my father's preferred place to cross the river, and luckily there was also a boat nearby, which was anchored down by a weight. It was very small, perhaps two and a half metres long by maybe a metre wide, and had a flat bottom; the sides were only forty centimetres above the water level. Vic was vainly trying to keep me from moving about; the drum was taking in water every time I moved. The sight of the water approaching the top of our vessel was making me increasingly alarmed, and I finally started calling for our father. The river was moving slowly; but the water had already carried us a few metres from the bank. My cries attracted the attention of my father, and you can imagine his surprise at seeing his boys navigating the river inside a lime drum! He came to our rescue as fast as he could, fully aware that we could fall into the crocodile-infested water. Despite his handicapped leg, he ran with all his might, his face contorted by his effort to save his sons. I still remember his eyes meeting mine from fifty metres apart. He got to the riverbank, jumped in the boat, and reached out to the drum; he then grabbed us one at a time, and pulled us out of the barrel into the safety of the boat. How can I ever forget these film-like scenes?

When we were safely on dry land, my father's reaction was an unexpected one. Instead of directing his anger towards my brother, he took it out on me, and I had to take several hard smacks on my bottom. As well as having a very sore behind, I was perplexed as to why only I was punished. Today, eighty years later, I still wonder why it was I, then only three and-a-half, who was held responsible for what happened: he did not touch Vic; surely he was the more responsible, even if this was because he was five years older than me. However, my brother's tendency to get himself into inconsiderate and often dangerous situations had revealed itself as a prevalent part of his character, and remained with him for the rest of his life. This negative aspect of his personality was for him (and others) the cause of many serious and unpleasant events.

From his infant years, Vic's character appeared different from mine in many respects: he was more independent, self-centred and egotistical. He also had a congenital tendency to alter the truth. As he was untrustworthy, no one could ever be sure if he would keep an appointment or a promise. He also was extremely courageous, and he would do anything to make people talk about him. He liked to build himself up as an eccentric, and derived immense pleasure from surprising everyone with his unexpected contrivances, which were usually completely unpredictable.

Christmas 1926 was different to the rest. My mother's empty place at the table was so evident that the air of festivity was forced and unnatural. For Christmas presents, Laura got a primitive flat musical keyboard, I got a ball that could bounce unexpectedly anywhere (as in those days they were not made perfectly round), and Vic got a compressed-air rifle. My sister and I immediately started to quarrel, as we both wanted the musical keyboard. To keep me quiet, father told me he would make a wooden rifle for me, and I was overjoyed when he kept his promise within a few days.

One day, a bird with the most beautiful metallic colours I had ever seen made its nest in a hole in a nearby tree. My father noted my interest in the bird, and asked me whether I would like it. After my affirmative reply, he began the job of capturing it; but what he then did greatly surprised me, and is a lesson that I still remember today. He pulled a hair from the tail of the mule, which was idling under a nearby tree, and made an almost invisible running knot at one end of it. He then skilfully placed the knot around the entrance of the bird's nest. To my joy, the bird was captured on the afternoon of the same day. It was pecking furiously at my father's fingers, but he did not seem to feel any pain, as he was smiling happily at me. It was a kingfisher and had a very sharp beak. As soon as the bird was handed to me, it proceeded to give me the same treatment, and I immediately lost interest in it. I was glad when father took it back from me, and let it go free.

However, I had learnt that the hair of a mule is very strong, and is capable of resisting the sharp tugs and movements of birds and other small mammals, perhaps even as large as a rabbit. I always have thought that my father had learnt this technique in Argentina, as I have never heard of it in Italy. It is probably used to capture the numerous multicoloured parrots which make nests in the holes of trees.

A short time after the capture of the kingfisher, my father had the opportunity to employ this technique again. This time the victim was a black mole rat, which had unfortunately chosen to dwell near us. As they burrow underground, mole rats have the habit of feeding on the roots of any plant that they come across. If the rodent chooses to establish itself near your home, you should try to get rid of it by all means. Otherwise it will start to proliferate and build an underground colony, and this would be very dangerous for all nearby plants. However, attacking the home of this rodent with a spade can prove a highly laborious task, as you may only succeed in unearthing several cul-de-sacs. There are several amusing accounts on the subject of removing these rodents. One suggests employing a cat, and this sounds like a good alternative. However, if there are a large number of the rodents then the cat may eventually tire of this source of nourishment!

All of these events formed our early lives, and they could have only have happened in that vast, free place. We were ourselves part of it: men, insects, animals, flowers and forests. As the days went by, our father taught us little tricks that he deemed necessary for living in that environment. Although they seemed banal at times, the pleasant manner of his teaching spurred us on. It also provoked us to consider all the aspects of the encounters we had with the insects and mammals of our neighbourhood; for example, in order to capture a dragonfly that had settled on a stalk, you had to get your hand near the insect. You also had to move very slowly in order not to alarm it when trying to grab its wings. This was in fact the same tactic used by the leopard to capture its pray, albeit in a different manner. My father taught us that the best way to hide from an animal is to remain immobile, and if you wish to approach it you must move very slowly indeed. Perhaps the best time to approach an animal unnoticed is when it is eating.

There was then a relatively quiet period, which you could say was the calm before the storm, and there are only a few events worth mentioning. One happened when I was a small child, and affected me so deeply that it often returns in my sleep. As there was a lack of Somali labour, my father had engaged a number of Ethiopian workmen for his farm. The new labourers were very different to the Somali in appearance and manners; they seemed like savages in comparison. They had thick curly black hair that was very long and pointed in all directions; together with their black shiny eyes, it gave them a devilish appearance that scared me deeply. When I looked at them, I could see nothing else but a huge mass of hair with two large eyes underneath it, which made them seem twice as big as they really were. My father told me that the Ethiopians had never seen a white man before meeting him, and they were obviously very curious about the difference in skin colour. They also wanted to look at a white child at close quarters, and always tried to come near me and touch me. They would all do this at the same time, baring their incredibly white teeth. They would touch my thin, light hair, so different from their own. From their repeated desire to put their hands on me, I gathered they would seize me at any moment. On a couple of occasions, despite my screams of fear, my father was delayed, and I had to endure a few moments of stress and terror. As a result, I have suffered from a terrible nightmare for forty-five years, which only stopped after I had been living in England for some time. It was always the same: a black figure appeared, and stared malevolently at me, with black, shiny eyes. He did not move, but was poised as if he wanted to jump on me. At this point I was immobilised by the terror the figure inspired in me. I was waiting for an attack that would never come, and would suffer this deep state of panic until I woke up, sweaty and exhausted, with a galloping heart. The nightmare was so lifelike that I decided to ask my wife Sally for help: I asked her to wake me if she noticed that my breathing was becoming louder and faster, and stop me facing this nightmare.

Once, true to himself, Vic accidentally shot a Somali woman with his air rifle. Obviously this type of weapon is not very dangerous, as the projectile does not travel quickly enough to penetrate – unless it hits an eye. Luckily, on that occasion the woman was only moderately hurt. Nevertheless, she caused a great fracas and reported the matter to the police, who paid my father a visit. I do not know exactly how the matter ended; but I can only presume that it was settled with a monetary payment. Shortly after this, my father had the novel idea of having dinner outside in the fresh air, like a sort of picnic. During the day he instructed us to collect enough firewood to last about three hours and, hopefully, provide the necessary light and warmth for the duration of the dinner. This dinner was another event that was destined to remain forever impressed on my young memory as a nightmare.

The place chosen for the dinner was about two hundred metres from home, at the edge of the forest near where we had the terrifying encounter with the leopard: it needed to be this far away in case any sparks from the fire should fall upon the straw roof of the hut. My father took his omnipresent revolver and the carbine along with him, just in case. I was allowed to stay up past my usual bedtime for the first time. However, I was indifferent to this privilege, as I would have preferred to be in bed: after all, I was less than four years old. A little while later, after we had started dinner, we noticed the appearance of some jackals on the other side of the fire, which started to bark incessantly; apparently they were calling some more jackals, as their number slowly continued to increase. Eventually there were about a hundred of them, in addition to a number of hyenas, and we could not hear each other talk over the din they were making. Finally, our father got up, went to the other side of the bonfire, and fired two rounds of his carbine in the air, causing the beasts to stampede. However, they returned a few at a time, running back and forth. They were less noisy now, but kept their eyes fixed on us constantly. Their continuous background presence became disturbing, spoiling the atmosphere of our evening, and after a while we decided to call it a night, and went home, taking a few stumps of burning wood with us as a precaution. I later heard of a superstition that claims that an assemblage of a great number of canines is a bad omen. The canine group includes the African hunting dog, which are always in a pack, and are always hungry.

However, this is certainly not the reason for the bad memories I have of that night. Maybe the real reason is that I unconsciously connect my father with this event, which is one of the few vivid recollections I have of him alive. I feel that the red light emanating from that bonfire is like a beacon that unites us. When I think of him and the destruction of my family I always become sad, and remember a dream that never came true: I wanted to live my infant life surrounded by the love of my family. The fact that this dream never materialised is my nightmare.

I think it is opportune to write something about the very common African hyena. She has a very keen sense of smell, and can easily discover dead bodies from a distance. She is a very intelligent animal, more dangerous for women and children than men as she can distinguish between a man and a woman. If, for example, she meets a woman who is going to collect water somewhere on her own, she would consider her as prey and would not hesitate to try and kill her for a meal. I personally know of cases where this has happened.

On one occasion during a hunting trip I met one face to face. I expected the animal to try to evade an encounter, but that was not to be. Separated by a distance of twenty-five metres I understood that she was not scared – she fixed me with a glare and was obviously considering whether or not to have a meal at my expense.

Naturally I was armed. I did not like her interest in me, and was tempted to send her to the Creator with a shot in the heart, but on that occasion I decided to let her live. Another characteristic of the hyena is that it can smell anyone who has been buried underground and will try to excavate it, so in Somaliland people tend to put stones on top of the graves to prevent hyenas from getting to the dead bodies.

Perhaps the omen was significant. My father had not been feeling well for some time, but had typically ignored his illness. He was not the type of man to fuss, and thought that he would simply shake it off. Nobody knew what was the matter with him, and I am sure that he did not know himself; it could have been anything from a banal fever to an attack of malaria. I can guess the course of events: after some time, and realising that the sickness was not subsiding, my father must have concluded that he did have malaria. As it was the common practice for Europeans under those circumstances, he must have started to take quinine (he would have surely discarded the option to go and see a doctor, as the nearest was in the capital, and this meant a few days' travel, therefore losing valuable working time). However, one morning father left home in a rather more serious condition; it must have been bad, as he did not pay us any attention. When he came back that evening he walked straight past me and went to bed; I remember it well, as it was one of the last times that I saw him alive. When the night set in, we all retired under the dim light of the paraffin light. I slept next to my father's double bed, and in the middle of the night awoke to the sound of his voice. He was standing near the headboard and was speaking with a loud voice. He was delirious with despair: we were extremely isolated, and he knew that there was nothing that his three children could do. After a little while, everything was silent, and I fell asleep immediately.

Immediately after I had woken up, my brother took me outside. Our father had died. After I saw him awake, I did not know if he had gone back to sleep or died on the ground. At that age I could not understand the tragedy that had taken place in the hut that night. Years later, my brother told me that he had seen our father die, as he had also been awake that night. However, I never asked him whether he had died in the bed, or on the ground. I do not know why, as I have always wanted to know what happened in my father's last moments.

We then faced much trouble and danger. Some of the farm workers came to enquire, as they knew he was ill and he had not turned up for work. The news then spread rapidly amongst the Somali and Ethiopian workers, and immediately a crowd formed in front of our house. However, they were afraid to enter in case the giant was in fact still alive, and came out of the door to confront them. When a few more courageous ones decided to enter, a tremendous scramble followed, and there was suddenly a huge throng of people, grabbing all they could, then running out of the house. Vic realised what was going on, but was not in any condition to stop them; in fact, he stopped me from going inside when I tried to save my wooden rifle that father had made for me as a Christmas present. In the hut there were many things that were much sought after by the natives: articles of clothing, suits, sheets and mattresses; a full armoury: rifles, carbines, revolvers and ammunition; a travelling trunk, where my father had apparently kept all of his savings. We watched the sacking (that lasted all day long) from the kitchen. They took everything, even searching the furthest corners in the hope of finding a last hidden treasure. They even stripped my father of his night-shirt, leaving his naked body on the bare ground in the middle of the bedroom.

At sunset, the last workers finally left the house. They had not molested us in any way, as we had not tried to stop them. We were then completely alone, with not a living soul for kilometres around, only the calls of the turtledoves breaking the absolute silence around us. A night of terror was about to begin. Vic had hoped that someone would come to our aid; but his hopes vanished with the advancing darkness. Nobody cared about us, not even the Somali families; although they lived some distance away, they were fully aware of our predicament and our danger. In fact, we could not even go inside the hut, which was completely empty apart for our father's body. We were also far too scared to spend the night at the mercy of all the predators of the forest.

Compassion is essentially a Christian principle, and at that moment all Christians were far from us. We accepted the only alternative we had: take refuge in the kitchen. It was about ten metres from the house, and was a primitive construction. The walls were made of small wooden poles, five centimetres in diameter by about two metres high. They were planted into the ground, close to one another, and held together by long strips of intertwined bark. The roof was a replica of the main hut, and was made from straw, formed into a pyramid shape, kept in place by the same bark strips. The floor was simply pressed earth, and covered a surface of roughly five square metres. There was no door, and this allowed any animals searching for scraps of leftover food to come and go freely during the night. Father had never considered that a kitchen door was necessary; but ironically, that decision could have cost the lives of his children. A few silent hours passed without cause for alarm. Then, in the distance, we heard the hunting calls of a pack of hyenas. Vic whispered to Laura and me, and instructed us not to speak. The hyenas approached to about one hundred metres from our hut and then retreated, clearly unaware of our presence. All around us we could hear bursts of their high pitched hysterical laughs, which they do from time to time. This terrifying pattern continued throughout the night. The situation was dangerous because the hyenas could be attracted by the smell of my father's corpse. Then they would discover us, and that would be the end. However, our luck held out.

At sunrise we were cold and tired, as we had been lying on the hard ground. The morning passed with only the occasional visit of some Somali to check that they had not missed anything the day before, and they did not even notice us. The day was long and slow in our solitude: we had no food, and Vic did not know what to do. Everything seemed impossible; we were isolated and helpless. Although he was still very young, Vic realised that my father's corpse was a serious danger. Putrefaction is rapid in Africa due to the heat, and the scavengers are all too quick to capitalise. The second night was just as terrifying as the first: the famished hyenas began to circle again, and it was only by a miracle that they did not find my father's corpse. We were sure that someone was protecting us, and if this was true, it must have been my mother. Eventually the night passed, and the next morning was the third day after the death of my father, and we prepared to spend it in the same appalling conditions. Suddenly, at about eleven o'clock, some missionaries arrived. Their timely arrival at such a critical moment has always remained a mystery. I will never know if they had learnt of the death of my father from the beat of the tam tam, or if they had simply been in the area and decided to pay us a visit. You cannot imagine their consternation when they saw the inside of the house. They then fed us, gave us water, and buried my father. My father's final resting place is the small cemetery of Genale.

The departure from the house signalled that our African adventure and our family's dream were drawing to a conclusion. In the hut where I was born and lived for nearly five years, we left behind many memories of happy days of when we were altogether, when mother was still alive. For the time being, our immediate troubles were over.

Chapter 2

When we got to the capital, the missionaries put my brother and me in a bedroom in the nuns' ward; but my sister Laura was not so lucky. As she was the only white Christian female child in that institution, she had to sleep in the general dormitory with the Somali destitute, in the company of those who possessed nothing, and were dependent on charity. It did not seem right to me. What a disaster! We were categorised in the lowest of classes due to our age, and this social rank that was to remain with us for the rest of our infancy marked a black spot on my pride. When I think back to those unpleasant years, a shameful feeling arises that makes me want to avoid thinking or talking about them, even to my wife. My sister found herself in a cultural environment that was foreign to her. She found herself completely cut off from her brothers, whom she would see only very occasionally. She was exposed to this contrasting environment only a few days after the death of our father, and it was a traumatic experience at her tender age. The decision to ignore Laura's European roots seemed to be taken very lightly by the missionaries of the Consolata, and it was a decision that had a deep scarring effect on my sister. I must admit, as a result of this arbitrary action, I feel a strong resentment against the principles of that Catholic society, which has never been placated.

What else could we have expected from the missionaries? I think that they were unreasonable, but should they have treated us as affluent members of society? Remember that we had nothing apart from the clothes that we were wearing; yet, it seemed so unjust that only a short time before we were a happy family, full of love for each other and content with what we had; barely a few weeks after, both of our parents were gone, and whatever was left was brutally stolen from us in front of our eyes. We then found ourselves separated from our sister and living amongst strangers who, with all their goodness, were at liberty to decide what to do with our lives. Maybe fate was unkind to us, not the missionaries. However, does fate exist? I do not know who was unjust, but I know my negative feelings were and still are very strong. My resentment remains and shall do for ever.

However, I must admit that there were pleasant times in the two years with the nuns of the Consolata. The missionary order originated from Piedmont, so most of the fathers were Piedmontese. All of them knew my father well as he was one of their fellow countrymen. The Mother Superior of the Mogadishu Mission was also a member of the Italian Royal Family, thus enhancing the mission's prestige. In 1926, the Crown Prince of Italy visited Somalia and the Mother Superior. She asked the Crown Prince if he would be Vic's godfather; he was taking his First Communion and Confirmation. The Prince agreed, which was and still is an honour for our family.

Most of the nuns had also known my mother and soon suggested that they should visit her grave. However, this innocent idea led to an unpleasant surprise for both the nuns and myself. I was then about five years old, and I did not understand the meaning of the words 'death' and 'cemetery'; after all, my father had told me that my mother had departed for a long trip, and I thought I would see her again one day. I assumed that she would be at the cemetery, and had no idea that it was a place where the dead were buried. I was also vaguely puzzled as to why I was the only one invited to visit the cemetery. I do not know if Laura had ever been to the grave of my mother, but I think somebody must have taken Vic there at some time; it was not far away, maybe three hundred metres from the mission, and we walked. The sea, which was about fifty metres away, almost completely circumscribed the cemetery, and eternally filled it with the sound of its waves. There were only a small number of graves: maybe sixty. The perimeter surrounding the cemetery consisted of a white wall about three metres high, with only one entrance. In the first grave on the left of the entrance lay my mother.

I remember it well: it was built of cement, or lime, and was roughly one metre high by two metres in length. Its design was unusual, and resembled a small country house. The roof slanted down on both sides to encourage precipitation runoff, and was altogether similar to a house that could have been made by children of a primary school. One of the nuns told me that my mother was inside the little house. They were not prepared for what happened afterwards: I threw myself at the grave, trying to penetrate the cover of cement that was encasing it, but it would not budge. I tried another place, but was again denied, and I started to call to my mother loudly, hoping that she would appear and put an end to my hysterics. At this point the nuns recovered from their shock and attempted to intervene, but as they were unable to grab or stop me they only succeeded in creating an even greater confusion. In the end they managed to get hold of me, and only by slapping me and dragging me away violently did they manage to remove me from the cemetery. This was the only true goodbye I said to my mother. However, the matter did not end there.

The next day, still full of sorrow and grief, I attempted to take my life in a very unusual way. I had heard that the African sun could kill a European if he remained exposed to its rays for a long period, without the protection of a colonial helmet. A large number of Europeans in those days did not understand about the debilitating effects of sunstroke; in any case, all of them tried to avoid the sun as much as possible without a helmet. This helmet had an interior of banana leaves, which combined lightness and anti-conduction properties, and made it particularly suited for hot temperatures. However, although it was extremely light, it caused your forehead to almost continually sweat, and forced you to remove it occasionally to dry your brow.

My attempt to kill myself was made easier by the existence of a large terrace on the same floor as my bedroom. The front of it faced the sea, which was maybe half a kilometre away, and on the left-hand side there was an enclosed roof, used for storing grain. This porch was also the coolest spot of the terrace due to the shadows that the roof created, and the nuns knew that they could always find me there when I went missing. It was my favourite spot, a place where I could enjoy the sight of the incredible expanse of the deep blue sea without needing anyone's company. It was near lunchtime when I attempted to take my life. I simply took off my helmet and lay down, with my head on the then hot cement of the terrace. I did not realise it, but the time I had chosen to kill myself probably saved my life. Due to the heat during the day, nobody ever entered the terrace unless they had to, and therefore my absence went unnoticed until lunchtime. I was probably exposed to the sun for maybe thirty minutes, until the nuns realised I was absent at lunch, and came to look for me. I was damaged mainly by the prolonged contact between my head and the scorching cement. My attempt to reunite myself with my mother had only partially succeeded, as when the nuns found me I was in a coma, and remained so for a few days. When I awoke, I was surprised to be in a marvellous unknown place. It was a hospital bedroom, brilliantly white, with a large, comfortable bed. I was alone in the room, but had been attended to with great care; shortly afterwards I awoke, and there was much rejoicing as I was welcomed back to the world of the living. However, I was not happy, and during the next few weeks the state of my health was precarious. I seemed to be prone to any illness: measles, mumps, scarlet fever – I contracted them all.

Due to the lack of any contact from our Italian relatives, the mission soon decided to send all three of us to an orphan asylum in Turin. We left the African continent sometime during April 1929.

We were transported to the ship in Mogadishu the same way our mother was transported from it in 1920. However, as we were smaller and lighter, my sister and I could fit in the same chair, and a Somali porter carried us across the shallow water to the waiting ship. Our nanny Mumina, who was living near the centre of the town, came to the landing jetty to say goodbye to us. After the death of our father, she had never failed to visit us regularly at the mission. She followed us through the water, crying as she held my hand, until she could continue no further, as the seas were a little rough that day. The moment my nanny let go of my hand, I said goodbye to Africa and all that it meant to me, and felt a pang of sorrow in the pit of my stomach. That young Somali girl was to prove far more affectionate than some of the people that I would meet in my own country. My farewell to her and Africa has remained clear in my mind. Even now, after so many years, the memories of those moments never fail to fill my heart with sorrow and sadness. I know that Mumina felt as if she was really our mother; she knew all the circumstances of my family's last years, and had filled the role of the foster-mother perfectly, creating a strong emotional bond with each one of us. I consider the compassion that she possessed to be a very precious thing in Africa. This was the last time I ever saw her.

We encountered very hostile seas on our voyage, and all of the ship's crew suffered from severe seasickness. Luckily children are immune to its effects, so we three had no trouble. At our arrival in Italy there was a 'nice surprise' waiting for us. Our relatives had finally managed to contact the Somali authorities, and had travelled from Rome to come and meet us at Naples. They had assumed that we would need some protection from the cold of April, and at the command of our grandmother had searched their wardrobes for whatever they could find for us. However, their clothes were more likely to envelop us than to dress us. The knitwear in particular had very gaudy colours, and sleeves that were far too long, perhaps more suitable for a carnival. Still, these were our only choice and our grandmother insisted that we put them on. The colonial helmets that we were still wearing accentuated our ridiculous appearance, and completed the amusing scene. Our grandmother insisted we wore them, as she had decided that it was necessary to protect our brains from the cold. Our group soon attracted the attention of some Neapolitan street urchins, and a small crowd gathered around, which was altogether too much for us: we were unable to understand why our presence had aroused so much attention and hilarity. The urchins were apparently enjoying it no end, and were making signs at us from a short distance away. Fashion was not an issue in Africa, and there people dressed how they felt like, or any way they could. The resulting appearance made no difference, as nobody cared.

Anyway, from this first meeting the gulf that was created by two generations' difference was already apparent, and was to widen as time went by. Soon the novelty of our arrival wore off. After my grandmother had met the sons and daughter of her daughter, and my uncles had met the children of their sister; the honeymoon seemed to disintegrate. They forgot that my mother had ever existed, and her memory did not have any effect on decisions made concerning us. Although I was very young, I understood that I was not their son, and that I was also alone.

Our grandmother became increasingly intolerant of our presence in her home. She never missed any opportunity to point out our shortcomings – real or imaginary. Her continuous observations and comments were doubtlessly due to her lack of affection for us. We all suffered from her hostility for different reasons: Vic was considered intolerable due to his strange, eccentric personality, and she had no intention of putting up with him from the beginning. The austerity of the thirties combined with a matriarch of the 1860s' generation cancelled all my brother's hopes of gaining the affection of my granny. I felt that my unpardonable defect was that I was the 'spitting image' of my father: a mortal enemy of my grandmother as he was responsible for the death of her daughter. My chances of getting into her good books were doomed from day one. However, Laura's unpopularity was perhaps for the most whimsical reason: Granny said that she shouted like and had the attitude of a monkey. The matriarch supported this parallel with a great conviction, backed up by a strange theory of hers: our mother had gone to Africa when she was expecting Laura, and at some point her daughter had acquired the habits and speech of the local monkeys.

It soon became apparent that our father had left us with some twenty-seven thousand liras, and in those days you could buy three apartments with that amount of money. In addition to the five hundred liras per annum that came from my father's medal for valour, the interest amounted annually to nine hundred liras. This was enough to allow for just one of us to stay with one of our uncles. Laura was selected, and the orphanage beckoned for my brother and me. We accepted this decision without resentment, as it would have been impossible for our relatives to maintain all three of us for a long period of time. Vittorio was fortunate enough to be sent to an orphanage that was run by priests, as he was older than the average child in our group. He then trained as a cabinetmaker and studied in a State school. After five years he left the institute and joined the Navy. I did not see him again for a long time. I was not so lucky, and the nine-year period that I would like to forget was about to start.

Even though the story of the orphanage is short, it is not easy for me to describe; however, I believe that this narrative would be largely incomplete if I excluded this part of my life, and this view is shared by many of my friends. The humiliation created by that place made me determined never to speak to anyone about this unpleasant era, and I have kept those years a secret from everyone, including my wife of forty years. An inferiority complex sometimes affects me even today when I think of those times. I am near the end of my existence, but still feel a deep sense of discomfort if anyone tries to investigate my infant years: I wish that this chapter of my life had never happened. My daughter Linda tries to probe every now and then, but I have always discouraged her. Maybe now she will understand my reticence.

The first institute (I want to refer to it in this way) had the reverberating title of Institute di Pedagogia Scientifica (Institute of Scientific Pedagogy). It was financed by the State, but managed privately by a General Director, and I remember him well: I remember his false and insincere attitude well also, along with his many 'good intentions'. His behaviour never provided any sort of relief, and gave us nothing to trust. He was an arrant buffoon. He always used theatrical words that were empty of meaning, and was capable of fooling anyone with his bluffs and his strong personality. He was responsible for all of our suffering.

Initially, the novelty of the new life in a community was not so bad, and the institute was located in an incredibly luxurious villa; I do not know how the General Director had managed to rent the Villa Torlonia, which was one of the most beautiful palatial constructions in Rome, and was of inestimable value. It belonged to one of the oldest patrician Roman families, and was located in the Gianicolo: a well-known aristocratic district in the capital of Italy.

It may sound incredible, but I can say that the Villa of Prince Torlonia was my first place of residence at the beginning of my nine orphanage years (1931–1939). There were enormous rooms everywhere, which later were transformed into a refectory and dormitories. The centrepiece of all this was an elaborate marble staircase. Beautiful paintings of angels and cherubs adorned the walls and ceilings of every room, and you would eventually develop a stiff neck from turning to admire them. The entry gate was electric (in 1930), and could be operated automatically from a distance. At the top of the palace there were two vast terraces at different levels; the ground floor was immense, and commanded a dominating view of Rome. It was basically a huge garden, half covered by gravel and the other half planted with trees. During the spring and summer evenings, it was used to hold large receptions. The General Director also used to have dinner there with his family on most summer evenings. This part of the villa was completely separated from us.

For the first two years, the personnel who took care of us were all women. Although the relationship between our governess and us was not particularly affectionate, a woman is by nature inclined to deal with children in a motherly way. Therefore, all seemed to be reasonably satisfactory. The villa's pretentious exterior was ideal for luring in naive potential clients, and the General Director exploited this perfectly. A sufficient number of children flowed in from ignorant estranged families, who were often living on the poverty line. These boys were utilised for dubious purposes and illicit gain without consultation. The word 'orphanage' is the simplest term for an establishment that houses destitute children without a sufficient family (mistreatment is also closely associated with this word). Therefore most parties prefer to call them 'colleges' or 'institutes', in an endeavour to mask the sadness and misery that exists within the walls. As our 'elite' institute had the grand title of 'The Institute of Scientific Pedagogy', it certainly laid a cunning trap for the unwary. I have taken the trouble to look up the word 'pedagogy' in a dictionary. What I found brought a sorry laugh to my lips. It read: 'Theory aiming at determining the ends of the educational process and to the more suitable ways to achieve them'. That was the supposed purpose of our institute. The prestige of Villa Torlonia was a suitable lure to not just attract the children of the poor, but also the affluent who wished to get rid of unwanted, embarrassing burdens in a way that appeased their conscience.

With this in mind, the General Director had come up with an idea to improve the deficient or mentally disabled sons of the well-to-do. But how? Well, the theory was that once these unhappy children entered into the institute, they would associate with stable children like us, all with calculated equilibrium. The handicapped children were then expected to improve through gradual interaction with 'normal' subjects. Of course, this simple solution did not always work out. What always did work out was the amount of money that regularly flowed into the pockets of the General Director.

However, the formula was not entirely wrong, and a few children did show signs of improvement. The only other way to improve the children would be by using sophisticated medical equipment; but this would have meant a cut in pay for the Director, and that was the last thing he was prepared to sacrifice. An honest and conscientious man would not have hesitated to cut back for the benefit of the children; but he did not possess either of these attributes. He announced that he wanted to help intellectually insufficient children as part of his noble crusade. A likely story. As the gladiators in ancient Rome used to say: 'Your death, my life'. Although it is rather disturbing, I will recall an example:

One day a new child arrived to stay with us. He was the ten-year-old son of a very rich Ethiopian Ras, and was severely mentally unbalanced. We promptly nicknamed him Gigi the Abyssinian. However, although his brain was somewhat dormant, his sexual appetite certainly was not, and on his first night he made an excursion into the bed of the child in the adjacent bed. The boy was obviously alarmed, and shouted loudly, awaking everyone in the dorm. Poor Gigi was incapable of understanding our explanations as to why he should not go into other people's beds, and the following night he repeated the advance. Naturally, after this we all refused to sleep anywhere near him, and as the institute did not have the facilities or the resources to treat Gigi properly, the General Director had no choice but to return him home. This must have been very annoying for the General Director, as he consequentially forfeited the prominent Ethiopian's money; however, if he had had the correct means of treatment available, then he too would have benefited.

After this occurrence, the honeymoon at Villa Torlonia was over, as the general approach was changed drastically. The General Director discharged all governesses and substituted them with male personnel. He hired these people without any hesitation and did not enquire about the schooling, background or mental condition of the applicants. As long as they received their meagre wages then everyone was happy. Except for us, of course.

In the meantime the General Director had managed to rent a number of other institutes at good prices, regardless of their locations. After two years at Villa Torlonia, I was among the first to be transferred, and found myself in an orphanage on the periphery of Rome at La Magliana. This was one of the worst experiences of my infant years. My infancy spanned two distinct periods, and the first of these was from 1932 to 1934. During this period not one person paid a visit to me. However, even worse than this were the episodes of serious uncontested maltreatment, which were inflicted on all the children by the personnel who were supposed to care for us. This situation arose from the lack of interest and absenteeism of the General Director, who left us at the mercy of our direct superiors. On Sunday relatives were allowed to visit the children, and they seized the opportunity to take them out of the institute and have a welcome Sunday lunch together. Alternatively, they arrived armed with parcels of food and comics, which were devoured with much relish. I felt very humiliated to be the only child who never had any visitors on Sundays.

On some weeks I was the only child left in the institute, while all the others went out for the day. Everyone had somebody who loved them; several of them, more fortunate than I, still had a mother.

The situation was much worse during the bitter winter. My discomfort became more severe as I was less adequately dressed for winter and suffered the cold more than my wretched companions, although all were in some amount of pain. There was a tube about half a metre in diameter which jutted out from a wall adjacent to the kitchen and discharged the warm smoke generated by the cookers. It went through all the neighbouring rooms to the kitchen, and we gathered there during these winter months to keep warm. We tried to generate heat by staying close to one another: much like sparrows gathered under a convex roofing tile on a cold winter's night.

At these times, I could not refrain from comparing my past life with the present. I compared the sweet caresses of my mother and father to the constant unjustified beatings from strangers, and the warm vast lands of my Africa to the poverty and the squalid cold winters of Italy. Only my infinite pride and self-respect prevented me from begging my relatives to come and visit. I wish that they could have done this of their own free will, and convinced me that there was still someone with a heart; but this was only a dream, a forlorn hope of mine. When I stayed with my relatives at Christmas, I always told them that I did not need anything in spite of my squalid appearance; I also always told them that everything was fine at La Magliana. If they had any feelings for me, they would have read the sorrow in my face, and the malnutrition that prevented my otherwise growing body from developing.

Sometimes I went to stay with one of my uncles at Christmas. He had three children and the gap between us was painstakingly evident. I was never jealous of their life, and I was genuinely happy for the presents that the children received. I never touched their toys and never tried to play with them: I was content with their happiness. I often think that my relatives only gave presents to be noticed by others, and their mind was only satisfied by the gratitude of the recipient. However, my potential gratitude was worthless, so there would never be a present for me. I have always tried not to disturb my relatives or make them remorseful for abandoning me. I believe I have been successful, and I am sure that when my grandmother went to the Almighty she was ashamed. I am also sure that there were some accounts to settle when she faced my mother.

In order to understand the magnitude of my humiliation, it is perhaps necessary to mention some cases of ill treatment that I suffered at La Magliana. To counteract the harshness of that life, we all agreed to adopt a 'Fortitude Conduct Code', and we pledged: 'Everything unpleasant that is happening to us, in the circumstances, is accepted as inevitable'. From then on, our general attitude was: here nobody ever cries; we never invoke anyone, neither our mothers nor God; here we do not steal; here we never say please, we never say thank you; here we never ask for anything; here nobody owns anything, jealousy does not exist, envy does not exist; here you must never whimper, you must never complain, you must never have weaknesses, as nobody will ever help you. With this pledge, we were ready to accept anything destiny threw at us.

In the orphanage, the discipline was far too strict for our tender and impressionable age; military discipline was a walk in the park in comparison. If a soldier breached a fairly serious rule, his punishment would have been far less harsh than the beatings that we had to endure.

During summertime, we were forced to take a siesta after lunch. However, it was they who really wanted the nap, as their bellies were fit to burst. With our half-empty unsatisfied stomachs, sleep was the last thing on our minds. This compulsory afternoon rest lasted four hours, from one to five o'clock; during this time, our masters warned us not to move or even whisper, in order not to disturb their slumber. Their idleness severely tested our patience in the heat of the summer months. In the circumstances, it was only possible to hold a whispered conversation with the person adjacent to your bed. In order to enforce these strict rules, each afternoon our superior would choose one of us to act as a guardian, with the task of taking note and reporting anyone who spoke during this period. The chosen boy was then assumed to have a superior position over the other boys, and had the chance to exact revenge over any enemies. At five o'clock, after getting up from our beds, we had to stand in a row in front of both the well-rested teacher and the 'guardian'. The guilty boy was then named, and would receive his punishment on the spot in front of everyone. I will tell you of one case in particular, which has remained impressed in my memory due to the severity of the punishment. I can still remember the name of the boy: Pasquale Fumi, of Nettuno.

He was nine or ten years old, and had a very mild and vaguely meek character. Anyway, he was called from the row of boys and was accused of attempting to speak with the person in the adjacent bed. As soon as he reached the teacher, the man delivered a kick on his bottom so powerful that it lifted the boy clean off the ground. Still unsatisfied, the villain then pelted him with a hail of punches and kicks as he lay prostrated on the floor. Even our code of fortitude was not enough to stop the wretched boy crying to his mother, and then God. He urinated in his pants in pain and fear; meanwhile the coward kept cursing and beating him, completely carried away with sadistic pleasure. Unfortunately the boy had also broken our code, so he was derided for some time, in order to help him become stronger.

The same people who were supposed to care for us and teach us proper manners carried out this violence. They were nothing but cowards who took every opportunity, every excuse, to vent their vicious temperament and satisfy their craving for violence. They constantly took full advantage of us, knowing that we were not in a position to defend ourselves: they were all aged well over twenty, and in view of our inferior physical strength, any attempt at self-defence was impossible, although a few of us had tried it. Most of the time, when we knew we were about to receive a beating, our only defence was to throw ourselves to the ground and adopt the 'hedgehog position'. This involved bending the knees and bringing them up to the chin, with the hands trying to protect the back of the head and the arms guarding the side of the face. In this position, with the body tensed, it was possible to bear the blows to a certain extent until the bastard got tired. Our tormentors took the hedgehog position as a sort of challenge, and they would try to aim their blows at the uncovered parts of the body, in order to hurt us as much as possible.

A member of staff once surprised me whilst I was plucking wild apples from a tree outside our enclosure. These apples were small – perhaps a little bigger than a cherry – and were not suitable for sale; they would have barely been suitable for pigs. However, I received a few strong kicks to my backside, and was locked in my bedroom as a bonus. I remained a prisoner all day in the cold murky autumn, and was deprived of my lunch and dinner. Even though the food was largely insufficient, I was desperately hungry. I really thought I was going to die that day; but in honour of our code, I accepted my punishment with great stubbornness. I often wonder what my parents would have thought had they known what had befallen their son.

Only a person who was intent on personal gain and considered themselves to be a god would engage a bunch of rude lackey-guardians. Had the State only provided us with the simple State education that we required, it would have saved not only a lot of physical suffering, but also our dignity. Attempting to uphold this was the only thing that kept us going.

We often used a boxing match to solve conflicts that were considered comparatively serious. They would be held in the lavatories, which were fairly large – more or less the size of a boxing ring – and we observed the traditional rules, but obviously could not use gloves. Any unorthodox techniques were considered to be a sign of fear (for example, head blows or kicks) and resulted in instant disqualification. No allowances were made for differences in weight and age: if a boy had the courage to face an older or heavier adversary, then it was up to him. Everyone was admitted to view these fights, and we would decide who was the winner at the end of the bout.

No relationship in the orphanage was based on mutual affection: we were united by the circumstances, the environment and the rules We were all in the same boat, but friendships were rare; nearly every one of us was completely uninterested in the welfare of others. However, during my stay in the institute at La Magliana, I met a boy who has had a noticeable influence on my adult life. He was the same age as me, and was literally dropped into the institute: one day someone 'deposited' him at the entrance of the orphanage and abandoned him there. His name was Dante Leoni, and we guessed that he must have either come from a family of acrobats or a circus, as he possessed an uncommon ability to walk on stilts and perform other tricks. However, he would never speak of his background, so we guessed that it must have been hard, or disagreeable. His manner gave the impression that he was a lot more mature than the rest of us; in addition, his often sombre expression and detached attitude seemed to indicate that something unpleasant had happened in his young life. He would also never take part in team games, but was always keen to play something more individual, such as cards.

On our return to the orphanage after the Christmas holidays, most of us had money in our pockets, as we had intentionally paid a visit to our relatives (we all knew that they would understand the purpose of this visit, and would usually hand over some coins). Dante was feeling a little more sociable with all this money floating around, and would always profit due to a few simple card tricks (and perhaps a little bit of cheating). His tricks were never malicious, and simply indicated that he had been raised specifically for the circus life. He was also blessed in another way: he was a master of Graeco-Roman wrestling, and constantly defeated everybody with an adroit move called the *ancata* (a heaving hip throw employing one's back muscles). If this move is properly executed, it always results in a spectacular victory, and is virtually impossible to counteract. I asked Dante to teach me this particular move, and in true honour to our ethos of equality, he agreed. I practised with him for several days until I was also able to execute it equally as well as him, or perhaps even better. This episode is important, as the *ancata* has proved decisive in many of my fights. Dante and I came to blows twice over the course of the years; however, we only used our fists, as wrestling was forbidden. I lost the first encounter; but was victorious in the second, as it was four years later and I had grown considerably larger than him. At the end of our time in the orphanage we went our separate ways, and I never saw that likeable boy again.

We only had two teachers at the orphanage: one was called Mr Rossi and taught music, and the other teacher, whose name escapes me, taught the remaining subjects. Mr Rossi was blind from birth, and had obtained a diploma from the prestigious Academy for the Blind in Rome. He was very able, and guided us by reading Braille scriptures. He taught us how to sing the beautiful aria from *Nabucco*, the Mameli hymn, and many other beautiful regimental war songs (even today, I still remember their words).

One day, for some reason, Mr Rossi lost his patience with us during his lesson. After telling us to be silent (which we did immediately) he then added with a commanding voice, 'Shut up, all you sons of whores.' None of us had said a word. We all looked at each other whilst shrugging our shoulders with our palms skyward as if to say, 'What is going on?' I tried to work out what had happened when reflecting on the insult later. Mr Rossi had already obtained silence from us before uttering those inopportune words; therefore they were unnecessary. After having called us 'sons of whores', he paused for a long time, as if he wanted to savour the effect of his insult on us (I had to ask somebody older than me to explain the insult's meaning, as I was too young to understand). I think that it was a vent for his sorry state of mind, in a moment of weakness. He must have been brooding in his darkness beforehand. I truly believe that it was not directed at us, and was simply an utterance against his unfortunate way of life. I really do not think that he wanted to insult anybody.

In spite of this unpleasant incident, Mr Rossi was not a bad person. I thought of him when I returned to Italy at the end of the last war, and made some enquires in Rome. A friend of mine from college told me that he had been seen playing the accordion, on the pavement of Piazza Maggiore. I would have liked to say hello to him and thank him for all the help that he gave to me; in addition, I also would have liked to help him in whatever way I could. However, I never did find him.

He was very much on the same level as us boys, but his way of thinking was quite avant-garde. We represented the lowest strata of society, therefore *vae victis*! Our ransom must come with our will to re-emerge anew. We did not want anything except respect and understanding during our difficult phase, and then eventually we would be ready to reintegrate into society. I think that the Italian Government should have taken care of us in a more fatherly way; it should have monitored these orphanages more closely, and attempted to recognise the unscrupulous sadists that made our lives a misery. I was one of the children who suffered humiliation, hunger and many beatings as a result of the poorly run orphanage system.

In 1934, our orphanage was deemed a guinea pig for experimental vaccinations against tuberculosis, which was then a disease widely known for being highly infectious and contagious. However, it was impossible to defeat it completely. In those days everyone believed tuberculosis to be even more contagious than HIV is today: its transmission could occur by breathing the air in the same room as the infected patient, or by direct contact. If someone caught tuberculosis then they would have to be completely isolated from their family and friends. This was always a problem, as hospitals would rarely admit someone with this disease, and the rest of the family had no choice but to look after the sick person, with inevitable results. This dilemma was a typical example of the nightmares that were a reality in those times.

In the fifties, the battle was won against tuberculosis with the development of the streptomycin and vaccination. This breakthrough was only made possible with the assistance of people who agreed to act as guinea pigs. Some of these people were idealists, and others did it for pecuniary gain; but all fully understood the risks involved. We, of course, did not. So one day, during the spring of 1934, four bold young doctors (they could have been male nurses, or medical university students, we did not know) came to visit us in the classroom. The teacher interrupted the lesson, and the four smiling young men told us (all aged between eight and twelve years) that they had come to carry out an experimental vaccination against tuberculosis. Without further ado, they produced some serum and syringes, and injected us on the arm. The untried formula could easily have contained a strain of dormant tuberculosis bacillus. Luckily, nobody was infected, thank God. It must have been someone with no sense of responsibility or humanity that authorised these experiments on a classroom of young boys. We were not asked for our consent; I am sure they would have asked grown men if they were prepared to take this chance for the good of humankind.

The year 1935 found our General Director in serious financial difficulty; he was close to bankruptcy, and was forced to leave Rome and rent cheaper accommodation that was large enough to house about seventy children. As the present area was too costly, the most enticing alternative was to leave the Lazio region altogether. In the words of Prophet Mohammed: 'If the mountain does not come to you, you go to the mountain.' This advice was taken literally. Half the inhabitants of La Magliana found themselves at the top of a mountain in a small isolated village, in the Campania region; to save on both rent and maintenance he had moved about half of the children to a region poorer than Lazio. However, his funding would remain the same, and the crafty fellow would make a tidy profit at our expense. In addition to all this, the rustic dialect of the area was difficult to understand, as we were used to speaking modern Italian.

The run-down castle that was our new abode clearly showed

that we were in a less prominent region than before. It was a formidable construction, cold and austere. In the centre, there was a yard that had been used as a parade and drill area for the troops of a now forgotten potentate, large enough for horses and mules. Outside the castle, the walls still bore the scars of cannonballs from battles of long ago. It dominated the highest part of the rocky mountain, and the hawks that had taken residence in the abandoned high tower circled even further above our heads. Not even the powerful spirit of youth could cheer up these gloomy surroundings. At one side of the castle the mountain slanted away and there were wide embankments, made by workers generations before. These farmers had planted them with olive trees, which were the only existing life on what was otherwise a barren and perilous descent. At the foot of the mountain, a small brook signalled that you were leaving that bland habitat. The entire mountainside was off-limit to us, and the General Director had warned us that anyone found on that part of the mountain would be severely punished.

The small village nearby was more than one hundred kilometres from Rome, so even the more fortunate who once had the pleasure of their mother's visits were deprived of this privilege. We were now all completely isolated, and all equally as famished; in order to obtain vital food we were forced to take the risk of venturing into the forbidden area: this was the only place in which we could partially satisfy our hunger, and we visited there in the hope of finding even a single olive that had escaped the eye of the usually thorough pickers; the rain sometimes unearthed them after they had been buried by a careless foot. The olives were black, wrinkled and bitter; but when found, were promptly gnawed down to the stone. The barren part of mountain also offered other temptations, and we often picked a handful of wild peas, which we called *terette* (available only during springtime). If we were lucky, we could also grab some strawberries or blackberries, or even a few stalks of asparagus: how they managed to grow there, nobody knew.

The municipal school that we attended was another big disadvantage. There were thirty-five children packed into a small classroom, and it was virtually impossible to cater for everyone's needs. As our superiors were not even slightly interested in our welfare, the teaching was vague and incoherent. Therefore it was incredibly difficult to advance from one level to the other.

During the winter months our discomfort increased. Our clothes were insufficient to protect us from the cold, whilst our pangs of hunger were stronger. In November someone discovered that a tree inside the enclosure produced a profusion of edible acorns. From then on we picked a good quantity of them every day. Somebody suggested that they would be better to eat if they were roasted; but to avoid them exploding in your face, you must first make an incision on their shell. They had a very acrid and pungent taste; but we soon got used to them, and they lasted for over two months. I still remember the Christmas of 1936, sitting around a little fire on one side of the courtyard. My friends and I roasted acorns one after the other, whilst laughing merrily and forgetting our troubles; it was an example of the strength of our spirits, and not once did we show a moment of weakness.

However, two days after Christmas, one of our companions died. His name was Salvatore Russo, and he was eleven years old. He had thought differently from the rest of us, and believed that it would have been more beneficial to rummage through the garbage for cabbage stalks rather than to eat acorns. He guarded this secret fiercely, as he believed that we would try to compete with him for the rotting food. It was never clear whether Russo had washed the stalks before eating them; however, he caught severe typhoid, which killed him within three days. The General Director should have reported the death to the medical authorities, in case there was danger of an epidemic; but he was afraid that the conditions that he was subjecting us to would be exposed.

One thing was certain: our friend Russo should not have been worried about competition for the garbage, and every one of us was shocked to learn that one of the boys had sunk so low. On the same day as his death, we were all lined up in a row in the courtyard, with the coffin of our dead companion in front of us. The cold and the rain increased our sadness. As was customary, they called the name of Salvatore Russo. 'PRESENT' we answered altogether, and Salvatore had departed to a better place.

The death of our companion was traumatic for all of us. All of a sudden, we did not feel inclined to eat acorns, and we decided it would be more appropriate to abstain as a mark of respect. The owner reclaimed the castle soon after Salvatore's death, and we returned to the orphanage at La Magliana. However, our return was short-lived, and we were soon moved again to a prestigious villa at Tivoli.

* * *

Tivoli, about twenty kilometres east of Rome, was then a small town of about fifty-two thousand inhabitants. It was famous for being an administrative centre during the Roman Empire.

The size of the property indicated that the owner must have been very rich; however, as the land surrounding it was infertile, it cannot have been a very profitable investment. The owner must have decided to rent it to our General Director and wait for a better opportunity. Although it was certainly an impressive building, it was still not as luxurious as the Villa Torlonia; nevertheless, it still had all the necessary facilities and was perfectly capable of hosting us.

It was enclosed by a high white wall, and the gate connected the villa to the main road, which ran adjacent for a short distance. From this road it was possible to have a view of the countryside, and a fraction of the nearby college. The villa was erected in the lower part of the property, as it was built on a stony hill. It was easy to hide ourselves in its vast expanse of promontories and winding ravines; what we also found was that it was impossible for our superiors to completely control us, and we enjoyed some previously unknown liberty at this picturesque place. They seemed to be content as long as we did not disturb their sleep.

One day, due to a fortuitous incident, the General Director had to finally end the 'pedagogic experiment' that he had run for so long. During the summer of 1937, a teacher was enjoying beating a boy inside our compound, not far from the entrance. Luckily, some influential inhabitants of the small town near to us were in the habit of taking a walk along the main road that skirted our college, and the loud yells and cries of the wretched child attracted the attention of one of these passers-by. The man approached the entrance to the college and witnessed the brutal act. He protested against the violence, but the arrogant reply of the teacher resulted in a fierce argument between the pair. Our superior, who was used to believing that he had the right to beat whoever he liked, would not tolerate any form of external intervention; instead, he uttered more and more aggressive insults as he continued to punch and kick the boy.

His bad manners deeply offended the gentleman who had tried to defend our companion and he promised to return to demand an account of his behaviour. We learnt soon afterwards that the man held a high position in the Ministry, and after a short time an inspection was ordered to investigate the conditions and treatment of the inmates of the College of Scientific Pedagogy. When the Ministry's inspector arrived, he firstly asked to inspect all the inmates of the college. Our teachers had a worried look on their faces. They told us that the boys with the best appearance must be positioned on the front row, whilst those with the worn garments and shoes with holes must hide in the back rows. However, we were all hoping that the inspectors would spot the holes in our shoes, and they did: the thoroughness of their inspection thwarted all attempts to hide the miserable conditions in which we had lived for years. The Ministry closed down the college and we were moved to another institute in Rome, where we finally found conditions that were suitable for human beings. It also included a State school, and provided food that was sufficient for growing boys. The children that went to this school lived with their families, and we were finally treated as equal members of society. This was the kind of establishment that I wished I could have gone to in the first place. However, I managed to finish my academic preparations just in time.

Chapter 3

It was 1940, and the cannons were thundering. My uncles had already applied on my behalf for my enrolment in the Italian Air Force. My application was accepted, and I left the institute on my seventeenth birthday. The next day, I belonged to the military.

Contrary to what people generally believe, I found this life very enjoyable, much easier and freer than college. The nightmare had ended: I had a job and had reached the age when I assumed full responsibility for myself, and could plan my own future. As time goes by, my recollection of my infancy becomes less incisive and more distant, and the details of the worst times are now almost forgotten. I rarely remember the happy times now; but when I do, I feel a strong sense of nostalgia, mixed with a tinge of sadness. Those times are gone; but not forgotten.

After fourteen months of training at the Aeronautical Military School, I passed my final exams and was a qualified 'Airman Electrician Specialist', trained for aeronautical telecommunications. Just after this, I received a letter from the Ministry of Military Aeronautics, which invited me to choose a post on one of the two hot spots of that time: the Russian Front or the North African Front. In 1941, no one in Italy doubted that the Italo-German Axis would be victorious. At first, I was tempted to choose the Russian Front, although I could not ascertain why that part of the world attracted me so much. On the other hand, I had a vague presentiment that was holding me back, so my mind was unsettled with regards to the Russian campaign. Several nights passed in trying to solve my dilemma, and I eventually opted for the warmth of my Africa. It emerged to be the best choice, as I contributed to the war in the comfortable African climate, instead of the minus forty temperatures of the Russian winter. However, I was still in for a few sad surprises, and shifts in morale, from the enthusiasm of our ongoing advance in 1941, to our defeat in Egypt a year later. What followed was the general capitulation of the Italo-German forces on 11th March 1943.

We briefly flew at a low height over the Libyan coast, and I had a splendid view of thousands of date palms, inducing memories of my youth. I recognised the familiar immense uninhabited spaces, and the light colour of the sandy soil, so similar to that of Somalia; finally, I had come back home! We camped in a tent on the first night, in a palm grove. Before going inside to lie down, I enjoyed the sight of the full moon shining in a clear sky of stars. The soft sandy soil muffled every sound; even the noise of faraway vehicle engines, or the occasional low-flying aircraft was subdued. In the peaceful silence, the only distinct echo was that of dogs from a nearby Arab village. I greatly enjoyed my first night in Africa for over twelve years. It also placated my strong nostalgic yearnings, and I almost forgot the serious nature of my visit. The love that I have for the desert (or semi-desert, like the arid African forests) is a peculiar aspect of my personality – the woods of Europe mean nothing to me in comparison. However, I am not the only one to possess this love of the desert: I share this affinity with all those who have been living on or near this serene place for a long period. Maybe it is the sense of security that comes from the constant solitude and perennial silence that is found only there.

At the beginning of 1941, the war seemed to be favouring the Italo-German forces, as the Germans appeared invincible. We could never have predicted Stalingrad, which subverted the North African situation and effectively altered the outcome of the war. We were concentrating on capturing Alexandria for the time being, and nobody could have guessed that our country would be defeated in a few months. I would soon see the loss of the same soil (Libya) that my father crossed with the Italian Army and captured in 1911. My return symbolised the gap between the two wars; two different periods; two generations under the same flag. I do not intend to describe battle strategies to which I could not directly contribute (due my specialised role); I also do not want to give myself a starring role in a collective effort. I contributed to the war as adequately as millions of other soldiers, but no more; in my opinion, the glory should be reserved for the infantry, the tank crews, and the artillery on the front line. We were nothing compared to them, as we enjoyed all of the privileges of the Air Force. The risk was still only occasional for even the bombers (when operating in normal circumstances). The Navy also enjoyed many privileges (with the exception of the submarines), and supports this point: the brunt of the war is borne by the infantry. As we were considered the specialists, we were deployed only at emergency airports near the front line, an example of this being Fuca, which was only thirty kilometres away from El Alamein.

At the start of October 1942, the 8th Army started the attack on El Alamein. I was located just behind the line in one of the emergency airfields. It was very small, and there were only two squadrons of Italian fighters stationed there: the heavy bombers that were used to attack Alexandria or Suez came from the rear fields. It was also very exposed, and there was no cover from the constant machine-gun fire of our enemies. This was why there were only a small number of planes in the area. Our task was to try and reduce the dominance of the opposition's air force; but the odds were stacked against us. There were an overawing number of enemy fighters, and they were far quicker than us; as if this was not enough, the English Spitfires were equipped with eight machine-guns with twenty-millimetre cannons, in comparison to our seven of twelve millimetres. Another task of our fighters was to fly over the front line to establish our presence and encourage the hopeless soldiers on the ground, who would raise their arms in salute.

From aircraft to tanks, the difference in quality and quantity was too great for us to have any real chance. In these uneven conditions, there was no hope of our troops defending themselves adequately in the flat terrain of the Libyan Desert, and the inevitable result was our surrender. There was often no choice, as there was an advancing sea of English tanks ready to literally squash them. I will give an example of the difference in equipment.

Our army was equipped with hand-grenades which had aluminium outer shells. Inside was a lead envelope that contained hundreds of little spheres of lead, similar to the balls found in shotgun cartridges. These relatively primitive weapons were no match for the pineapple hand-grenades of the opposition. They were made of cast-iron, criss-crossed by grooves, forming lethal metal squares which fragmented at the moment of the explosion, with deadly consequences for anyone in a twenty-metre radius.

This state of affairs was deeply humiliating for our army, as was surrendering. We faced the contempt of the Germans for our meagre support in the African campaign, and later, English jokes concerning our courage and withdrawal. Our marine supply lines had become too hazardous, and those by land, too stretched. Our Navy decided not to risk any more large ships to Egypt, as they were slow and vulnerable to enemy aircraft. Instead, the Generals in Rome decided to transport supplies to our troops in Egypt on barges that were forty metres long, and only required a crew of two or three; they had foolishly thought that the enemy navy would not consider the barges even worth a torpedo. This childish logic was soon proved highly inaccurate; the English Generals knew we were desperate to supply the Egyptian front, and attacked the small fleet with fury. They torpedoed every one of the barges, and sank the majority of them, killing most of the men. The unlucky troops that were chosen for this foolish experiment were the San Marco Battalion Marines, who were armed with only a single machine-gun per boat. However, they undertook their suicidal task with courage and belief. Many of their young corpses were washed ashore on Egypt's coast a few days after the attack.

Since the beginning of June 1942, it had been rumoured that there was a substantial German movement. Unknown to us, they had begun to withdraw from the Egyptian front five months ago to meet a hazard that was right on our shoulders: the imminent landing of American troops, expected on the Algerian coast. British propaganda, via the radio, tried to turn us against the Germans, and suggested that the Germans were abandoning Egypt, and us. However, we knew that the Germans were trying to fight the war on their own – a stark contrast to the English, who used troops of different origins to fight for them. This was the common view before the start of the British offensive in Egypt in October 1942.

After the beginning of this offensive came the order to withdraw eighty kilometres up to the port of Marsa Matruk, which the indigenous population had completely evacuated. On 3rd November 1942, as we awaited the outcome of the ongoing battle, I met a friend of mine from the aeronautics course. His name was Mascherin, and he had also been withdrawn from another emergency airfield on the front line. I remembered him well, as he had the cherubic face of a young child. He now stood before me two years later, and his pale, tired, aged face shocked me, as I am sure mine shocked him. After sharing a tin of beef, he told me that the front had been broken at several points, and he had just managed to escape the encirclement; he also said that Libya had been lost, and that swarms of British tanks were advancing. We then had to say our goodbyes, as he was retreating with another unit.

The next day it was rainy, indicating the beginning of the monsoons in North Africa. The clouds were scattered, and passed by quickly, giving me a sensation of sadness. The ever-present enemy were flying unusually high; but there were no bombing attempts. At last, the order to abandon the post arrived – the enemy forces were advancing more rapidly than envisaged, and as my companion Mascherin told me, the tanks were indeed very close. There was no panic within the men. Our aeronautic unit, which by that time had no planes left, tagged along behind the withdrawing column of troops, and became part of them for one thousand kilometres, from Egypt to Tunisia. The entourage included hundreds of thousands of men, and a variety of transport. There were also remote detachments of men coming in from the vast lateral perimeter of the Egyptian front, who had nothing to do with the front line, but had been necessary to protect the lateral wings of our front, converging to escape otherwise inevitable destruction. The main road was macadamised up to Tripoli, and would permit a rapid advance when not overcrowded; however, due to the vast number of men and vehicles on the road, it was impossible to move at much more than walking pace. Thousands of diesel lorries carried hundreds of men and tons of artillery north; an equal number of lorries carried a similar load south, on the opposite side of the road (I have never known why they were going south). I was amazed to see military lorries going in both directions, full of soldiers armed to the teeth with quadruple-barrelled anti-aircraft guns, in case of an aerial attack (there were also single-barrelled machine-guns on the lorries in case of an attack from the roadside). All these vehicles were in an endless line, travelling at a very slow speed: so slow it was possible to talk to the soldiers going in the opposite direction, if you shouted over the loud diesel engines.

It was an incomparable and unique experience at my tender age of nineteen, and I considered myself privileged to be part of that huge concentration of forces retreating from Egypt. Everyone was dusty and tired; but all were disciplined and obedient, united by the same flag and the defence of our families back in Italy. Some of the vehicles were manned by the Combat SS, who were the equivalent of the military police. They had nothing to do with the political SS, who were later accused of massacres. They used motorcycles to move up and down the road amongst the traffic, and made sure everyone observed the strict rule not to overtake, or they would face death. They promised that they would immediately put anyone 'to the sword' who attempted to overtake another vehicle. 'Put to the sword' roughly meant a bullet through the head, and the vehicle thrown off the road, then set alight. Without any major incident, we passed the Libyan–Egyptian border and were back finally on Libyan soil, and in Italian territory.

When we were about twenty kilometres from the Bardia embankment, we witnessed a battle between our anti-aircraft guns and British bombers. The embankment was part of the road that went from the Egyptian lowland to the Libyan highland of Cirenaica. It was the one and only road in these mountains; it had been constructed by digging up the rocky slopes, and its outer edge hung over the sheer drop below. The road rose steeply with long tortuous bends, which were necessary to reduce the sharp gradient and enabled the heavy vehicles to climb the several kilometres' rise at a very slow speed. The road was a prime objective for the English bombers, but was very difficult to hit due to its narrowness; had they been successful, they would have cut off our only retreat and secured their immediate victory. This would also have shortened the Tunisian campaign by about six months.

The embankment was packed full of anti-aircraft artillery that protected the road from enemy fire. The bombers made several passes over the road, each time unloading their deadly cargo of heavy bombs. However, due to the concentrated fire of our guns, the aircraft had to operate from a very high altitude, and missed the narrow road every time. Eventually they retreated to their base, and we managed to get to the top unscathed. At the summit the road was flat, and the vehicles could travel at a higher speed. All army units now split up and dispersed themselves over the flat highland. After this they reassembled and took up battle positions again. This elevated position was to our temporary advantage, as it allowed us to control the advance of the enemy and hold the front for another month. At the same time, we gave the Germans the opportunity to engage the American Army on the new front created behind our shoulders, in Tunisia.

I wish to tell you of something that I feel is relevant and worthy of mention. It concerns the area near Barce, which I passed through during our retreat.

Barce (or Marj) is a small Libyan town near Benghazi and the Mediterranean coast. During the Fascist Era, Mussolini chose the surrounding territory as a starting base to establish twenty million Italians in Libya, with the intention of transforming this area into a miniature Italy. Substantial oil fields in the area were already known to our researchers So before the Second World War, the Italian Government transferred an initial thirty thousand families from all over Italy to the Barce region. Each family was allocated a plot of this fertile land: Mussolini's plan was to establish the beginning of a large agricultural centre. The centre gradually developed, and there was a steady influx of Italian immigrants, all with the intent of recreating the famous Libyan granaries of the Roman Empire. However, when I passed through this same area perhaps a year after this prosperity, I found the estates abandoned. All the doors were wide open, and everything had been removed by the former occupants and taken to the zone behind the front.

The exodus was for a good reason. The absence of all of the men created a dangerous situation for the women, who were left at home to look after the children. They were therefore at the mercy of the advancing troops, with disastrous effects. The farmers believed that the advancing British were civilised enough to respect the undefended female civilians; but this was not the case. Due to the miscellaneous ethnic composition of the troops, they were difficult to control, and they systematically raped the women that they found cowering in their homes. Whilst I am making this point, I wish you to note that our troops have never abused a conquered population in this way. The Italian and German disciplinary action against this sort of violence would have been of the utmost severity. Our troops knew this, and did not dare to break these laws. I can safely say that during my six years in the Army, I never heard one case of civilian abuse from our side.

The (mainly Australian) troops continued to advance, and simply abandoned the areas that they passed through. They were soon replaced by Arab civilians, who repeated the atrocities of their predecessors. After the first retreat of 1941, the Italians reoccupied that territory, and the Arabs paid a high price for their inhumane behaviour. The farmers' wives left that area for ever when the Italians lost that territory again in 1942. On a more peculiar note, the Italian government offered one million liras cash on the spot to anyone who would marry one of those unfortunate women.

The retreat brought me to Benghazi, Sirte, and finally Tripoli: a trip of about one thousand kilometres. The British fighter planes did not trouble us at all, so the long trip back was almost like a holiday. We stopped wherever we happened to be at the end of the day, enjoying the pleasant climate and the peace of the desert, as the front line was many miles away. This was the advantage of being in a small aeronautical unit: we did not receive many orders from the Army, and enjoyed almost complete autonomy. Our only instructions were to wait for further instructions once we had reached Tripoli. We passed the Tunisian frontier about a month after the order to retreat from El Alamein; but the trip was no longer a retreat. The Axis Army and Air Force were taking up new positions, and preparing once more to oppose the British and American advance; this time on two different fronts. It was the last few days of the year 1942. At that time, we received an order that all the vehicles must not proceed any more in long columns, as was the case during the retreat in Egypt. We were travelling along the road to Tunisia, smaller territory than Libya, and it was dangerous.

The enemy's air force base was across two fronts (Algeria and Libya), which permitted them to efficiently control the restricted territory. Their aeroplanes could easily see us from every angle. In these circumstances, it became prudent to travel only at night with the lights off. We therefore hid the vehicles during the day under nearby trees. The light from the stars was sufficient to enable us to see the road for just a few metres ahead, so we advanced very slowly. The enemy, from the sky, even if they did not see moving lights, knew that on the road beneath there were hundreds of vehicles in transit. Below, we could hear them pass, and sometimes we could even see them flying at low altitude, not more than a hundred metres from the ground. For this night hunting, the English had reserved heavy bomber aeroplanes, the famous four-engine type, which instead of using machine-guns like the Spitfires did during the day, preferred to drop thousands of kilos of small bombs on our heads at night. During this night march, sometimes along the road far away some German vehicles also in transit opened fire with four-barrelled machine-guns when they flew over, and this was a signal to all nearby vehicles on the road to stop and allow the occupants to disperse into the countryside. On one occasion, I saw an aeroplane flying very low and was tempted to fire against it with my rifle, but one of my companions informed me that if I did, they would kill me instantly, so naturally I chose not to open fire. The supply-lines by sea were suspended, as the Straits of Sicily were completely controlled by the Allied forces, so all supplies had to arrive by air. The Germans used several six-engine aeroplanes for this task, and each of these managed to carry either one Super Tiger tank with a 105mm cannon, or three hundred fully equipped troops. It was a superhuman effort, but was still insufficient to fuel the requirements of the Tunisian perimeter, and there was no hope of winning the last stage of the North African Campaign. In fact, we only held out for another six months.

In the first days of March 1943, the American troops from the Algerian side managed to break through the German front near Bizerta. The American success came after many hard month-long battles against the Germans who, as usual, fought for every metre of terrain with exemplary tenacity. We were very surprised the Germans yielded on the Bizerta front.

A week before Easter, the Commonwealth troops attempted to break through our lines, without success. This was why we were surprised that the Germans yielded at Bizerta. Although the war was practically lost, I wish to clarify some situations on the Tunisian fronts at that time. The Germans held one of the fronts against the Americans on the Algerian side. The Italians held one of their fronts against the British 8th Army on the Libyan side. After the American occupation of Morocco and Algeria, France declared the general mobilisation of both these two provinces, which were then under their control. This enabled more than two million Algerian and Moroccan troops to join the Allies at the front line. We were then outnumbered by the enemy four or five to one.

In any case, we were pleased that our line had not buckled. After all, we had done better than the Germans had done in Tunisia. However, the Libyan terrain greatly differed from that of Tunisia. The Tunisian terrain was much more mountainous, and many spots were inaccessible to the armoured vehicles of the enemy. We had lighter artillery and were much more mobile, so we could quite easily combat the Allied tanks, and neutralised their threat for a long period.

After breaking through the German lines, the Americans were

now uncontested and advanced rapidly to Tunis. We received orders to abandon the El Auina airport immediately, and proceed to the Capo Bon peninsula, which was about one hundred kilometres further north. However, in order to get to Cape Bon, we had to go through Tunis, where a revolt was taking place. The French civilian population of Tunis and its surrounding areas had wrongly thought that our troops were now incapable of defending themselves, and they had set about attacking our soldiers. They then attacked all the recovering Italian and German patients in the hospital. After brief and decisive battles on the roads, we re-occupied and held the town until the troops went through. They soon arrived undisturbed at the Capo Bon peninsula.

At the extreme end of Capo Bon was a rocky mountain that dominated the coast down below. On its side were numerous natural caverns and caves of different sizes, ideal for hiding in. In case of a long battle the largest of these was transformed into a storeroom. There was also a vast plain on one side of the mountain, suitable for an emergency landing; it was even sufficient for a heavy bomber. However, this area was not to be used as an airbase, as it would be impossible to defend due to its open nature; its primary purpose was to evacuate some VIP personnel who would be very useful to the remainder of the war effort. The secondary purpose was to try and prevent the enemy capturing the Italian Army flag; but at this stage, this would only be possible through an aerial evacuation. Five Bersaglieri waited at the edge of the field for the arrival of an aircraft which would carry them to safety. The notion of an uncertain future once more confirmed the dedication and courage of the Italian-German Air Force.

This was our only remaining emergency airport in Tunisia, and was situated in a completely exposed spot, without any ground-to-air defences. As this was the last remaining territory in our hands, the enemy aircraft soon located the airport. From our elevated position we had a worrying view.

About thirty kilometres away, between Pantelleria Island and the Tunisian coast, was a vast semicircle of stationary American and English Naval units, ready to open fire. We were in a very difficult situation indeed, as they were observing us closely on radar and through their binoculars; the Italian aircraft would obviously have to fly over that part of the sea, and they would see us switching on our landing lights. However, two planes had already managed to land. The first was a German Junker long-range bomber, and without wasting any time, it collected the VIPs and the Bersaglieri who were escorting the Italian flag to safety.

The second aircraft was an Italian S-84, also a long-range bomber. After it had landed, something very odd happened: it turned around and stood in the take-off position. The pilot had apparently received incorrect information regarding the military situation in Tunisia, and had maybe thought that we had been captured or had surrendered. However, he had obeyed his orders and attempted to land to save the Italian flag (which had already been saved by the Junker). There is also another reason for the pilot's peculiar behaviour; but I must travel back in time slightly to explain it. In 1941 we captured the port of Tobruk, along with a large quantity of victuals and a number of British Army transport vehicles. These vehicles were taken over by the Italian and German armies but were still painted the usual British colonial brown. The pilot from the Italian aircraft saw these vehicles, and would not come out from his cockpit, believing that he was facing the enemy. Our officers were tired of waiting for the pilot, and decided to go and meet him, so they jumped in their vehicles and headed towards the stationary aeroplane. The suspicious pilot's doubts were confirmed when he saw the British vehicles approaching, and he took off immediately, and zoomed away. One hour after this peculiar event, we were waiting on the dark airfield listening for enemy planes. By then we were veterans, and our ears were able to distinguish the sound of our planes from those of the enemy. After a while, we heard a German plane approaching. Unfortunately, when we switched on the landing lights we also attracted a patrolling English fighter. Despite our warning on the radio, the German pilot was still determined to land. There was no moon and the night was very dark: it was impossible to distinguish one aircraft from the other. Gradually the British fighter managed to get close to the German aircraft, and was in an ideal position to attack; however, he waited until the German pilot attempted to land and switched on his lights. It was then a very easy target, and the British plane released a brief burst from his machine-guns. The German aircraft crashed to the ground in flames, killing its crew instantly, and effectively ending the chances of any more planes landing. We were then completely severed from our Fatherland.

We waited for orders at the top of Capo Bon. We were bewildered and disbanded, and there were not enough of us to organise a serious defence; on top of this, our food store was nearly empty, and the English seemed to be very aware of this. Their aeroplanes bombarded us with thousands of brightly coloured pamphlets, all in Italian. They told us that resistance was futile, and tempted us with descriptions of the food that we would enjoy if we surrendered; there were vivid pictures of bread, butter, marmalade, tea and much more. They also suggested that we should not destroy our means of transport, as the Allies were short of vehicles. If we did this, it would mean marching for hundreds of kilometres to reach the prisoner clearing point, and we would be accompanied by the Moroccan troops. The Germans asked us why we were not destroying our vehicles. We told them of the march, and the unappealing escort: going by the evidence of previous Moroccan behaviour, we sure they would see to it that most of us did not make it to the prisoner clearing points. The Germans made their views very clear: they called us Italian shit. I believed our decision was a rational one, and thought that the extreme patriotism of the Germans was decisively stupid. The later events proved that we had acted with pragmatism and intelligence. However, the Germans destroyed all of their vehicles, and many preferred suicide to surrender.

A few hours before the British Army arrived to capture us, the Italian command gave the order to open the stores That enabled us to make use of whatever remained, and prevented it from falling into the hands of the English. However, it later became evident that the British did not intend to use our provisions, and after we were loaded into lorries, an armed sentry exchanged our wristwatches for food. Soon we did not even know the time of day. After we reached the clearing centre at Tunis, the English began to use their vehicles. But the Italian drivers were sharper than the Germans, and they removed some vital parts from the diesel engines of our vehicles rendering them useless. We had avoided the long march, and prevented the British from using our property. However, soon they would have run out of fuel anyway, as there was no supply of diesel in that area.

After we arrived at the great clearing camp at Tunis, some quite unpleasant incidents occurred between our troops and the Germans. Before they were properly organised, the Allies threw a large number of Italian and German prisoners together in a large space on the periphery of the town. They then directed lorries filled with provisions into the camp, without an organised distribution system. It was every man for himself, and there was now an explosive situation between our troops and the Germans. There was no order, no discipline and no guarantee of future provisions. The rations that had been confiscated from our army now arrived in our vehicles (those that we had not yet sabotaged). The choice not to destroy our provisions and vehicles was now paying dividends; however, the Germans, with their customary arrogance, were still proud that they had destroyed their supplies, and despised our decision to save ours, even though it would be these provisions that would now save them. During the war they treated us as insignificant Cinderellas, and would often tell us to 'shut-up', backed up by a menacing wave of their pistols. Now they tried to take possession of the cases that arrived at the centre, so they could consume them in their own groups. The two parties quickly crowded round the lorries, and the assault began as soon as they were stopped. We then set about removing the essential parts of the engines once again. Some Italians had the good luck to obtain a few cases of food; but a group of Germans had the gall to try and take them. However, it soon became evident that our men were far more aggressive than those from the other side of the Alps. They told them that their pistols were no longer there to help them now, and taught them a lesson that they will not forget for as long as they live.

When we were moved from camp to camp, I was always on the first lorry to depart. One day I was in the company of two friends whom I had met in Tunisia prior to our capture. We had managed to stash a small quantity of food, which we had claimed from the stores just before the surrender, and this was very precious to us, considering the irregular meals. Finally we arrived at the infamous Costantina camp. It was vast, big enough to hold about a thousand prisoners, who were all held captive by several rows of steel and masses of barbed wire. It was also easy to join: all you had to do was go through the main gates, and you would be a guest until the end of the war.

The camp had acquired a very bad reputation as a result of the maltreatment inflicted by the Moroccan troops, who adopted a repressive and downright brutal attitude towards the inmates. Many of the prisoners who were unfortunate enough to end up here never saw Italy or their families again. The Moroccans also systematically stole all garments and food sent to the prisoners by the Americans. Everything was pilfered except the meats as the Koran instructs all Muslims to abstain from anything that is slaughtered in the wrong fashion. They will only eat animals that have had their throats sliced whilst pronouncing the words: 'With the will of Allah.' However, they did not hesitate to confiscate the clothing, so the wretched Italian prisoners were transformed into a bunch of ragamuffins and famished beggars. The prisoners at Costantina endured the same treatment as those in the German extermination camps, and received a different one from those in the more civilised parts of Europe.

My two friends and I seriously considered remaining in that place, but were altogether undecided whether this was the correct decision. However, one day I discovered them eating some of our little reserve of food behind my back; this made me conclude that their morals were far different to mine, and without any comment or goodbye, I jumped onto one of the outbound lorries, and never saw them again.

During the first part of that day, my bad luck continued. We fell into the hands of some Moroccans, who ordered us to step down from the lorry and form a long queue. We then were marched for thirty kilometres, kindly accompanied by the Moroccan troops and their fixed bayonets. Even though it was a gruelling encounter, the sight of the Moroccans was a source of mirth throughout the whole march: the bayonets and rifles were so big that they dwarfed the small Arab soldiers!

Some of the Italian prisoners were carrying very heavy bundles of food, which they were obviously very reluctant to abandon. After several kilometres of marching, one began to stagger, and soon fell to the ground. I can assure you that he did not get any sympathy from the Moroccan escort, who convinced him to get up by hitting him on the back with the butt of his rifle. If he had been unable to get up, then he surely would have been executed on the roadside, as the Moroccans had no intention of herding along a slow prisoner. Soon another man started to wobble and flopped to the ground. As he was making an effort to rise, he was struck sharply between the shoulders with the rifle. Knowing that every fall would merit a blow, he was forced to drop the twenty-litre can of olive oil that had been in his possession since the time of his capture. Maybe he was dreaming of twenty-litres' worth of roasted chickens. They would be a long time coming.

I heard much later that the Trento Division, who were captured on the internal side of Tunisia, had been marched for hundreds of kilometres. With some help from the Moroccan bayonets, most of them died by the roadside.

At about five o'clock in the afternoon, we arrived at a classified post, which was full of lorries. It was a British base that was assigned to sort the transiting prisoners; some of them, the luckier ones, were even sent to America. Here we were handed over to the English, thank God. We learnt that we would stay together as a unit and be transferred to England to work in the agricultural sections, which were of high importance in wartime. The Germans were separated from us and sent elsewhere. After letting us go hungry for the day, the English had a surprise for us. They had prepared a warm meal; but I forget what it was. From the time of our surrender, our meals had consisted of what we called in military jargon 'emergency rations', i.e. hard biscuits and tinned meat, which can be consumed without a mess-tin, so this unexpected treat was extremely welcome. However, the generous British initiative had inadvertently created some distress for those who had lost their mess-tin and spoon. The soldiers without those utensils risked exclusion from the dinner, and after an arduous day of marching without food, the last thing the prisoners wanted was this unexpected obstacle. They were forced to find a solution, or go without dinner, and I can only assume that they borrowed the utensils from a kind soul. However, most were so excited about the unexpected meal that they momentarily forgot about the plight of others.

The British had organised the distribution of our dinner in two distinct lines about ten metres apart: one Italian, and one German. The line of the Germans was strangely more disciplined, and they consequently ate far more quickly and efficiently than the Italians. We ended up finishing two hours later than the Germans, and I can only assume that this was because there were far more of us. Also, many Italians were waiting for their companions to finish in order to borrow their utensils. At the end of it all, our bellies were full and peace was re-established, so everyone went to look for a space on the grass on which to pass the night.

The slightly sloping ground was uncomfortable to sleep on. At every unconscious movement my body slid a little further down, and after a few hours I awoke a metre away from my original spot. That night's sleep was insufficient for people who were as fatigued as we were, although we were certainly not complaining. We formed small groups of friends that evening; the general idea was to stick with people you knew, as there would be much moral support required for the long days ahead. It is remarkable how completely different characters unite under strange circumstances, even though these superficial relationships would not stand even the first serious test. Quarrels often leave a bitter taste in one's mouth, as I experienced when I discovered my friends eating our meagre reserve of food. It is always hardest to find loyalty when you need it most. Rather than sharing my loyalty with those whose personalities were unknown, I decided that I would be better off on my own.

A few groups of people still found time to discuss the events of the day in murmured undertones, which collectively sounded like a mass prayer. The problems and obstacles that faced us were always worth discussing, even if it meant losing some precious sleep. The main subject of the whispering was the awkward business with the Moroccan troops; but also, more positive thoughts for the now altogether brighter future.

Once more that night, the African sky did not disappoint me. I exchanged a wink with the brilliant stars over us; there was not a cloud in the sky, and the moon was shining on our grass carpet. Our garments were light colonial attire, and nobody complained of not having a blanket; it was not needed, the warm nights of April were on our side. Someone pulled out a mouth organ and started playing. Everyone knows how pleasant and relaxing the sound from this simple instrument can be, and this player knew his business. The unknown minstrel began the marvellous music of *La Paloma*: sad and sentimental, very appropriate for the moment and the mood of the listeners. The murmuring and whispering stopped and, as if by magic, everybody began to listen. I was sure that the thoughts of my companions were far away, with their families, their towns and villages, and as to when and if they would see them again. These thoughts did not concern me. I had an advantage over my companions: my sentiments were easier to manage than the majority of others'. My thoughts could not wander back to those who were waiting for me, as there was no one. That magic moment lasted as long as the tune and after that there was only complete silence, observed by all. That April night remained in my memory, like my youth in Somaliland by the Uebi Scebeli River with my family, but very few other events did.

Chapter 4

The following morning we all climbed on lorries again, and off we went. The next few days were continuous travelling, alternating between lorry and train; fortunately, the train carriages were open, so we could view the sprawling panorama throughout the journey. However, the rations were reduced to one meal a day, and it was not a warm one. This diet lasted for weeks, and you cannot imagine how tough it was. Luckily, my physique coped well in that testing period: I was one metre seventy-five tall, and when I arrived in Britain my weight was down to fifty kilos (this would be similar to an inmate of a German concentration camp). Our situation was severely testing, and I am pleased to say that I survived without falling ill once. The factor that saved most of us was undoubtedly the African climate; in any other place, such as Northern Europe or Russia, most of us would surely have perished. However, there was always the danger of malaria, especially in Constantina, which we passed through briefly. In that period we prayed that our strength would not fail us, as it would have meant certain death at the hands of the Moroccan rabble.

A British sentry armed with a rifle would stroll back and forth along every couple of wagons. He knew very well there was nothing to guard. They were all elderly, and we could see that they felt sorry for us; there seemed to be a mutual understanding that did not need to be expressed in words. We did not consider them as enemies by this time, but fellow soldiers, just a bit more fortunate to be on the winning side; we never received any abuse or one bad word. They observed Christian principles, and displayed typical European civility (later I learnt that the English prisoners in Italy had been treated with equal respect).

Eventually we reached the port of Algiers, where groups of prisoners had arrived from all over the territory. Allied ships were littered on the seabed of the port, confirmed by the ghostly image of their topsails poking out of the water. This in itself confirmed that the efforts of our torpedo planes had been successful when trying to hinder the Allied landing in Algeria, and took me back to the period in Sardinia with my bomber squadron. We were all young and enthusiastic, fresh from military school, ready to join one of the various battles. As demonstrated by the Algiers anchorage, we had achieved satisfactory results.

I was loaded onto a large cargo ship with about four thousand other prisoners. The convoy was of about thirty vessels, and was escorted by a number of warships. They did not allow us above deck when the ship left the African coast, and as soon as we were in the hold we began to acquaint ourselves with our new travelling companions. I met a fellow called Cumpare Fuonzu, who stood out because he had served an eight-year prison sentence for killing his wife; but I do not remember why. He was a natural storyteller, and would entertain us during those long days in the hold by telling us tales from a book that he had read in jail. These stories were interminable, and the English sentry could not understand what he had to say that was so interesting. He was about forty years old, and became very popular with us, a sort of paternal figure, whose experience you could learn from.

He gave good advice to us youngsters by telling us of his wrongdoings before and after his prison sentence, and soon became our mentor, instructing us on fighting techniques. He maintained that it was always good to have a knife at hand; he even went so far as to give us the specifications. He told us that the best weapon had a triangular blade, a very sharp point, and must be no longer than ten centimetres. After this, he drew one out to show us (all of our weapons were supposed to have been confiscated). His advice was to pierce the buttocks of your opponent, no deeper than two centimetres, if possible. At this depth it would not be fatal, but is a very effective deterrent; the wound prevents the recipient from sitting down for a substantial period, and takes a very long time to heal. They will therefore be forced to rest face down, as any pressure on the rump will be likely to break the stitches. Master Alfonso asserted that this punishment always had a prolonged psychological effect on the other man, and greatly reduced the chances of another quarrel with that particular person.

A massive wooden grille that weighed at least a ton held us prisoners in the hold, and was controlled by a chain attached to a capstan. During the day this grille was usually open; but an armed sentry always blocked our route to the deck. From ten to eleven o'clock we were allowed onto the deck for one hour of fresh air; but we were not too grateful, as the May air over the Atlantic was not especially agreeable. As we had come from Africa, our garments were not thick enough to repel the cold that blew right through us; therefore most of us preferred to stay below deck.

Every time the submarine alert was sounded, the sentinel immediately switched the capstan on and the grille slammed shut. We were then enclosed within the hold without any chance of escape. On one occasion we could hear the explosion of depth charges that were deployed by English torpedo boats. This alert lasted for a long hour, and if a torpedo from a German U-boat had hit us, it would have been curtains. During these explosions we crowded round the grille to ask the sentry what was going on above. He reassured us that he would open the grille if the ship was sinking; but I was sure that he would not keep his promise if a torpedo hit us. I moved away from the crowd as I considered their pleas to be useless: the grille would remain closed. I leaned against the bulkhead and prepared myself to die, pondering how long it would take to drown in the cold waters of the Atlantic. It was a terrible and terrifying experience. Gradually the explosions became more and more distant, until all was silent, and I am here to tell the tale.

The sailors told us that the trip from Algiers to Scotland would have taken five days in peacetime. However, to avoid German attacks we had to sail towards Canada, and then turn toward Britain. The entire voyage took eleven days, and was quite tranquil apart from the experience described above.

On 11th May 1943, our ship entered the port of Glasgow. Although it was a cold day, the sun was shining. We observed the harbour and wharf curiously, and the first thing that we noted was the absence of people; apart from the sailors of our ship, there was no one around. This was peculiar, and some of us thought that everyone must have been evacuated due to German bombardments. However, this was not the case; there was no trace of bombing, or any form of destruction around the harbour, which is normally the primary target when attacking a port. Later, someone told us that the Germans had practically ignored Glasgow as far as bombing was concerned. This strategy has always remained an unsolved mystery to me.

After docking we were put into a column of four rows, four thousand prisoners long. We marched for a few kilometres and then crossed a large avenue, where we saw the famous red double-decker buses for the first time. I can still remember the people in the buses eyeing our colonial uniforms with curiosity. When in a complete unit we displayed a range of different uniforms, including the Army, Air Force and Navy. Our destination was the Glasgow football ground, where a hot bath and POW uniforms were waiting for us. They were fairly similar to the British Army uniforms, but ours were a red-brown colour. There was a thirty-five-centimetre yellow or blue recognition patch on our back, and a smaller one on our thigh. We were also given a pair of heavy shoes, which were in fact the same as those used by the British Army, and a brand-new undergarment, made of pure wool. To complete the Christmas-esque presentation, we had a knapsack to keep all our equipment in, as well as all the other hardware and mess-tin. It really was a comforting sensation to receive such treatment, and after the distribution was completed, the 'icing on the cake' arrived: a warm meal. It was a dream after weeks of malnutrition.

All our worries seemed to be over, including the war. In the year 1943, we could already consider ourselves survivors. After that welcome meal, they directed us to the stands, where every prisoner stretched out over four seats: ample space for a person to sleep on. One thing that was very irritating was the angle of the sun, which seemed settled low on the horizon, and would not go down. As nobody had a watch, we could only guess the time, and we estimated it to be about five or six o'clock. Why would the sun not set? In the end, somebody solved the puzzle: in a place as far north as Scotland, night would only last a short period in the summer months; in any case, the nights are never completely dark, and the remaining light is enough to permit reading, albeit with some difficulty. Some of us preferred not to go to sleep at all, as in a few hours it would be light again, and this meant another day of work, travelling or, worst of all, walking.

The first concentration camp I was sent to was about three kilometres from the periphery of the famous university city of Oxford. They put me in an army hut, together with twenty-nine companions. It had twelve barracks, and was occupied by three hundred and fifty prisoners. We slept in bunk beds, which were warm, comfortable, spacious, and easy to keep clean. Two simple and efficient coal stoves provided adequate warmth during the winter.

The English authorities were treating us with respect and consideration. They provided everything necessary to make our temporary stay in their country pleasant, and did not even show much preference to their own troops! They really were great people, and even though they gave a lot, they considered their hospitality customary. Contrary to what most of us believed (like the tales of their famous five daily meals), I learnt afterwards that they had suffered a lot in their past, especially in the time of industrialisation. I discovered that after the First World War some children of poor families were going to school shoeless in winter, with their feet in direct contact with the ice on the road. I learnt this from a reliable Welsh companion at work, who assured me that it was a common occurrence in those days. I also discovered that in the same epoch England had one of the highest rates of tuberculosis in Western Europe, due mainly to malnutrition. I believe that this miserable past has moulded the English into the great people that they are today.

I would advise anyone that visits England to pay a visit to the old coal mines in the Midlands. The 'Black Country' is perhaps the most unadulterated reflection of the hard times that this country has seen: even the houses that the coal miners lived and suffered in are still untouched.

The entrance to the mine was a hole in the ground with a diameter of about three or four metres. Every morning the miners would be loaded into a basket and lowered into the terrible darkness, where they would remain all day. In the winter, when the nights were long, the miners would not see daylight for months. Boys and girls still at a tender age were also sent to work in the mine, in order to try and slightly improve their miserable lives financially. The age at which they started work was usually left to their father's discretion; but it was possible for a child to start working at the ridiculous age of seven. Girls were no exception: all members of the family had to contribute to their poverty-stricken lives. The young were usually employed to carry the caskets of coal produced by their fathers to a collection point; from there, the coal was forwarded to different destinations for consumption. Only once you see the entrance to the mine can you even begin to grasp the inhumane and horrific practices of the Industrial Revolution, and spare a thought for the mothers and fathers who had given life to their children and did everything they could to help them; but then saw them slowly deteriorate into ill health and general hardship. The sight of thousands of houses that were made for those unlucky workers is almost as depressing and saddening: small red brick houses packed next to each other, with just about enough space to sleep in; two small bedrooms, cold but humid, filled with melancholy children; a miserable kitchen, transformed into a living area because of its comparative warmth, the place where the family spent most of their monotonous evenings. It also had another important use in the wintertime: it was used to dry the washing that was permanently stained by the filth of the mine.

A blacksmith was a common occupation in the coal mines; however, if he wanted to keep his precious job, he had to produce a chain of about a thousand rings at the end of each day, and these had to be heavy enough to be used for a ship's capstan or anchor. They were bent by forge and hammer to hold them together, and to maintain this level of production it was necessary to work for sixteen hours a day, six days a week.

I am stating these facts in order to refute the myth that the English have always been rich people with fat bellies who lie around all day, as they have nothing better to do. However, I was not to enjoy the tasks that the English set for us. We were working in the agricultural sections, and I only had a very limited knowledge of this type of work, and no experience. The English expected us to help them produce food for their nation in exchange for our upkeep until the end of the war. I had never even seen a bull before, as I had lived for the majority of my life in Rome, and certainly did not know how to use a hoe or any other agricultural equipment. I would almost certainly severely reduce the efficiency of the whole operation, and I prepared myself to tell the Camp Commandant of this unfortunate problem. However, I need not have worried. We were ordered to form groups of ten prisoners, and we were each accompanied by a sentry and a civilian, who told us how to do the simple work on the perimeter of the field.

The first assignment of my group was to clean the small drainage canals around the cultivated fields. These canals were about one metre wide by eighty centimetres deep, and at the bottom there was a small amount of stagnant water, caused by the build-up of grass, mud and small shrubs. Our job was to restore the steady flow of rainwater by removing all of this debris. The entire area needed the same maintenance; but to treat all of it would have taken about forty years! The owner said that the last serious maintenance to these canals was during the First World War. On that occasion, German POWs had carried out the work.

One of our fellow prisoners had died and when we visited the cemetery near the camp, we were surprised to see tombstones with German inscriptions. They were the tombs of eighteen German prisoners who died during the previous war, doing exactly the same work as us. A question immediately came to my mind: which other nationalities would clean these canals in future wars? They may also leave some dead behind, and they again will be forgotten, and become irrelevant.

Relations with my barrack companions were completely and mutually distanced; no one was interested in being any more than generally civil, and this attitude remained during the years we were together. As for the inmates of the other barracks, I occasionally exchanged a few words now and then, as you would with the tenants of a large apartment block in a city. In that place nobody possessed anything, and if you did it was yours: there was no need to share it with anyone else.

Once a week on Sunday, they counted us to make certain we were all present. After the count and before our release, we went through the ritual salute to the Fatherland, symbolically represented by the King and the Duce. To the call: 'Salute the King', we all replied together: 'Hail the King'. To the call: 'Salute the Duce' (Duce – from the Latin *Dux*, the same root as *inducere*: Leader – Commander), we would reply: 'To us', with the traditional fascist salute: the extension of the right arm and hand at ninety degrees. It was quite an impressive ceremony, and gave an impression of great discipline and homogeneity to the occasional passer-by. The English always observed this ceremony with curiosity, and did not have any objection to it, as it did not concern them.

At the beginning of my stay at that camp, a fellow Roman prisoner in the bunk next to me called Trani unexpectedly gave me a lesson in altruism. His way of seeing things never crossed my mind during my years in the orphanage, and was a lesson for which I was very grateful. Trani was a persistent cigarette smoker, and in accordance with terms of the Geneva Convention we had the right to forty cigarettes a week. I thought it only natural that

I should sell my ration of cigarettes, as I was a non-smoker, and with the money obtained I could buy a couple of bottles of beer at the prison canteen, or perhaps some cake. I offered my cigarettes to Trani; but he rebuked me. He pointed out that smoking was not essential to survival, but eating reasonably was. Cigarettes were obviously not as important as eating, and to deprive himself of the little food money he had to buy my cigarettes could have severely jeopardised his health. I found his argument convincing: I had no right to take advantage of the situation, so I decided to always give him my cigarettes for nothing, and renounce my two bottles of beer.

From that moment on I understood the true meaning of altruism. I believe that I always had sacrificial characteristics in me, but I needed an incident like this to bring them to the surface. Aided by a book on the subject, I analysed what had happened more deeply, and came to realise that true satisfaction in life does not come from receiving, but from giving. However, Trani soon repaid me.

Trani was much older than I, and had his own story to tell. He told me that when he was in action in North Africa a bullet entered his chest and pierced one of his lungs. Aided by the dry Libyan climate, the wound eventually healed, although not easily. He was captured while he was still in hospital, and was obviously very resentful about this. The wound still occasionally troubled him, and he would constantly curse the war (and those that had sent him into it). He hoped that he would not get any worse and die in a place as cold and as humid as England, where he would join our comrade and the German soldiers in the cemetery.

The POW leader, an Italian Army sergeant, had the idea of putting together a group of improvised amateur actors to perform in a theatre, which would offer some diversion from the everyday monotony. He was therefore looking for volunteers to act in his production. The thespian life never really appealed to me: I never liked the idea of impersonating something I was not. However, the sergeant had noticed me – a beardless youngster, with a slim body: exactly what he was looking for, and I believe he did not even pause for a moment to think what effect his proposition would have. He marched straight up to me while I was talking with Trani, and suggested that I should fill the role of a beautiful girl, heroine of the comedy *Arsenic and Old Lace*. The consequences of playing a woman could certainly have been serious in an environment without women; what was more, it could have raised serious doubts about my masculinity! The sergeant's words appalled me; however, before I could answer, Trani interrupted indignantly. He excitedly told the sergeant that the Romans were notorious for having the sword at hand to strike people down, and were not renowned for dressing up like women. I thought the retort was quite adequate and required no further comment. The sergeant obviously had expected that kind of reply – he laughed loudly and went away.

Anyway, another young man eventually played the part of the beautiful woman, and the play was a great success. He was much broader, with wide wrestler's shoulders, and there was nothing feminine about him whatsoever.

Our mess was fitted with a radio receiver that the English had not confiscated, and we could listen to the war bulletins. Every evening after dinner, most of us would crowd round it, and hope for a turnaround in fortunes.

Our camp must have been located beneath a transit point for an Allied bomber unit, as hundreds of aircraft would fly over us in formation, and head in the direction of Central Europe; somehow, with a pang in my chest, I sensed the imminent surrender of Italy. A short while later we heard the news of our capitulation, and the camp fell under a cloud of silence that lasted several days. The gloomy atmosphere gradually disappeared, and life slowly returned to normal. The prisoners soon divided themselves in two groups: in one, all the die-hards who would not accept defeat; in the other, those who thought that it was better this way, as the end of the war would mean the possibility of going home. After Italy's elimination, there were no immediate changes in our life; however, there was a feeling in the air that English attitudes were changing. We were sure that there would be some sort of important news soon.

Towards the end of 1943, I had an unpleasant experience. It all began with a quarrel I had with the civilian who was accompanying our group, and the perennial sentry. The civilian was from Eastern Europe, and was responsible for checking that we were doing our work correctly, as he answered to the owner of the land. He also spoke good Italian, and was in the habit of stopping for an occasional conversation with us as we worked. However, he did not have the same view of our situation as the English, and unfortunately was only too keen to express his attitude and feelings towards us. As an East European refugee, he understandably had a strong resentment towards the Germans, and consequently towards us too. Unlike the English, who never discussed the war with us, he often talked about England as if it was his country, and boasted about 'their' victory.

Our gang of ten prisoners was divided again into five groups of two: one to use the pickaxe, the other the shovel. One day, whilst I was pausing to take a moment's rest, the assistant insinuated that the Italian troops preferred surrender to combat. This implication was met by an insult, and I also told him to think about the disaster of his own country, and requested that he not discuss matters of this nature with Italian prisoners, as the regulations were very clear concerning his relations with us. That evening coming back from work, the sentry stopped me at the gate, took me to the small camp prison, and locked me up.

I firstly wish to explain that this prison was not like the regular confinement where they detained ordinary criminals: this place was only for minor military infractions. The maximum prison sentence in these cases was never more than twenty-eight days; but particularly serious cases guaranteed a stern regime of bread and water for two days, alternated with normal meals every third day.

The Camp Commandant was Colonel Warren, an English officer with a prominent moustache. He would often caress this moustache, particularly when he was reflecting on something. During the First World War the Germans had taken him prisoner, and he was given a very bad time. He had a reputation for great severity; one reason for this was that the Germans had always harshly punished any English prisoner that quarrelled with German personnel. He now always looked for revenge, and exacted it on anyone who was unfortunate enough to cross his path. The next morning I myself was brought to him, and he was graced with a military ceremony that really was a sight to behold. I was flanked by two English soldiers, who sharply clicked their heels and saluted the Colonel. I had been told by other prisoners who had witnessed the same spectacle to watch for the Colonel caressing his moustache, as each caress equalled seven days in prison; sometimes he used both hands to save time! The assistant then accused me of refusing to work, and the Colonel listened to my argument with the help of an interpreter. He had a paternal look about him and did not seem menacing at all, and after having denied the accusations against me, and observing the good-natured face of the Colonel, I had the feeling that I was out of trouble. However, after some deep thought, he lifted his hand to reach his lethal moustache. I counted four caresses: it was the maximum sentence, and in addition, he gave me seven days of bread and water. He had fixed me a nice holiday! However, the next day, when I was supposed to start my bread and water regime, I had a pleasant surprise. The sentry on duty brought me a normal meal instead of the prescribed bread and water, and a very abundant one at that. He told me to consume the meal as quickly as possible in case one of his superiors discovered it. I responded with a grateful gesture, pleased that there was some comradeship between one soldier and another, even if they were from opposing nations. However, when different sentries were on duty the following days, I still received the same generous meal, and I suspected that the Colonel had perhaps renounced his order to ration me.

The routine in the eight prison cells was generally the same as those adopted in the normal camp. At five-thirty every morning the sentry on duty would enter the building and allow the inmates to visit the lavatory. We would then proceed to clean out the barracks. The toilets were all located in one room, and the inmates had the opportunity to converse for a little while; after thirty minutes, the sentry would return and again lock all the prisoners in their respective cells. We would then be served breakfast through a small window in the door of our rooms.

During my term there was only one other man in the prison. He was a rogue and a habitual client of the building, and was likely to have been a criminal in Italy; it was also very possible that he was one of the convicts released when we were forced to retreat. There was an assortment of his type among us who openly bragged about their wrongdoings. They had clearly not learnt from their mistakes, and always carried a knife to gain respect, steal and look menacing. I had also heard reports from other prisoners in African camps of attacks on young prisoners with sexual intent. These attacks often took place in the toilets, and were quite frequent, not to mention dangerous. Therefore groups of friends had formed associations, and went to the lavatories en masse during the night.

His name was Rabaglino, and his cell was at the other end of the prison barrack, on a diagonal line from my own. He was about four inches taller than me at six foot one, and ten to fifteen kilograms heavier (I then weighed about sixty-two kilos). My physical condition was excellent, and the doctor said that I was one of the fittest people in the camp. Weight for weight, I think I could have held my own with anyone in the camp, unless he was a professional wrestler. Unknown to me, Rabaglino had chosen me to be his 'wife'. He had noticed the sentry's half-hour absence every morning after having opened our cells and he had made a plan to sexually assault me. But he would find a nasty surprise waiting for him.

As usual, the English sentry left the barracks, and we were on our own. I finished dressing, and was about to go to the toilets to wash my face, when I bumped into Rabaglino at the door of my cell. He did not waste any time, grabbing my arms and twisting, trying to turn me around. Although he had taken me by surprise, I recovered quickly, and went into action. I put my arm around his waist, ready for my usual 'ancata' attack. The stupid man fell for it: he mistook my embrace for a submission or an amorous advance, and relaxed his grip. I then bent my knees and when I stood up Rabaglino found himself forty centimetres off the ground, and could do nothing. I rolled his body onto my hip joint and despatched him onto the floor in a spectacular manner. He fell onto my feet with the scared look of a thrashed dog: he had never expected such an energetic reaction from someone as slim as me, and was lucky that I was still too naive to finish him off the in the way that he deserved. I was still abiding by the laws of the orphanage, where the rule was never to hit a man lying on the ground. Rabaglino picked himself up and quickly left my cell, without looking back once.

Our lack of experience in the agricultural field sometimes ended in a comical farce. It was sometimes possible to go and live outside the camp with the English landowner, who would provide separate accommodation. There were many advantages for the prisoners who chose to adopt this arrangement. Firstly, he would become part of the host family. The farmer relied on the young arms of the prisoners, and often gave them his maximum confidence; in some cases, he would go as far as lending the prisoner a double-barrelled gun to go hunting for pheasants and rabbits in the evenings. These lucky prisoners occasionally came to visit the camp on weekends to catch up with their friends, and would try to persuade them to attempt to adopt the same life that they were enjoying. They would describe their life as almost the same as being in your own family, with an abundance of food, and sometimes even short love affairs! We would listen to them eagerly; but I was not entirely convinced: what bothered me was the fact that they had to get up at three o'clock every morning, and my good sense told me that this should be avoided, especially in the cold, dark winter months. One of their numerous early morning tasks was to milk a hundred cows. Frankly, I had the impression that our friends were trying to convince themselves rather than us that they had made the right decision.

They maintained that their only unpleasant job was looking after the bull; if you were not careful then you could be in a lot of trouble. In addition to cleaning him, there was also the precarious task of encouraging the beast to come out of the shed to keep the cows company. It sounds simple, but the beast is an enemy to everything that moves, with the exception of his cows. After he had enjoyed his period of freedom, which lasted from morning to late afternoon, he would have to be put back, and this was just as dangerous and difficult. However, one friend joked that there was no need to be scared of the bull; all you had to do was keep a fork near at hand, and he told us that nothing would happen to you if you followed these rules:

After having removed the chain from his nose, you must immediately rest the pointed end of the fork between his horns, and pace slowly backwards when he pushes. Never make sudden movements, as the animal is very irascible, and would take any sudden movement as an attack. Never lose your nerve and try to flee, otherwise the animal may think that he has defeated you, and would then certainly attack. (Before I continue, I must say something whilst on the subject of the agricultural tools used in England. The shovels, forks and God knows what other similar paraphernalia all had short handles. This compelled the poor person who was using a tool to bend down for the duration of the job, and when he rose, he felt as if his back had been virtually broken.) Anyway, in this operation, the short length of the fork handle meant that you had a very uncomfortable close-up view of the beast. English bulls are all first class and are enormous. They would often pass our enclosure whilst they were under the restraint of their yoke, but they were still very intimidating. They observe the environment with their reddened eyes, and from their hostile look it is clear that they are not fond of our presence; if they were given the opportunity, then it is evident that they would like to do nothing better than stick their horns between your bones. I have already mentioned that you should show a bull no fear, and I have an example of what could happen to you, as told by one of these men who had left the camp.

Once during the operation of taking the bull out of the shed, the helper noticed that it was in a worse mood than usual, and as he was pushing harder, the fork broke. With his defence gone, he turned and fled. Until things went wrong, he and the beast had reached a field of beetroot that was near the cowshed and was very muddy. Before he got even one metre away, the bull hit him like a train, throwing him several metres away. He started to roll in the mud and screamed for help; but none arrived. The beast kept trying to gore him with his horns, but luckily only succeeded in rolling him over and over. The man was now completely covered in mud, and only the whites of his eyes were visible. At last the farmer arrived with a spare fork, and by this time he must have uprooted more than fifteen square metres of beetroot. The courageous farmer then managed to secure the bull with the point of the fork, and surely saved the life of his desperate helper. After he had finished, I said thanks, but I prefer the tranquillity of the camp! I had also remembered the story of the city mouse (which has a life full of trouble), and the country mouse (which has a peaceful life) that I had learnt at primary school, and when I recounted it in Napolitan dialect, it provoked uncontrollable laughter from all who were present.

Occasionally during our working day we ourselves encountered bulls freely roaming in the fields. After this story we gave them the maximum respect they deserved: even though there was a wooden gate between us, it was always a good idea to keep an eye on these unpredictable animals. The first rule was never to walk across the middle of their field when crossing it, as you would have little chance of making it to the fence. When a bull is with his cows, it is possible to pass comparatively near him; let us say thirty metres. At this distance, he will be undecided whether to attack you or remain with the herd. However, it is still not a good idea to stray far from the gate, and if he begins to paw the ground threateningly with his front hoof, you know you are in danger. It is then time to start for the nearest gate at full speed. I often heard stories of prisoners who did not show the bull maximum respect, and landed themselves in trouble. They found themselves being chased by a ton of angry bull, and had to break the hundred-metre world record to escape them. In spite of the seriousness, these stories always brought laughter from the listeners – all you could picture was the poor bastard running for his life, with an angry bull in pursuit!

Half a century later, I was reading the English *Daily Telegraph* newspaper, just after writing this episode on the bull. The paper reported that a man had been gored to death by a bull against a car. He had tried to reach his car before the beast did, but without success. This image is not so amusing, and the victim is only one of the numerous victims of bulls over the years.

I have one more story concerning animals and our lack of agricultural experience, which is not quite as morbid, and this time concerns a Venetian prisoner. He agreed to take care of two or three hundred piglets that belonged to a British breeder, as he was convinced that it was a prime opportunity to improve the standard of his life. The food we got at the camp was good enough for a normal life, but nothing compared to what he would get at the house of the breeder.

Unlike others who had external jobs, our Venetian companion came back to the barracks every evening. He went to work on a bicycle every day. It was fifteen kilometres away through the English farmland; he said that the ride put him in a good mood. However, he soon realised that the quoted number of piglets was no exaggeration, and told us they had taken him for their adopted mother. Every time he passed their enclosure, they would squeak loudly to try and get some more food. Even from afar, the blessed little beasts were able to smell him, and would squeal with excitement; he wondered how they could have such sensitive noses. After a year on that job, he felt as though he was turning into a pig himself. When he heard the yelps of the piglets and the grunts of the sows, his hairs would stand on end, just like theirs did. He was often tempted to turn the bike around and head for the safety of the camp. The beasts always knew when their mother was coming, and he would always be greeted by the noise of three hundred little rumps rushing to meet him.

However, the family were very nice as usual, and every morning at ten o'clock work was suspended, and he was invited in for a substantial bowl of Scotch broth, a very nourishing soup. He would then immediately forget his stressful work and tell himself to be more patient, even if he did know that he now had a permanent porcine smell, which hung around him and penetrated the thick wool of his prisoner's uniform. He would be fed again in the evening, just to make sure that he did not forget about the advantages of his situation. When I was transferred from this camp, my Venetian companion was still taking care of his piglets.

For us the war was over. However, we still had to consider our loyalty to our ex-ally, Germany; but this area was very unstable. Our relationship over the past four years had been characterised by a number of regular incidents, mostly negative occurrences. Witnesses that were present at these scenes would always look at the bad side of them instead of seeing them for what they were, giving the impression of an emerging gulf between the two forces. For instance, if a German soldier was guarding the water pump and refused an Italian soldier access to it, it would be perceived as an act of hostility, even though the German was merely obeying orders. The Italian would then report the incident as an act of resentment, and would widen the gulf between the two forces even further. However, there was evidence suggesting that the Germans always favoured their own troops over ours.

One instance was when the Italian ship *Il Conte Rosso* sank in the straits between Sicily and Libya. My friend Cucciardi from the Air Force assured me that the German soldiers fought the Italians in the water in order to get the best fragments of the ship, and our men were repelled every time they tried to grab a scrap. Another example was on the Russian front, where half-empty German lorries refused to pick up Italians during the retreat over the freezing plains, thereby condemning them to certain death.

There was never any real friendship between the Germans and us. They mostly displayed an endemic arrogance, probably fuelled by the fact that they had superior armaments to ours. It is true they had some spectacular victories, which awarded them some acclaim; but it did not give them the excuse to behave the way that they did, and our resentment was aroused entirely by this air of supremacy. However, the war came first, and we put these differences aside. If we had been victorious, then all would have been forgotten.

* * *

At the end of 1944, our situation in the camp changed drastically. The British Army authorities asked who wanted to co-operate with them until the end of the war; by this they meant working closely with them and not sabotaging any of their operations. In exchange, they offered the liberty to leave the camp at any time after working hours and at weekends. The decision was difficult: either remain loyal to our roots and companions that had fallen, or co-operate with our enemy. Half the members of our camp chose not to co-operate, and at first I was inclined to do this as well. However, after debating the matter at length with myself, I decided that co-operation would be the pragmatic option. Once again, the British commanders showed great experience in handling and neutralising a potentially dangerous situation. Early in the morning, two days after our decision, the group that had decided not to co-operate were loaded into lorries and driven to the railway station. They were then taken to a Scottish camp.

Those of us who had remained in the camp continued to work as before. It was then September 1944, and the beginning of autumn, when the rain becomes more persistent and the sky is always grey. We then participated in a new agricultural experiment, which was called the campaign of the potato. The potato is as valuable in Britain as wheat is in Italy. Before the autumn frost starts, it is necessary to provide cover and protection for this vital product, as in some areas of Scotland the ground may begin to harden as early as September. The great Irish potato famine is a harsh reminder of the crop's importance.

Potato picking is a tiring, backbreaking job. I would certainly not recommend it as a good occupation, nor would I choose it over the majority of other professions. Firstly you must remove the potatoes from the ground by hand, one at a time. You must then clean the mud off with your fingers, and then put it into a container that will transport it to the silos, where it is dried. The discomfort obviously arises from the hunched position that you must adopt all day; your back is constantly screaming for you to straighten up. However, the English farmer, who understood the difficulty of the job, devised an ingenious scheme to reduce the monotony and speed the whole process up. Occasionally he would be assigned groups of women from the Forces to assist with agricultural production. They were called 'land girls'. At the start of every morning, he would put ten of the young girls at every alternate row of potatoes, about ten metres in front of the men. This was a real-life situation of the donkey and the carrot, and the shrewd farmer knew exactly what would happen. The prisoners had a prime view of the girls' backsides, and were eager to catch up with them and liaise; on the other hand, the girls, seeing the funny side, also quickened their tempo in order to keep away from the men. When they reached the end of the field, the two groups were separated again, and the procedure was repeated. Naturally, everyone was aware of the scheme; but it made the day more interesting for everyone. The English farmer always watched the scene with his ever-present smug smile, as his ingenious idea had become a source of great mirth in the camp.

Two months after the potato picking, the beginning of November marked the commencement of the sugar beet season. To harvest sugar beet requires a different technique but it is not as difficult as picking potatoes, as it is possible to grab it by its tuft and pull it out of the ground. The unpleasant side is the bitter cold, and if it has been a frosty night, the dewdrops become solid ice. Grabbing the tufts of leaves with the bare hands then becomes a painful operation, as the hands become frozen, which renders the fingers immobile. Under these conditions it was necessary to stop at frequent intervals to restore the circulation of blood to the hands, and to achieve this we used a simple exercise that we were all familiar with: we rotated our stretched arms rapidly for a few minutes, and then slapped them under our armpits several times, until the blood began to flow again.

The country seemed much more silent in the early morning during the autumn and winter months, and only the ravens would welcome us into the day with their croaking from the tops of the trees. It is difficult to describe the state of my melancholy mind at the beginning of those long working days; no apparent reason could justify the heaviness that pervaded my spirit, except maybe the vague feeling of a useless, wasted life. The distant barking of a dog or the feeble bellowing of faraway cows would also sometimes reach us through the early morning fog. Often a persistent drizzling greeted us; we were never sure whether it was rain, or condensed fog turned heavy and transformed into small drops of water, something that is indeed neither rain nor fog They were long and dark days.

This is not a very happy picture. Maybe with a bit of luck the fog would clear during the day; but there was no chance of even one isolated ray of sun. I could not avoid thinking that picking that sugar beet in a place so far away from our beloved sun was a waste of time. Some poet in our ranks wrote some verse, later recorded by our camp journal:

> Oh immense drills,
> Interminable file,
> Talk thou hoe,
> No,
> Talk thou shovel.

During the weekends, the prisoners who were more dextrous with their hands were very busy making small objects, which they could then sell to the English. They made silver rings from English half-crowns, cigarette lighters from scraps of downed aircraft, and many other sought-after souvenirs.

The rest of us were never bored. The diversity of the jobs and the vitality of our youth always ensured that we worked with a good heart, whatever the conditions. With youth on our side we were always happy, and never talked of our eventual return to Italy, as the military service in our country probably would not differ much from our life in England. I dare say that most might have even chosen the life we had at that moment, as we could not have hoped for anything much better.

I met a neighbour of mine in Rome after returning from England, and he told me that his years as a prisoner of war were the happiest of his life, and he would have been happy to remain one. He had a boss who guaranteed food, clothes and accommodation: what else did you need? What was more, the food was always in large portions, and the work assured physical fitness all year round.

As for my own physical condition, I know for sure that my body had never worked so efficiently, and it never let me down. I maintained a weight of sixty-two kilos, a height of one hundred and seventy-five centimetres. It was at this time when I was assigned to unload some anthracite coal from railway trucks, and then my body was tested as never before. I was sent to a strange place; I have never worked out what it was – it could have been a railway station, but there were hardly ever any trains. It could have also been a factory that produced gas for the lights of the nearby small village.

A man who looked after the place explained to me what I had to do. We were in front of a railway truck loaded with nine tons of anthracite, and it had to be unloaded as soon as possible to make space for other trucks, which were also full with the same material. It then had to be transferred to the ground next to a furnace, three metres away from the truck. (For reasons unknown to me, the furnace was alight day and night.) The truck was filled with coal up to the top of its sides, one metre and a half high. Anthracite is the best mineral coal, and the type that is extracted from the English mines is some of the best in the world. It is hard and heavy, and produces the highest temperature when burnt. Naturally, it is also the most expensive.

After climbing on the truck, I immediately realised that shovelling coal required a different technique to shovelling soil; this mineral comes in hard blocks weighing roughly three hundred grams, and I could see that it would be difficult to penetrate with the shovel, so I faced a problem that I was unable to solve. I also did not know how much they expected me to do in a day: maybe half a truck would be sufficient. I thought that four and a half tons would be a good day's work.

Another truck about two metres away from mine was also waiting to be unloaded. Before I started to work, an elderly man of maybe sixty-five years of age climbed onto the other truck and started to unload the coal. I immediately took this as a challenge: two equal trucks, in one truck an elderly English man, in the other a young Italian. The Englishman was small, and wore a beret à la Andy Capp, which was the fashion in those days with labourers and railway workers. He looked to be very good-natured, but did not speak to me. I don't think he was interested in my progress, and minded his own business which suited me. There must have been a particularly efficient way to unload the coal, but I was unaware of it. I simply tried to shovel as fast as I could along the top of the coal surface, believing that this was the logical way to do it; however, this turned out to be the wrong technique.

I never stopped: I was always on the attack with my shovel, and kept taking sneaky looks at the progress of my imaginary adversary. I was very careful, as I did not want him to see me looking at him; but every time I lifted my head to see how he progressing, he was always motionless, looking down at his unloaded coal. I soon realised that he was also always slightly ahead of me. It was like a scene from a Charlie Chaplin movie, as though he anticipated my every glance round, and every time I turned I always found him in a rigid position, leaning on his shovel. I was certain that he wanted to give me the impression that he was taking it easy.

At the end of the first day, after a gruelling coal-shovelling competition, I had managed (with difficulty) to unload nine tons from seven in the morning to four in the afternoon. I had worked indefatigably, hardly ever stopping, and there was no limit to my energy. I had even sustained the same rhythm as the old man; but he had still finished unloading his truck some fifteen minutes before me. I looked like a chimney sweep, and a little before five o'clock the Englishman came along and told me that I could have a warm shower. Whilst he was saying this, he smiled and handed me a bar of good-quality soap. This was a nice present, considering that at the camp we only used laundry soap. I appreciated the gesture and was about to thank him; but he disappeared, and I went to take my shower. I have never seen a showerhead with such a large perforated nozzle: it had a diameter of about twenty-five centimetres and its effect was similar to that of a small rainstorm. However, it was very warm, and very nice.

The morning after there was a similar scene: the old man and I, each on our own truck, and I prepared for the same imaginary challenge as the day before. After about one hour of work, my companion interrupted me, addressing me as 'my son'; indeed, he could easily have been even my grandfather, and he told me in kind voice that my method was all wrong. He explained that the first thing to do was to excavate a hole under my feet, large enough to be able to use the shovel all around it. The hole should be near the side door in order to keep it accessible; in addition, it should also be deep enough to reach the floor of the truck. When your feet are on the floor, you can open the door freely. This massive heavy door opened outwards, and would remain hanging there on two solid hinges. It was then easier to slide the shovel on the wooden floor of the truck under the coal, which could then be deposited out of the door. I calculated that by using this system I would be able to unload nine tons of coal a day easily, and in fifteen days I would have shifted a hundred and thirty-five tons. After this I felt very satisfied.

Every day the Englishman would thank me and hand me a fresh bar of soap, which I put aside. The offering of the shower and the soap was a kind gesture, and demonstrated the compassion of the English. I did not expect these offerings; but I welcomed them.

In 1945 I said goodbye to all agricultural work, and together with another fifty companions was allocated small jobs that were suited to our trades e.g. carpenters, electricians, pipe-fitters, plumbers, etc. Our group went to live in the small village of Wallingford.

The barracks in which we stayed were adjacent to the last house of the village. This house was occupied by a seventy-five-year-old man and his wife, and only a metre-high wall separated us. They had an apple tree in their garden, and some of its fruitful branches hung over into our enclosure. This tree cemented our friendship with the couple next door; they said that we could pick as many apples as we liked, provided that we took care not to damage the branches.

Our showers were located in a separate barrack, which was made of corrugated iron. It was only possible to have a hot shower on Saturdays, as warm water was not available the rest of the week. Whilst showering, many prisoners would sing, and bang on the corrugated iron sheeting, creating a happy atmosphere. This happened every Saturday. I was the only Italian capable of taking a cold shower during the winter months, and with the icy weather outside I can assure you that it was not easy. For this reason, I had gained a bit of an eccentric reputation.

The majority of my companions at that time were from Northern Italy. They would often sing Alpine choral songs with much gusto, and I would always join them. We got into the habit of singing every night, and with their help I learnt all of the songs from the north; I even learnt them in their dialect, especially the Venetian ones, which I particularly liked. These choruses are beautiful, especially when sung by robust masculine voices, and they helped to pass the evenings. Although we were at the end of the village, everyone heard our singing, particularly the elderly couple.

We were then all virtually free, and in the summer would walk everywhere, if the weather permitted. Our favourite place was the countryside near our camp, which was a pleasant and tranquil area; in addition, we could also pick blackberries, which are abundant in England. One Sunday, I was on one of these walks with a companion of mine, and we witnessed something very unusual: a rabbit hunt with the assistance of a reaping and binding machine. By sheer coincidence, we found ourselves near a piece of land they were about to harvest. There was a group of about ten hunters, all armed with double-barrelled shotguns. The land was in the shape of a rough square, the size of four football grounds, and was full of ripe corn, ready for cutting. We sensed that something unusual was about to happen, and decided to stay and watch. The machine began to move in concentric circles, cutting and leaving behind sheaves of corn, which a vehicle collected. After the first rotation a small path was left in the corn.

In England, as in Australia, there were millions of rabbits that severely damaged crops, and were considered a major pest (but children still loved them; often as much as their teddy bears). They were particularly fond of corn, cauliflower and the Savoy cabbage. Naturally, the farmer declared war on the rabbit, and if he had had his way would have eliminated all of them; however, the animals are small and difficult to flush out, so it was impossible to control their numbers. Whilst I am on this subject, I must add that the English farmers had a great deal of help from the Italian POWs in their battle against rabbits. Instead of using shotguns like the farmers, the prisoners would use snares, which they placed at the entrance of the rabbits' burrows during their working time in the fields. The prisoners hunting with this method had a lot of success, probably helped by the incentive of succulent roast rabbit.

It seems that the rabbits never stopped eating, day and night, and they caused the farmers great frustration. The ears of corn at harvest time were an attractive asylum for the rabbits, and although you could not see them, you could guess where they were by the movement of the corn shoots. Anyway, after the machine had completed cutting the first circle, the hunters positioned themselves in this area, with their shotguns at the ready. The harvesting machine continued to cut the corn in ever decreasing circles; but the rabbits, who were not as quick with their wits as they were with their legs, stayed put. Eventually the uncut corn must have covered an area of only about fifteen metres in diameter, and the poor rabbits were now so terrified by the machine that they decided to make a run for the woods. After the massacre there were no survivors. It was maybe necessary; but it was not a very pleasant sight.

* * *

With the capitulation of the Germans, a large number of them now started to arrive in England. They were not prepared for the surprise of finding large numbers of Italian prisoners, and gave each other searching looks, not knowing what to assume. However, the truce between us was now at an end, and they were full of resentment; they accused us of having betrayed them, and said that we were the reason why they had lost the war. Two years before they had chosen not to surrender honourably to a superior enemy; but now the 'invincible armada' had no choice but to surrender if they wanted to live, just as the Italians had done previously for the same reason.

The English soon realised that they had underestimated the latent hostility between the Germans and us. They also made the mistake of putting us in close proximity to each other, and after a short while they separated the two factions in a hurry (there had been a number of serious incidents). Gradually, the German prisoners started to replace us, and we began to be sent home, starting with the oldest prisoners.

A year after the first repatriations, all that was left was a scanty group of twenty youngsters; but finally our turn came. Before leaving the place that we had worked in for so many years, we returned to the store to give our tools back, where we had a pleasant surprise. The people who worked there were very surprised that we were still in England, as we had not seen them for a long time; they thought that all of the Italians had gone home. The whole crew came to the exit gate to wave goodbye, and said that they were very pleased to have seen us again, even if it was for the last time. They also added that they greatly preferred us to the Germans.

Their goodbye moved us all. We could not help thinking that they never considered the Italians as their enemy, and this was one of my fondest memories of the English, ending this period of my life on a positive note. My goodbye to the charming couple was very friendly as well, but this was not to be the last time that we saw each other...

Sixteen years later I was married, and returned to England to meet my wife's family. I had told her about the time I had spent in England as a prisoner of war, and expressed my desire to pay a visit to the lovely old couple.

My wife's brother was living in Didcot, which happened to be one of the places I had worked in as a POW; it also happened to be a few kilometres from Wallingford, and I took advantage of the coincidence. As we drove through Wallingford, I told Sally that I recognised everything; it had not changed a bit in sixteen years, and as we approached my old barracks I began to excitedly ask myself if the couple were still alive. At that very moment a man came out of the house, and I recognised him immediately. We stopped and got out of the car, and he looked extremely surprised to see the occupants of a car with a foreign number-plate walking towards him. I introduced myself as a former occupant of the barracks, and he was extremely pleased to see me; he added that I was the only ex-prisoner that had returned to see him. I enquired about his wife, but straightaway guessed from the sorrow on his face that she was no longer with him, and he told me that she had died some years before. He now lived alone at the age of ninety-two.

He asked me if I would like to take at a look at the old barracks from his garden, which was an unexpected but welcome offer, and I accepted (I still could not believe that after sixteen years they had not destroyed the barracks to make way for something more useful). He took us through the house and into the garden, and I went straight to the low wall which once separated us. As I leant over the wall, I remembered the old times with our host and his charming wife at his side, encouraging us to take as many apples as we wanted. A little to the left stood the old apple tree itself; to the right, the old showers, which were now silent; and a little further on, our old barracks, the doors wide open as we had left them sixteen years ago. Everything was quiet. A squirrel rushed across the grass a mere ten metres from where we were standing, and upon seeing us stopped to observe our faces for little while, unafraid, then disappeared. Nothing was more eloquent than that silence and that sense of abandonment, especially for someone full of memories like me. It was an indication of the inexorable passing of the years, and I compared the light-hearted carefree life of when you are twenty to the maturity of an adult. On these occasions my nostalgic personality cannot avoid recalling my friends of those times. Where are they now?

Just before we left our friend, he told us of the deep regret that he felt when we left. He said that it was nice to have us near every day, always singing, always full of life. When we left, he said, he lost a little of his own life. He could not have given us a better compliment.

On 11th May 1946 – exactly three years after I had arrived – we departed from Southampton. The return voyage to Naples took only five days – a big difference to the outward journey of eleven.

The first thing we saw upon docking at Naples was a dirty shabbily dressed woman. She was running back and forth along the wharf, covering the entire length of the ship, and constantly shouting a name. I thought that she was maybe a mother who had lost a son in the war, and probably greeted the arrival of every ship in the hope of finding him.

In spite of the evident disorganisation in the town, we were greeted with a welcome of some sort. A band was arranged on the wharf, and was sarcastically playing the *Piave Song*, with particular emphasis on the part: 'and the Piave whispered: no stranger will pass from here.' A word of explanation is required here.

In the First World War, in the autumn of 1917, the Austrians attacked the Italian troops in the Alps with all of their might. Our troops were forced to withdraw, and were heading to what looked likely to be a disastrous defeat. However, the Italians managed to regroup on the banks of the River Piave, held the Austrian drive, and drove them back, regaining all of the lost terrain in the process. The resultant euphoria was overwhelming, and in 1918 an Italian songwriter called A.E. Mario composed a song to hail our soldiers. The end of each verse ends with the words: 'and the Piave whispered: no stranger will pass from here.' The song is still very famous in Italy today.

The sarcastic repetition of this line reminded us that we had been unable to prevent the strangers from entering our country. From the ship's deck, we could now see many strangers, passing by the thousand. Maybe the band was implying that in this country, we were now the only strangers.

Another ship had arrived at almost the same time to us, this time full of ex-prisoners from North Africa. As soon as they got their feet on dry land they did not waste any time, and immediately tried to attack some Moroccan troops, who were in a camp near the port. Unfortunately for the Italians, the Moroccans were protected by some barbed wire, so all they could do was scream abuse at them from the outside. On our ship we had been told of the barbarities that occurred in the infamous Constantine Camp, which I had avoided by mere chance. There were stories of attempted sodomy at bayonet-point, which soon prompted a revolt in the camp. During this uprising the prisoners had even managed to temporarily take over the town of Constantine. At this point I was busy with something and missed the details of this episode, so I did not find out whether the American troops had intervened and re-established Moroccan control.

As I mentioned earlier, the only food distributed by the Moroccans was tinned meat. This is why these prisoners from North Africa and veterans from Germany were receiving special treatment. As we waited for clearing and discharge (for several days) we listened to their sad stories of abuse and maltreatment. Now that they were back on Italian soil, it was impossible for them to repress their anger.

Chapter 5

I went straight to Rome and looked forward to meeting my relatives. However, I knew that I would be an extra mouth to feed, and was not expecting the reception of someone who had won a billion dollars on the lottery. There was no chance that I could make any financial contribution; nevertheless, I had no alternative but to grit my teeth and go ahead with it, and I prayed that one of the Saints who protects us would at least provide a roof over my head.

When I arrived at the house of one of my uncles, I realised immediately that I would be a burden, and did not know what to do. I was completely unprepared for reality, and was at risk of falling into poverty, which would be very hard to get out of later. It was time to make use of my inheritance, which was nine thousand liras: now equal to one month's salary. I could not help bitterly thinking that at one time that amount would have bought me an apartment, and would surely have got me out of the trouble I was in.

I soon found a job with the Ministry of Aeronautics as a clerk, which was a ridiculous job for me but it was all that was available at the time.

A few months later Vittorio came back from a POW camp in Kenya. However, his health was poor in comparison, and he had to spend one month in a military hospital. He decided to continue his career in the Navy, and thus avoided all of the trouble that I had. I could see by his decision that he had better foresight than me in those chaotic circumstances, wisely deciding to stay under the financial shield of the Navy, and wait for a better opportunity.

His dream was to return to Africa, and in 1948 he heard that Britain's Labour Government was setting up some development projects in the colony of Kenya and the protectorate of Tanganyika; he also heard that they were planning to employ some specialised personnel from Italy, and there was a good chance of getting a thirty-month contract in Kenya. Vic did not waste any time: he decided to go, and asked me if I would like to go with him.

The pay was fearfully low; however, I would have a period of eighteen months with financial cover – albeit very bad cover – to find a job. I would also mature rapidly when exposed to a difficult life, which was very important to me. I felt that destiny pointed to Africa; in any case, I would have to start from scratch.

After a few months of preparation – and worrying that the British Government would change their mind – the day arrived. It was at the beginning of the year and was very cold, but all my cousins and friends in Rome still got together to see me off at the bus stop. I had taught them how to sing all the Alpine choruses in the northern dialect – obtaining good results – and had managed to discipline the high and low parts of their voices the same way my old friends had taught me. Now, at night, in the quiet streets of Rome, our group started to sing. I was leaving the neighbourhood where I had lived briefly, and was devoid of grudges, nostalgia, or even any great affection – my heart was indifferent. Soon all the windows started to open on both sides of the road, and it was clear that the people were enjoying our chorus, which was unusual for Rome. There were no protests or strong words, which are usually a primary aspect of the Roman spirit.

The flight to Kenya was made in a leftover four-engine bomber, and took seventeen hours, including a refuelling stop at Tobruk. There was little to see apart from a number of antelopes intent on searching out a final tuft of grass. It is difficult to understand how they can live without a drop of water. This place again reminded me of the events of six years earlier, and I still recognised the more important aspects of some areas; but did not feel any pangs of nostalgia. These were places that I had crossed during our advance in 1942, and I could still see some trenches, protected by sacks of white flour. I also remember this town's capture in the same year: mountains of marmalade in five-kilogram tins – a little bitter, but still delicious; millions of tins of meat, coffee, honey, tea, all taken by our troops, which I was proud to be part of; burnt tanks and armoured vehicles, British 88mm cannons with the barrels opened like flowers, sabotaged by the British before their surrender; deadly pineapple hand-grenades, brand-new rifles, cases of ammunition (I took a rifle and two thousand rounds of ammo, which I kept until we were captured in Tunisia). As I reminisced,

I also thought of the attack from British warplanes on two of our ships, which sank before my eyes. This happened eight months afterwards, when we were retreating.

Two hours later, the aircraft took off from Tobruk airport for the long stretch over the Sahara desert, which lasted six hours. It seems impossible that such an infinite expanse of red sand could be so real.

Finally the first stunted trees of the dry and rocky region of North Kenya appeared. This passage over the green waters of Lake Turkana is a spectacular view. After a short while we had entered the luxuriant highlands north of Nairobi, rich with constant water and fertile soil for the cultivation of all crops, including coffee and tea.

When I arrived in Kenya in 1949, the vast highlands named Kikuyu-land after the natives that lived there were almost entirely in the hands of the British. It has a very healthy climate and is ideal for raising children; consequently it is the first choice of settlers and farmers, although it can get quite cold in some months, especially at night. There are several rivers, all supplied by the snowy peaks of Mount Kenya. A few years after my arrival, this territory witnessed the Mau Mau uprising, and it gained independence in the 1960s.

At Nairobi airport the young customs officers began to check our luggage; however, they were soon discouraged by the pungent smell emanating from the socks belonging to the robust mountain men of our group. Typically organised British military personnel were then waiting for us with a list of our names and associated skills. We were divided into three groups, and the first group was assigned to an area on the periphery of Nairobi. This included Vittorio, and we were separated once again. I was in the second, and we were assigned to a place called Athi River, about seventeen kilometres away. The third group was effectively separated from all of us, and was dispatched four hundred kilometres away to an isolated area in the middle of the savannah, called Macchinnon Road. Until the end of their contract, their only company would be the beasts of the future Tsavo National Park. Tsavo had become famous after an event that occurred shortly after the turn of the century:

Two man-eating lions were following the progress of the railway being built there, and every night they would attack one of the camps, devouring at least one of the Indian labourers. The cunning beasts never repeated the attack on the same camp, therefore foiling any attempts to catch them. Sources estimated that they had killed over three hundred Indians before they were slain by the British head engineer of the project. Lieutenant Colonel J.H. Patterson, DSO, tells the true story of this saga in a book entitled *The Maneaters of Tsavo*.

The railway project was completed in 1906, and many thousands of Indians decided to stay in the three territories of East Africa (Kenya, Uganda and Tanganyika). The English encouraged more to immigrate, and today there is an increasingly vast number of Indians.

The railway is the backbone of Kenyan communications. It is 2,776 kilometres long, 2,600 kilometres of which is in Kenyan territory. It starts in Mombasa then continues through Nairobi, Jinja, and finally Port Bell, in Uganda. A section branches out at Voi to Arusha in Tanganyika (now Tanzania); from Nairobi another reaches to Mount Kenya; and at Nakuro is the important fork to Kisumo and other secondary destinations.

European residence was beneficial to the Africans in some ways, but eventually they wanted them out. They had about 130,000 square kilometres, and the Europeans had about 105,000. However, the Europeans were established in the best, most healthy sectors, and hostility was inevitable, especially from the Kikuyu tribe. Before the Second World War they formed the Kenyan National Union, headed by Jomo Kenyatta. It was dissolved in 1941.

The colonial authorities created a ministry so the Africans were under the illusion that they had some power. However, the Mau Mau (a faction of the Kikuyu), under the command of Dedan Kimuti, began a hostile revolt in 1952, with the primary goal of independence. The British declared a state of emergency, and were very tough opposition. Nevertheless, Kenya became independent in 1963, and Kenyatta was President for fifteen years.

Athi River is aptly named after the small watercourse that flows through it during the rainy season; however, during the summer it never completely dries up, but leaves long patches of water, often deep enough to host crocodiles and hippopotami. These conditions are also ideal to attract a large number of other wild beasts.

My place of work was along the main road from Nairobi to the southern border of Tanganyika (150 kilometres away); my job was to repair and maintain the electrics of military lorries. Our encampment was in the middle of a plain that stretched away in three directions as far as the eye could see. The north faced Nairobi, and after about a kilometre you reached the edge of the Athi River. The reddish sand and sparse dry grass that surrounded us was the same that you find in most African savannah areas, but was not high enough to oppose any resistance to the hot winds during the dry season; thus, the wind kept creating whirlwinds of red sand, and sometimes the twisters would quickly grow into a worrying size, and then vanish into nothing after a few seconds. These sights gave me a real sense of desolation.

On Sundays I was often fed up of staying in the camp, and would have liked to pass a couple of hours in nature's company, sitting on the white, dry rocks of the river, enjoying the silence. However, this would have been very hazardous, as a pack of lions had taken up permanent residence in the neighbourhood, and had been spotted roaming around.

Any beasts in Kenya – even dangerous felines or hippopotami – were free to roam anywhere at will; it was possible to encounter them at the edge of town at night, or even in the centre of the city, and nothing more was thought of it (but you would still tell your friends). As we were right in the middle of the savannah, there was no reason for the British authorities to interfere with the beasts; in fact, it was entirely up to the person involved to get out of any trouble they found themselves in. However, if a beast killed someone in a small village, a professional hunter would hunt the culprit down and kill it.

Theoretically, the lions of the Athi River could enter our camp and eat someone any time they were hungry, and there was no insurance of any kind – it really was all at your own risk. The camp toilets were about one hundred metres from where we were sleeping, and if anyone wanted to visit them in the night, it was up to them to have a look around with the torch first. The possibility of a night encounter with a lion was underestimated because it had not happened – yet. The most friendly visitors to our camp were the antelopes.

As you have probably gathered, lions were present in a great number in the East African territories. Incidents with these felines were quite frequent, and usually happened around isolated African houses, in the savannah. However, not all of these cases were reported, so there were probably far more than everyone realised. During my thirty-one years in Africa I had numerous encounters with lions when I was unarmed, and on one occasion only good luck prevented me from a disastrous face-to-face encounter. I had been more careful at other times and proceeded with caution; consequently I became aware of their presence, and stopped just in time. In spite of my good luck, I still went through all of this with a great deal of fear.

A factor that indicated our lack of experience of this country was the attitudes of most people towards the local fauna; they never thought that lions could be present just beyond the doors of their homes. Having heard some of them talking, I was inclined to suspect that they had never heard of an animal called a 'lion', which only eats meat – mainly fresh meat. I did not know whether to admire or abhor their naivety: they would not hesitate even for a moment to go for a walk on the savannah, and on more than one occasion we witnessed the dramatic spectacle of lions chasing gazelles across the flat land (and what happened to the gazelles afterwards). In spite of the many warnings, some of them were in the habit of walking the three kilometres across this area to the Indian bazaar. At first they did this at weekends, or in the afternoons after working; but they became reassured by the lions' absence, and would start to stay later at the bazaar, maybe to nine or ten at night. Their naivety had no limits, and it was only a matter of time before their casual behaviour landed them in trouble.

A happy party was returning home one night at about ten o'clock. It was a full moon, and this is when a lion's eyesight is at its best. They were about three hundred metres away from the camp when they heard the roar of a group of lions which must have been hunting. I can assure you that no type or amount of hair gel can straighten the hair as much as a lion's roar at night. The men were now badly scared, and did not even have a torch to assist them in their flight. The lions appeared to have hostile intentions, and were following them. This time only good luck allowed them to return to the camp unhurt: they were lucky the lions were not in front of them. Three hundred metres was too far, especially since they kept tripping on the tufts of dry grass. The felines must have given up, perhaps hoping that somehow they could grab the prey with no extra effort. This was the first lesson.

Another group was travelling back from Nairobi in a lorry that the British had lent to them. It was also about ten o'clock, and they were forced to stop to repair a puncture, a little before they reached the bazaar. While they were changing the wheel, someone noticed that a lioness was nearing the lorry; the headlights and the people around them had probably attracted her. A general stampede ensued to get to the rear panel and climb onto the lorry. It was an Austin, which had higher sideboards than normal; luckily, the lioness, perhaps a little blinded by the lorry's headlights, could not understand where all the people had disappeared to; she obviously did not realise that they were in the lorry and all she had to do was simply jump up there and get them.

Naturally the wheel-change had to wait for a long time whilst the beast sniffed around the lorry, probably trying to solve the enigma of her disappearing dinner. In the meantime, our friends quietly cowered in the back of the lorry, where they remained for a long time after she had left.

I can also recollect a third scary encounter, once again due to our poor knowledge of the surroundings and animals' behaviour:

We heard that an African herdsman (who did not belong to the combative Masai tribe) had been confronted by a group of lions whilst he was looking after his herd of cows. He was alone and there was no chance of any help, so he had no choice but to retreat and abandon his cows. He was deeply overwhelmed by this fearful encounter, so much so that he refused to return to that place, therefore forfeiting his pay. Anyway, an Italian friend of ours told us that as the herd was out on the plain unsupervised, it was necessary to find the group of lions and kill them, so he asked us if we were interested. It was a formidable task. Surely a professional hunter with a large hunting rifle would have been more suited; but we did not hesitate for a moment – the invitation of adventure was too great and we formed an enthusiastic group of six.

However, our enthusiasm clouded our judgement, and we blundered rashly into the unrealistic project. Firstly, none of us had any experience of hunting big game; secondly, there was only one weapon between all six of us, which was my semi-automatic shotgun, which I had bought with my first salary. Now, the first rule in this type of hunt is that everyone should have at least a rifle each, not one shotgun between six. In case any of my readers do not know, I will now try to explain the difference between a rifle and a shotgun.

A shotgun is traditionally used to shoot birds. There is the double-barrelled variety, which may have the barrels side by side, or one on top of the other – the 'over and under shotgun'; and there is the semi-automatic, which can shoot five rounds in rapid succession. The inside of the barrels is as smooth as a mirror, and the bore is slightly 'choked' towards the far end – this is to prevent the shot from coming out at too much of an angle. You can also buy special single-ball ammunition, used to hunt medium-heavy game at close quarters (large antelopes or boars at about thirty or forty metres).

Hunters all over the world use the big-game rifle – in Africa, Asia, the Americas. There are three types: single-barrelled, double-barrelled, and single-barrelled semi-automatic. All shoot cartridges, which are stored underneath in the magazine. The inside of the barrel is spiralled to create a swirling effect on the bullet, thus keeping it stable through the air. To reload a single-barrelled rifle, you must slide the breechblock backwards then forwards: the backward movement despatches the old cartridge, and the forward one reloads a new one.

The double-barrelled variety looks very similar to a shotgun; but its bore is grooved in the fashion of an ordinary rifle. This gun – also called 'express' – is much heavier than a single-barrel, and employs very powerful ammunition to hunt elephants, rhinoceroses and lions, often from sixty to seventy metres away. When using the same ammunition, the express is more powerful than both types of single-barrel. The semi-automatic loses some of its power when expelling its cartridge, and has a dangerous tendency to jam – mainly due to defective cartridges – and for this reason is quite unpopular with professional hunters.

My gun was a weak semi-automatic, and was definitely very unsuitable for the task that lay ahead. Looking back on it now, I cannot understand how foolish it was to undertake such an impossible adventure. I think I got carried away with wanting to play the part of the 'professional hunter'.

Anyway, we chose to take an Emilian friend with us, as he claimed to be a weapons expert. He explained to us that this was because they were all made in his region (according to his logic, all people in Emilia were weapons experts). However, he advised us to use much bigger pellets (double zero), and told us as he was the commander of the expedition, he would execute all the lions.

We agreed, and hoped that if he missed, the lions would attack him! But I later learnt that they would just attack the nearest man.

The next Saturday, with the Emilian leading, we went to look for the missing herd of cows on the savannah. After a few hours of walking, we saw a group of fifteen cows which appeared to be grazing calmly. There was no sign of any herdsman, so the Emilian and three others decided to investigate, only to discover a slain cow. As the carcass was two days old, another companion and I decided not to waste any more time, and we left the group. But after a short while we heard screams coming from their direction, and we saw our friends running towards us. When they got to us they were gasping for breath and holding their sides; they then told us that we must leave, as the area was crowded with lions. The herdsman was nowhere to be seen; he had probably also fled when the lions slew the cow.

When nearing the herd, they had noticed that there were a number of calves lying down a short distance away. Everything seemed safe enough, so they walked quickly over, until they were about twenty metres away. At this point, the 'calves' got up, and began to walk towards them. Our friends froze. They now realised with terror that they were walking into a family of lions, males, females and cubs, which now stared intently at them, and the group of would-be big-game hunters made a fast turn, and an even faster sprint towards us, hence the screams that my companion and I had heard.

Upon reflection, I cannot understand why the lions did not attack such easy prey; maybe it is true that each of us does have a Saint to protect us. The only explanation I could think of is that their bellies were full: lions are well known for being reluctant to attack on a full stomach; in fact, they had not moved from the herd for three days. Why should they? They had all the food they wanted at their disposal.

We never did go back to the Italian who had assigned us the task. After that experience, we preferred to forget it altogether.

About three kilometres from us, on the road to Nairobi, a fork led off to our camp and the southern frontier of Tanzania. On one side of the fork two or three Indian families had taken up residence, and were giving the final touches to a shabby building, which included apartments and some shops. We passed the building every weekend when going to Nairobi with the lorry, and could observe the progress of the strange building. They were working hard to finish it, and it was clear that this fistful of pioneers were determined to assert themselves financially. It was a shabby construction, and they had even used sections of two-hundred litre oil barrels, which created enormous random red patches on the walls.

They had begun by planting tree trunks in the ground for the walls of the building. They then filled in the empty spaces in the trunks with sticky mud, typical of that area. Finally, a coat of whitewash finished the job. Any remaining holes were filled with tin sections from twenty-litre paraffin cans, painted red to stop them from rusting. The structure was far from a perfect square, and from a distance gave the impression of having just survived a tornado. The lack of financial commitment was clearly evident on the roof, which was made out of two by one metre corrugated iron sheets, also painted with red anti-rust paint.

This type of construction was very common in East Africa, and was home to mostly Africans and Indians, who were robust enough to live that kind of life. They did not need the comfort of a good modern construction to get by.

The Athi River location was ideal for the Indians, as they could intercept all traffic on their way to the coast or Tanganyika. Their main commodity was spice, which was mostly crammed into large boxes with low sides, while some were rammed into glass containers. They were kept tightly sealed to prevent the pungent aroma escaping, and this distinctive smell was typical of the Indian bazaars. Near the shops there were also hand-operated petrol and diesel pumps. Kerosene was also highly in demand, as thousands of people in this territory employed this form of lighting. The kerosene simply sat in twenty-litre tins on the floor. The Indians were very casual, as they had a virtual monopoly in this area.

Food and alcohol was also available. Beer was a principal attraction for not just the British personnel in the camp, but also us workers. A large paraffin refrigerator near the door ensured that it was chilled and completed the colourful shop, a simple place that was extremely convenient for those just passing, or those that had time for a cold beer. It was also somewhere where people could stop and chat, breaking the monotony of the four hundred-odd kilometres that separated them from the coast.

Our group included about sixteen quarrelsome Italians with very loose fists. They were born in Tunisia, and the British regarded them as the most aggressive Italian troops they encountered throughout the whole war. Unfortunately they were still very aggressive, and were always looking to land a blow on someone's nose, whether they deserved it or not.

There was also the usual group of scoundrels that you encounter in all four corners of the globe: an explosive mixture. This lot had decided that they needed to make some more money, so games of roulette and baccarat became a constant fixture in the mess-tent, and a miniature Wild West was born.

I soon learnt that it was necessary to adopt a decisive personality here, and if necessary counter violence with violence. If you were intimidating and decisive enough, then you could maybe hope to live in peace. However, during my thirty months at that place I was involved in four separate fist fights, and I knew that it was necessary to fight aggressively, or be judged a coward. Luckily my fists were hard when I was twenty, and during all my years in Africa I had to go to court three times for assault. Of the four fights at the Athi River, two of my adversaries had to go to the hospital, and the other two surrendered after the first punches had been thrown.

The British occasionally succeeded in astonishing me. They had assigned a number of Africans (I do not remember if they were the military or civilians) to empty twenty buckets from the camp's latrines every week. Even the Italians thought that this was an extremely humiliating operation, and it would have been much easier – and less troublesome – to have used a small part of the vast amount of space available to construct Turkish toilets, thus avoiding the resentment of the Africans for this degrading operation. It was this lack of respect that earned their resentment, and quickly the rumble of the revolt began to be heard in the sky of Kenya. Unfortunately the Mau Mau revolt was against all white people, not just the British. It began in 1952, but was already brewing towards the end of 1949, as the next episode shows.

There were two separate camps: one for the British, one for the Africans. Some of our workers had heard there was to be a display of tribal dances in the African camp, and asked them if they could attend the show, to which the Africans agreed. I would like to say that up to then our relations with the Africans had been good, although this was mainly because we did not have to work with them, and everyone minded their own business.

I had been to a few African dances before, and found them rather boring. They were extremely childish and repetitive, and I considered them to be a complete waste of time. However, a group of our workers had never experienced them before, and were very enthusiastic about the forthcoming show.

As the show went on they began detect some unrest on the part of the Africans, who kept throwing hostile looks at them. None of our workers knew a single word of the local language, and did not have a clue what was going on, so they just continued to sit quietly. They first suspected that the Africans were annoyed by their own copious consumption of their strong coconut liqueur; but the motive was much deeper than that. Some Good Samaritan Africans were trying to calm the bullies down, but without much success. They now had their hands on their pangas: large knives, similar to the machete or scimitar, that could cut sugar cane with a single stroke (or, on some rare occasions, human heads). There now seemed to be no easy solution for the Italians, but luckily one of the more reasonable Africans (seeing that a massacre was imminent) told the group to leave immediately, without even looking back. They only needed to be told once, and abandoned the spot with haste.

In retrospect, this episode was clearly one of the early stages of the Mau Mau revolt, but we did not realise it until later. In fact, our group had previously ignored the situation between the Africans and the British, and did not even suspect that there was any hidden animosity, which was soon to affect us as well.

My brother and I were only living about twenty kilometres apart, and we bought a robust second-hand motor car, which we converted to make it more suitable for cross-country hunting. Vic was also a cabinetmaker, and he refined the body. There were no doors on the front or back, so it was easier to get in and out in an emergency; there were also no side panels. The roof was supported by robust stanchions at both corners, and there was a square aperture at the front which served as an observation post and could be closed in case of rain. Canvas curtains would also keep us dry, which we could roll up to the roof when not in use. We copied the design from some motorcars that belonged to an English farmer; some were used for transport during the rainy season, others for hunting.

Vic bought his Winchester rifle for big-game hunting; this way, we had weapons suitable for not just dangerous animals, but also guinea fowl and partridges, all of which were abundant in this area. We formed a small group with others who shared our passion for hunting, and every weekend we would travel all around Kenya.

It was 1949, and there were only six million African inhabitants, sixty thousand Europeans and practically no tourists at all; what was more, there were practically no restrictions on travel and hunting. There were also hundreds of kilometres of beautiful sandy beaches, with clear, warm water, mostly uninhabited, with the exception of some small fishing villages. However, the coast held no attraction for us – our pleasure was to bivouac regularly and hunt on the savannah.

With the exception of the two-hundred kilometre road which ran from Nairobi to Nakuru, ending in Uganda (constructed by Italian POWs captured during the Somalian–Ethiopian campaign of 1940), there were no asphalt roads. The Italians were famous for constructing roads in Ethiopia, Eritrea and Somalia, so the Kenyan Colonial Office had requested that the job be assigned to them.

Eighty kilometres along this road was the Gil-Gil station, where my brother had passed six years as a prisoner of war, and we could not miss a visit there. We also paid a visit to the local cemetery, where some of Vic's companions who did not make it were buried, waiting to decompose into the African soil. As Vic pointed at some of the graves, he recounted a few anecdotes: the knife conflicts between the prisoners, which was aroused by Italy's capitulation; and the feats of a group of Sardinians, who had hunted buffalo with lances. They had also trained a small but enthusiastic crossbreed of mongrels to fight against the buffalo. Now this was no laughing matter, especially when you consider that the buffalo was in the top three animals responsible for all human deaths in Africa. The other two were the hippopotamus and crocodile. The attack was bloody, mainly because they had assaulted the buffalo calves and therefore had to answer to the mother. Vic told me that she had ignored the dogs and concentrated on the men. But the dogs would give her no respite, attacking her from every angle, trying to bite her legs (similar to the method of the Masai, which involves a group attack where it does not matter who dies – the fight goes on). Naturally, all of the Africans were full of admiration – they had never heard of such courageous white men.

The Italian prisoners working on the road erected a small church, as an eternal mark of their presence in the area. They chose a spot about thirty-five kilometres from Nairobi where the Kikuyu highland descends steeply towards the lowland and Lake Naivasha. The small building is no bigger than a city apartment, and is known as the church of the Italian prisoners. They have given life to the steep, inhospitable terrain; but due to the isolated position it is not frequented, except for occasional visits from tourists. When you look at it on a cold foggy day, in the middle of nowhere, situated halfway up the mountain, you can really feel a sense of dejection. However, it is looked after by the Nairobi Catholic Church, and can still be visited today. In fact, the frescoes of the Saints on the walls needed to be restored after twenty-five years, so an appeal was made in Italy to trace the original artist, and he was happy to return to Kenya and touch up his work.

It was a progressive period when all Africa had Italian prisoners; but unfortunately there were also some very serious and negative aspects.

The Italians taught the Africans how to transform wood into charcoal, and the disastrous consequences of this activity are now clearly visible fifty years after it began. Before the last World War, charcoal did not exist in Kenya; now it is produced in large quantities, and sold in sacks by hundreds of charcoal merchants particularly along the Nairobi–Nakuro road, where the prisoners used to reside. The signs of severe deforestation are now clearly visible in this part of the territory, and there is an increasing need for wood from the ever-expanding carpentry industry. However, the situation is no longer reversible.

The prisoners also devised many ways to obtain fresh meat from the copious stocks of animals around them. One was to make a snare from pieces of steel ropes which could be found in the military scrap yard, and after a while more contraptions appeared: traps, gins, lassoes, each time growing more sophisticated, more cruel. Some immobilised one leg of the animal, and if it were not found in time it would die in protracted agony. Nevertheless, the African population accepted these ideas with enthusiasm; for the first time ever they could obtain fresh meat without having to go long distances or use a bow and arrow, and the results were certain.

The war also caused another environmental disaster; but it was nothing to do with the prisoners. It involves fishing with explosives on the east coast of Africa, and I will deal with this problem later.

Most of the European residents of Kenya (mainly the rich English landowners and cattle breeders) were accustomed to meeting in Nairobi at weekends. They came from all parts of the territory, and brought their children, who were always beautiful and healthy, as they had been raised in an ideal climate; most were from the north-east, the most fertile part of the country, which received an abundant amount of rainfall. They were always extremely happy, but did not have time for anyone outside of their circles. During these two days all the hotels in Nairobi would be full, and there was a festive atmosphere with all the business the crammed wallets brought to the Indian shops. It was nice to be around the town during these weekends, and enjoy the rich air of exuberance. However, as far as I was concerned, I still preferred to satisfy my passion for hunting with my friends: for us, there was nothing better, and some of us believed that it would last for the rest of our lives. Any discomfort we encountered when in the pursuit of our hobby was treated with absolute nonchalance, a good example being our means of transport.

Before we bought the car, our only means of transport was the bus, and at that time it was exclusively for the use of Africans: towards the end of the forties racial separation was still enforced in the East African territories, and the Africans were liable to much persecution. The only way they were allowed to walk around at night was by carrying a lighted paraffin lamp, so they could be seen from a distance. If they were found without a lamp, or an unlit one, they would be arrested. The Europeans were not allowed to use the buses and if you were caught then you would also be going to the police station. However, our passion for hunting meant that we had to occasionally break the rules, and when we were out of town we would jump onto the bus, occupying a considerable amount of space; the buses were not very large, and with all of our equipment it usually meant that everyone had to squeeze together. We knew that our invasion would not cause any trouble as the Africans were always good-humoured when it came to such matters.

Our objective was to get away from Nairobi, and reach anywhere on the savannah near the Athi River, which was along the Nairobi–Mombasa road. All we took with us was the minimum we needed to survive for two days. We did not have any tents, and only took a two-litre water bottle each, some tinned food, and some ammunition. Each one of us wore an Australian military hat with a wide brim, supplied to us by the British Administration.

There were no trees in the savannah at Athi River, and the grass was sparse and low. On Saturdays we slept on the ground without blankets. We could not start a fire as there was no fuel, and the grass was teeming with ticks from the herds of Masai zebu. In other more fertile savannah areas you can rid the soil of parasites and tzetze fly by simply setting fire to the grass at yearly intervals. Luckily, ticks rarely attack humans in Africa; maybe this is because we emit a different odour from that of cows and other animals. However, I have heard of rare occasions when ticks have attacked people, and when they penetrate the skin with their head it is not easy to remove them; trying to pull them out will almost always leave the head anchored under the skin. But there is an easy way to ensure the entire thing is extracted: carefully touch the body of the tick with a lighted cigarette; this way it will die, and should come out easily. These parasites can carry serious infections, like typhoid, which can be fatal if neglected. I have seen Masai cows with their bellies literally covered with thousands of the pests, rendering it impossible to see the skin of the animal underneath.

At about three o'clock on Sunday, we would wait at the bus stop, hoping to be able to catch the return bus to Nairobi. I say 'hoping' because the return bus was a bit of a lottery: nobody could be sure if it would ever materialise.

Our hunting parties always consisted of the same group of friends, and one day we decided to make a visit to the source of the Tana, the largest river in Kenya. It begins in the Aberdare Mountains, and after 800 kilometres flows into the Indian Ocean, at the town of Malindi. On its upper and middle courses it receives water from many tributaries, and is peppered with rapids and waterfalls; the lower course then turns south and crosses a barren steppe region, where it almost dries up. Nevertheless, during the rainy season it is navigable for about 570 kilometres.

At its source the river is wide and crystal clear. We desperately wanted to bathe in it, but were worried about the possible presence of crocodiles. However, as the water was very shallow we decided that it would be very unlikely, and we enjoyed a refreshing bath.

Afterwards we met a man of about forty years (quite old for an African in those days), who had been a hunters' guide since he was a little boy. His name was Gela (Kiswahili for 'prison'). He told us there was an abundance of buffalo in that area and he knew where he could find them, so we hired him.

After walking for a few hours we finally found a solitary buffalo. We guessed that he must have been chased away from the herd by the younger buffalo when he was too old to assert his supremacy. As they live alone they can become very moody and very dangerous; very often they will attack on sight. However, this one had not seen us yet, and Vic did not waste any time – he shot it in the shoulder; but it tried to get up again. A man from our group then went over to the buffalo without thinking, intending to hack one of its rear legs off with a machete. He was lucky; although Vic had wounded the beast seriously, it still tried to get at its adversary when he was in range of its powerful horns, and a tragedy was prevented only by a successful second shot from Vic.

Afterwards Gela told us of an encounter he had with a solitary buffalo when he was much younger. He was a fair distance away from the beast, and because of this he did not consider it a threat; however, the beast attacked him, and Gela was sure that he was going to die: he was alone, and only had a knife to protect himself. He threw himself to the ground to avoid being gored by the buffalo's first charge; he must have already known that buffalo never trample on their adversaries, and it was this strange habit that gave him the chance to save his skin. Buffalo only kill by goring with their horns, and these curve inwards (as you may well know), so they cannot thrust directly forwards. Anyway, the buffalo was now lying down beside him, and trying to gore him by turning its head from side to side. But every time he did this, Gela delivered a blow to the beast with his pointed knife, and after each blow the animal would reel, but then come back even more determined. Their heads were now only a few centimetres apart, and the animal's eyes looked at Gela as if to say: 'You are mine and I will urinate on you.' (Buffalo sometimes do this after a victorious fight.) Now and then the beast would stand up and retreat a few paces; then it would change its mind and sit back down, before resuming the attack. This went on nearly all day.

Gela was now completely exhausted, and his reactions to the buffalo's attacks became slower and slower. When he had the chance he would try to stab the eyes with his knife. At long last the animal realised that the fight was impossible; he was covered in blood and was perhaps partially blinded, so he gave up and went away.

I was once watching a bullfight in Spain when the matador made a wrong move and fell to the ground. I noted that bulls, like buffalo, do not trample on their adversaries.

Soon our thirty months' contract was coming to an end. Nearly all of my companions had had enough of the Athi River and decided to return to Italy; only a handful of us wanted to stay.

It was time to start looking round for a new job, and this was not easy. In 1950 the economies of the British colonies were stagnant: there were no plans for expansion anywhere, no hotels, no new roads (which were badly needed). The local British enterprises were self-sufficient in every respect, and had no need for skilled European workers. The only people who were never worried about finding a job were the hundreds of British bureaucrats.

On completion of his contract with the War Department, my brother immediately found a job with the Coca Cola factory that was ideal for what he had in mind to do. This job could be considered as a parallel occupation.

As I have previously explained, Kenya was in a state of emergency as a result of the Mau Mau revolt. Coca Cola and all the other major companies, in response to an appeal from the Government, were agreeable to allowing their personnel, if they wished, to participate in the fight against the Mau Mau on a voluntary basis. Because of the initial surprise, the Mau Mau had killed many European families in a barbaric manner, exterminating women and young children.

Vittorio joined the police and worked with them on and off for two or three years.

Around Mount Kenya, besides the African police, there were also groups which were exclusively formed by the Kenya settlers, in addition to a Scottish regiment, the Black Watch. Vittorio's assignment was to take part in the siege of Mount Kenya. Every three miles there was a patrol of eighteen African policemen with a European in charge. The photograph of him illustrates the battledress he used during these operations, complete with Sten gun.

Part of Mount Kenya was considered to be out of bounds for the local population, and anyone found there would be shot on sight by the patrols. In one of Vittorio's letters to me, he explained that his patrol were aware there were Mau Mau within the out-of-bounds area who kept in contact with each other by way of the animal tracks, so his patrol used to ambush the animal tracks in order to kill them, or at least make it unsafe for them to continue to use the tracks.

Any person who was unemployed for more than two months was forced to leave the territory; if they refused they would be reported to their respective consul, who would almost certainly persuade them to be more co-operative. After a month of fruitless searching, my financial situation was very precarious indeed, and I was beginning to expect deportation; after this I would never have been allowed back into a British colony again. Even the Indians had a distinct advantage over us, as they had been in the country before we arrived. Eventually a member of the Italian Consulate in Tanganyika, whom I had contacted previously by telephone, advised me of a vacancy. However, I had to pass an interview with the general manger of a company that had a monopoly in the electricity business in both Tanganyika and Kenya. My financial resources were nearly gone, and I had to reach Dar-es-Salaam as quickly as possible for the interview. As I did not need any document to cross the border, I left immediately.

The Germans had constructed the railways when they were in control of Tanganyika. They were regular gauge, so they could be connected to those in other countries. However, the Kenyan ones were narrow gauge, so for the first 250 kilometres I had to take a bus up to Dodoma in Tanganyika; from here the train would take me to Dar-es-Salaam (capital of Tanganyika, on the Indian Ocean, 950 kilometres from Nairobi).

My first stop was a hotel in Arusha, in Tanganyika, which is about 50 kilometres from the Kenyan border, where I searched my pockets. It did not take very long, as all I had was the money for one day at the hotel and a ticket for the rest of the trip.

When I went to buy the ticket for the bus, the English clerk told me that there were no more seats available for the next day, and the next one was in three days' time. This was obviously no good for me, and I explained to the clerk that it was imperative for me to depart the next morning. Luckily the man was a reasonable person, and he told me to call at his house at seven o'clock, when he would hope to have a ticket for me. So at seven that evening I knocked at his door, and his wife opened it. Upon hearing why I was there, the woman flew into a rage with her husband; she became so irrational that she tried to engage me as an ally against her husband, whom she accused of extending his working hours until seven in the evening. She told me that he was too easily persuaded, and to make things even worse, he invited clients to his house. The situation was almost comical, as the woman repeatedly looked at me, waiting for my reply, and I simply tried to remain neutral, feeling rather awkward. In the end I did obtain that blessed railway ticket from a very embarrassed husband, who was so ashamed he did not look me in the face. I breathed a sigh of relief when I finally left the house.

At five o'clock the next morning I paid my hotel bill and left; for the time being I was not broke, although I was relying on getting a job in Dar-es-Salaam. However, there was a bad surprise on arrival at the bus stop.

Before describing this experience I have consulted many people, including my wife, on whether to mention it or not. It describes a terrible disease: leprosy. I thought that the description may be a little indecent, or perhaps a bit disrespectful to those who carry it. Every person I spoke to told me not to ignore any detail, as the book must be complete to maintain its authenticity. Here it is.

When I arrived at the bus stop, which was near the railway station, there were some thirty lepers waiting under the shade of a large mango tree. I had never seen so many together. They met every bus, hoping to scrape some charity. It was an appalling sight; there was a cloud of flies around them and we had to continually try and stop them from settling on us, right up until the train for Dar-es-Salaam arrived. I have to honestly say that the horror of their sores, covering every part of their body, left no space for feelings of pity: all of the passengers felt like running away from that place.

Until then my knowledge of the disease was only from what I had read in the Bible and some Roman records. Although these descriptions alone were enough to make me shiver, it was nothing compared to the impact that these wretched people made on me. Their disease was at a very advanced stage, at a state of irreversibility. It had begun to erode the extremities of the limbs and nose, and its slow progress condemns the person to a long and painful death. What was most disturbing was the absence of the fleshy part of the nose; in its place were two deep holes. It was impossible to stare them in the face; only after a big effort could anyone bring themselves to abandon their sense of repulsion for one of pity.

The leprosy bacillus is similar to tuberculosis. It can be contracted through sexual and casual contact, especially through a patient who is at an advanced stage. There are several reports of this from Christian missionaries who have dedicated their whole lives to the disease.

If it is treated in its early stages, then it more easy to cure than is widely believed. The direct application of sulphur to the sores, together with antibiotics, has proved to have success over the bacilli.

The long trip from Dodoma to Dar-es-Salaam, with East African Railways, was uneventful, apart from an occasional sight of some wild animals. All European seats were first class.

When I travelled on this service, the cutlery was made of solid silver, with the company logo engraved on them; but this show of prestige was not to last for long. After 1950 a less prosperous class of European traveller started to frequent the service, and the silver cutlery was replaced. Obviously some of the travellers thought that it was out of place in a poor country like Tanganyika, a museum piece worth pinching.

My interview with the General Manager of DARESCO (Dar-es-Salaam Electric Supply Company) was successful, and they became my new employers. I thought it was better to tell them about my lack of experience in this particular area – large industrial plants and petroleum pumping stations – but I was wrong to be so thorough. They appreciated my honesty; but the salary they offered me left much to be desired. However, I wish to add that I have always been grateful to my employers, and I understand that at the beginning of my recruitment I was fairly unskilled. Remembering this, I gave them my unconditional loyalty, and in return they had complete confidence in me.

At Athi River I had learned to get the most out of my staff, who were mostly Africans, and a few Indians. By encouraging them and showing a good example, I usually managed to obtain results that the Indian foremen very often could not. Corruption is the great plague of the Third World, and I told them I would not tolerate any act of dishonesty. I assured my men I would try to help them, and that they could rely on me at all times; as far as it was possible, I would also try to help them with their family difficulties and to protect them from any forms of abuse. They soon learnt that I kept my promises. Later I will tell you of two examples that prove my good faith.

I still possess a group picture of all the African staff in the company, which was given to me when I left Tanzania for good in 1972. When I look at that old picture I remember that we were all young once. Everyone had their own troubles then; but we still had maximum respect for each other.

One of the jobs entrusted to me was to take a monthly reading from the meters of the large industries. The majority of the company's income came from these industries, as they were the biggest consumers. It would have been very easy to tamper with these meters in exchange for a bribe from the client, so it was a job that required a reliable and trustworthy person.

I was still a young man, and it was a great satisfaction to see the changes and results I received after only a year's work; by this time I had more knowledge and confidence, and I greatly enjoyed myself. I also was getting to know Dar-es-Salaam well, and had travelled up-country a little. Here I would pass a very happy twenty-two years. I would meet my wife, and my two daughters Lucia and Linda would be born.

I noticed that Tanganyika had remained more or less the same since it had been under German rule (which had ended in 1914, at the start of the First World War). Most of the British citizens in the lower echelons of the civil service were living in houses left by the Germans, whilst the slightly more prosperous had established themselves in choice houses in the palm groves, and the even more well-to-do lived in exclusive properties on the seafront. Racial discrimination was improving but was still evident, and the Indian community lived in a sector on the town's periphery. However, the majority of the indigenous population lived in ramshackle huts some distance from the town centre. These miserable buildings had a wooden frame and walls of mud bricks. The roof was nearly always made of intertwined broom, or recycled sheets made from paraffin containers. The floor was simply compacted earth, and most huts did not have sanitary facilities or electricity.

Each community had different occupations: most of the British worked for the civil service and car dealers. The Indians had the monopoly in small businesses, and there were an ever-increasing number of shops dealing with literally everything: food, souvenirs, tools and pharmaceuticals. The Africans controlled the fish, fruit and vegetable market, and also made ivory and ebony carvings, some of which were very beautiful pieces of art. There were also quite a few motor mechanics, and some were very good. Others were very competent cabinetmakers, carpenters and electricians, whilst others were servants, generally working for European and Asian families.

In 1950 there were no modern asphalt roads in Tanganyika, apart from short stretches in the centre of some towns. Dirt roads connected most of the administrative centres, and they were in bad condition nearly all of the time: badly rutted during the dry season, and simply out of use during the wet season. To travel anywhere up-country of Dar-es-Salaam during the wet season was a major gamble; the danger was getting your car bogged down in an isolated stretch of road, where you would remain trapped for days, at the mercy of the weather.

Dar-es-Salaam is situated at the southern end of the Zanzibar canal. Back then it had a flourishing fishing industry, and the port area was enclosed by land, giving the numerous ships excellent protection. The entrance of the canal was roughly two kilometres in length, and varied from three hundred metres across at its widest point, to fifty metres at its narrowest. However, a cargo ship sunk by the Germans at the end of the First World War lay in this narrow section, and represented a serious obstacle to naval traffic. They had also sunk another ship in the port at the end of the bay; this act seemed to have no other purpose, except to be an annoying hindrance.

In the 1950s, an Italian firm specialising in reclaiming ship relics for their metal, won a contract to clear the two shipwrecks. The job was completed around 1955, and until then all ships had to wait for high tide to enter the harbour, and use two pilot ships to tow them in and out safely. As the job was in progress, the company inadvertently taught the Africans how to fish with explosives. Most underwater cuttings were usually done with oxygen flame, but to sever the large beams of the ship's main structure it was altogether quicker to use dynamite. The company had also employed a number of local labourers to help with the separation and loading of the cut iron.

Now, most people know that fish like to dwell in shipwrecks, and these two boats had been lying in the harbour for thirty-two years. After the first dynamite blast, something like five hundred kilos of dead fish came floating up to the surface. The African workers had never seen anything like it before, and stood there stupefied, staring at the fish. The company were unaware of the Tanganyikan laws, and rushed the fish to the African market. However, the police intercepted, and confiscated the fish.

The African labourers had now seen how easy it was to use explosives, and several of them left their jobs and became fishermen. But they did not realise how destructive this method was to the marine life; it would kill two thousand small fishes for every hundred of the large ones. Most of these fishermen obtained the dynamite illegally from the miners, and it was still possible to hear the explosions along the coast when I left the territory in 1972. Since then many more fishermen have abandoned their nets for explosives, further damaging the sensitive marine environment. It was also dangerous for the fishermen, and there were many reports of some novices who had lost their limbs – and sometimes their lives. Before the enterprise of reclaiming ships started, this type of fishing was never seen or heard of in this part of the world.

The canal of the port of Dar-es-Salaam is studded with small islands on both sides, none of them bigger than a few hundred square metres. However, there was no fresh water, and they were therefore uninhabitable. Some of them were sandy, with a sporadic palm tree, others were rocky, and some were a mixture of the two. On those that did have a combination of the two, there were some shrubs and some coarse, rough grass. This vegetation was just enough to sustain a colony of rats and snakes, two species that can survive in otherwise impossible surroundings by eating each other.

A few years later, I met some English boys and girls who had decided to pass a night under the stars on one of these islands. Some friends had taken them over by motorboat, and promised to collect them the next morning.

For the rest of the day they enjoyed themselves snorkelling and fishing; no one could have predicted that they would have anything other than a wonderful time. At sunset they sat down to eat some of the food that they had taken with them, laughing and joking, until it was dark.

At twilight they realised that they had company: a few rats were timidly coming over to the group; they must have smelt the food in the air. The girls were the first to shriek their disgust, and the rats disappeared in a flash; however, they returned later, in a much larger number. The boys tried to scare them away by waving shrubs at them, and for a while they were successful. Nevertheless, they kept coming back, each time more numerous, each time bolder, as the night got darker. Two of the boys had flashlights, and they could now see hundreds of pairs of eyes in the dark, moving back and forth, getting nearer, squeaking loudly. As time went by, it became obvious that the rats intended to attack them. The boys also got very scared, and went to join the girls in the sea, where the whole group remained until morning. In the meantime the rats ate everything that was edible on the ground, and then disappeared.

The youngsters breathed a sigh of relief when they finally saw their friends' motorboat arriving to fetch them. They left the island without hesitation, but with an exciting and frightening experience to recount.

(This story reminded me of another tale, told to me by a companion during the last war. His patrol had to camp near a fig plantation in Villa Cedro County, Sardinia, but they did not know that the place was infested by a large number of rats. It was summertime, and they had slept in the open, taking off some of their clothes, including their shoes and socks. During their sleep the rats had gnawed the nails and hard skin from their feet. They had done it with such delicacy that the soldiers did not realise what had happened until they woke up the next morning.)

The sandy island nearest to the open sea stood one metre higher than the highest tide, and was an ideal place for underwater fishing. However, sadly, all that you can see on the seabed now through the clear water is what looks like grey powder – this is all that remains of the once beautiful coral, destroyed by dynamite fishermen.

The island is also a rest stop for numerous flocks of migrating marine birds on their way to a distant destination. Other flocks also come to it every evening for a night's rest. Bird-watchers can observe their movement from the mainland at six o'clock; with a bit of luck it is also possible to watch the passing of giant fruit bats to destinations unknown to us.

On the mainland, on the north side of Dar-es-Salaam, there used to be a number of cemeteries and a crematorium, right next to one another. Each one was for a different religious group, and they had been there long before the First World War, when they were well outside the town. However, since then the town had grown considerably larger, and when it started nearing the cemeteries, each group built a new one elsewhere.

In 1962 Tanganyika gained independence, and in 1964 the country was renamed the United Republic of Tanzania. Shortly after this, the new Government notified the various embassies that they intended to reclaim the land that the old cemeteries stood on, and that everyone should arrange for their relatives' graves to be cleared.

The German Embassy acted immediately, and removed all of the graves in their area, transferring them to a more suitable place inland. The new cemetery (nearly all of which is occupied by soldiers) is now taken care of and visited by members of their own community. However, members of other non-Christian communities objected to the Government's decision, and refused to co-operate. The Government replied with a warning, and gave four months to remove all of the graves. The penalty for not adhering to this order would be arrest and imprisonment, which was not exactly an appealing prospect; the standard meal in Tanzanian prisons consisted of a main dish of sun-dried lake fish, accompanied by corn-meal mush (in Kiswahili this is called *posho*), and even the most hardened criminal would turn pale at the thought of having to live on these two ingredients for any length of time. Everyone in Tanzania knew what 'the Queen Elizabeth Hotel' (this is what the local prisons were known as) had to offer. You were not allowed shoes, and had to do anything the warden told you to, and most of the time his requests were pretty unpleasant.

The Government also threatened to flatten all of the remaining graves with tractors, and this was not a threat to be taken lightly; they had had enough of following orders and ideas from overseas administration, which had spurned their culture for a long time.

It is the custom of the tribes from East Africa, the Masai and the Kikuyu, to not have much respect for the dead, even for their own parents; they cannot understand how a dead body can invoke so much interest. They consider a corpse insignificant, and believe that the simplest solution is to feed it to the hyenas and jackals. The corpses are left far from their village to encourage the animals to deal with them; therefore they do not have to waste any wood on cremating them.

Other tribes, like the Wagogo (part of the Masai), prefer to bury their dead inside baobab trees. These giant trees are hollow, and when they are cut down it is often possible to find a number of human skeletons inside them. The trunk of an older baobab may have a circumference of over ten metres and a hole is cut a few metres up, just below the branches. The bodies are then thrown inside and sealed in as in a grave. My African workers believed that if you slept underneath these trees you would be woken with a slap in your face, administered by a ghost of the dead who demanded more respect. My friends assured me that this would happen if you insisted on using the tree as refuge.

In 1952 something started stirring in Tanzania. The Government wished to begin building the road network, and the contract was won by an Anglo-Italian company called Stirling Astaldi, which opened an office in Dar-es-Salaam. The two hundred-kilometre macadam road section would connect the capital to the important agricultural centre of Morogoro.

I thought carefully about this event. I was not happy with my current salary, and I decided to see if there was a chance to improve it with Stirling Astaldi. I was in luck, as they urgently needed an electrician to install the machinery in the main workshop, which carried out the maintenance of all the vehicles and heavy machinery for the road. My employers at DARESCO were not very happy with my sudden resignation, and would not accept it unless I abided by my contract, which meant that I had to give a month's notice. Alternatively, I could break the contract by paying them a month's salary, which I did, and we parted on good terms.

The Stirling Astaldi base camp was set up at Ubungu, about twenty kilometres from Dar-es-Salaam (the road would begin at Dar-es-Salaam). In this camp were the company offices, the main workshop, lodgings for the specialised workers, and the mess hall. Our sleeping quarters were supposed to be our home for the next four years, and consisted of two buildings with eight rooms each – two to a room. They were simple, cheap constructions, and the rough workmanship was envisaged to last the length of the four-year project. As they were bare apart from the beds, your personal belongings, such as shaving utensils, had to be placed on the floor.

This was, however, the only camp belonging to the company that was equipped with electric light. The workshop, living quarters and mess hall were all illuminated; but there were no lights outside.

The secondary camps, located a few kilometres apart along the road, were constructed in the same way as the main camp; but only the workshop had electricity, served by a small independent generator. The light for the living quarters was provided by small kerosene lamps; the only 'luxury' available in those smaller camps was the bath/showers. The roofs for the living quarters were made out of intertwined leaves of palm trees (*makuti*), and this material was often refuge for many unwelcome creatures, such as a large centipede, which had a horrible appearance and a venomous bite; and the occasional errant tarantula would appear under the bed, or even in the blanket. But these were not really a worry for seasoned post-war Italians such as us.

We came to hear of a report from the English engineers of the *parte contraria* office to the local government. This office was responsible for checking that the work met the specifications of the project planners, so that they could then authorise the payments. The report mentioned the adaptable and sacrificial nature of the Italian workers, which had helped the company to win this important contract; it also suggested that they had accepted to live and work under grievous conditions, which most other European nationals would probably have refused. As far as I was concerned, this view was in contrast to the lifestyles of the people who wrote the report, and I think it was certainly an exaggerated summary; but maybe it could have been relevant to people who were a little softer than we were.

(Some years later, Stirling Astaldi entered into a joint venture with a German road construction company, and the Germans offered some very attractive terms. This was because they were well behind schedule on the contract they had accepted two years before, and were now at risk of being penalised. Apparently, the reason for the delay was not because of any lack of expertise from the German workers, but because of their inability to obtain an honest day's work from the African staff. They retained about sixty specialised engineers and staff – including engineers and land surveyors – which they considered sufficient for the construction of the two hundred-kilometre road. Right at the beginning, the Germans raised an objection as to how Stirling Astaldi were to treat its Italian staff, and insisted on a separate bedroom for each worker, a bath/shower for each worker, electric lights twenty-four hours a day, a film twice a week, and other minor amenities.)

When observing my new Italian work colleagues, I realised that their behaviour was very similar to that of my old companions at Athi River, and I foresaw a number of fights. However, in spite of their hot temper, the group proved to be hard-working, disciplined and obedient – all essential characteristics for a productive day. Among us there were a small number of youngsters ready to accept the best Africa had to offer; every day there were different events, providing unlimited diversity. This was enough to make us forget the primary reason that we came to Africa; the majority of us had left our homes to save as much money as possible, and this seems logical when you bear in mind the hardships that the post-war family had to endure. These difficult days led us to accept any sacrifice, so we would not have to repeat them. However, the majority of the workers were middle-aged, and the fact that they did not have the slightest interest in the environment was, of course, natural.

It was clear to us that the financial prospects from this three-year job were not enough to stop us worrying about the future. Our major priority was to buy a house, and from our salary we knew that this job alone would not be enough, although with overtime it would give us more than the same job would pay in Italy.

Due to its proximity to Dar-es-Salaam, the Ubungu camp had become a convenient place to meet Italian residents of the city who were not working for the company. Some of them became very good friends, and we met with them every weekend. We had very similar opinions and ideas on the Italian post-war political climate, and this made our relationships even more interesting; all of our characters were also very similar.

It was during this period that I made my best friends for life, who have given much joy to my family and me. After fifty years we are still in contact with them, and I find it exhilarating that our friendship carries on through our children. (They all have one thing in common: being born and brought up in the Africa of the 1950s, a place so different from Italy.) Occasionally we would visit each other when on holiday in Italy, and that was simply marvellous. Our friendship was started and consolidated by our young wives, who shared common interests, and became stronger with the birth of our children, who were cared for by all, regardless of which family they belonged to.

My Milanese friend Pittaluga was gifted with considerable strength. In the last war he was a proud member of the marine unit MAS (Anti-Submarine Motorboats), who operated on the Aegean seas, and he never tired of recounting his adventures. He was an excellent and happy companion, always very sure of himself – maybe a little too much so: he was so naïve that he believed that he could confront a lion armed with only a good knife. Perhaps this was why he always carried a sharp hunting dagger on his belt...

One evening Pittaluga, two other friends and I were walking along the unfinished section of road, just outside the camp. We did not realise that we were approaching a group of lions about forty metres in front of us – until we heard their roars. Pittaluga did not lose his composure, and stuck to his instincts: he unsheathed his knife, dropped to his knees and took up a fighting position. I must say that we were all astonished, and I suspected that he did not have his wits about him. It looked like a joke; but it was not, it was a demonstration of how far the foolhardy courage and naivety of Pittaluga could stretch. He was lucky that the rest of us had more common sense than he had, and we pointed out to him how rash it would be to face one lion – let alone two – with only a knife. After hearing this he reluctantly gave up and came over to us. This incident caused a great stir in the camp and encouraged everyone to stop enjoying night walks.

Another great character, who could have come out of the pages of Jack London's books, is a Sardinian: Salvatore Vacca. He was a typical merchant navy seaman. This group were considered true seamen, as they wandered all of the exotic seas of the world, often in small and dilapidated ships. He was also a worthy representative of these 'sea-dogs' – as they are called – and had a long list of scuffles in the faraway ports of the South Seas. Resolute and aggressive, he was a true combat machine that was always ready to confront any adversary, no matter what their physical prowess or build: a true champion. He had also participated in the war, patrolling the Sardinian Straits in the Italian Navy. Vacca had all the characteristics of a Sardinian: a good heart, generous, courageous, loyal, reliable and true to his word. For these reasons, his family has always been very close to our hearts, and his wife Paola stood as godmother at Linda's christening (the youngest of my two daughters).

Salvatore and his pretty wife Paola had exceptional adventures during their eighteen years in Africa. These were years that were divided between jobs on land, and adventures on the South Seas.

For two years they had lived in a remote and uncomfortable place on the Mozambique border, where Salvatore had obtained a job. There the European population was almost non-existent; only a group of missionaries resided there. Paola was a petite woman, and soon fell ill due to their rough surroundings. She was within a breath of dying, and had no choice but to go to the doctor at the mission, who said that she was in urgent need of an operation. Unfortunately, he then went on to say that he was not experienced enough to perform it; he would have to operate with the assistance of a medical manual. He asked for written consent to operate, which also cleared him from any responsibility in case of a negative outcome. Salvatore and Paolo had no choice; there was not enough time for them to reach a hospital with competent surgeons. Thankfully there was no complication during the operation, and it was a complete success.

Eventually Salvatore found another job in Tanganyika, where he worked for an Italian gold miner for about a year. His job consisted of transporting gold-bearing sand to the watercourse by lorry, and then extracting the gold from it. Before leaving Africa for good, he worked in a diamond mine for three years, living nearby with Paola and his two children, Pinella and Gianfranco.

Another friend of mine is Fernando Rosato, from Abruzzi, whom I met when he was fifteen years of age; he was entrusted to me as a learner electrician. He was a strong-willed and intelligent boy, who has since made a success of his life. I have followed him and his work as if he were my younger brother, even after he left Africa. We chose him to stand with Paola as godparents to Linda.

Then there are our great friends Vera and Piero Mannini, with whom we have experienced so much together over the past fifty years. Piero was a specialised engineer, Workshop Manager of the Mercedes-Benz outlet in Dar-es-Salaam. He shared my passion for hunting and firearms. He also has always been a willing friend, a contributor of valid ideas, and ready to help with any work that required his professional versatility.

The Ubungu camp was surrounded with ordinary galvanised wire, which had the sole purpose of establishing its boundary; therefore, it would not prevent possible night incursions of the felines and hyenas. The toilet facilities were located in a separate building, and to reach them it was necessary to use a torch. Thus there was a strong possibility of accidentally stepping on a lethargic puff adder, which had the bad habit of wandering around during the night. It is the width of a man's arm and can reach up to a metre in length. This reptile is very common in Africa, and its venom sacs contain a higher quantity of poison than any other.

Our rooms were situated on the lower side of the camp, and just outside the fence was the dry bed of a watercourse. It was about six metres wide, and water only flowed during the wet season. As this area was of a semi-arid climate, our company decided to take advantage of this channel and build a dam, which was made very cheaply, using only stones, entwined plants and bedding sand. The store of water that was then created was useful for the camp; it could also be used to compress the soil on the road surface. After the first rains, the water reserve stretched three kilometres back, and in places reached a depth of four metres; this would then get shallower and shallower, until it disappeared altogether. To reach it you had to walk a short distance from the camp fence; because of soil erosion, the pathway was devoid of any vegetation – it probably had been fertile at one time. The right side of the dam joined up to some thick undergrowth, which ended after about thirty metres and made way for some luscious thick grass, reaching the height of about one and a half metres in places. A path had formed in the grass, about half a metre wide, and the place was very quiet; an ideal place for a feline ambush.

Something that surprised us was the existence of catfish in the lake. We were confused, because it was dry for most of the year, and as it was not connected with any other watercourse, we could not make out where they were coming from. Of course, I learnt much later that catfish have the peculiar habit (like frogs) of submerging themselves in the mud, until the water is sufficient to allow them to swim again. It is a robust, versatile fish, with a mouth that is way out of proportion with its body. It will eat anything that has the misfortune to fall in the water: larvae, insects, or even small mammals. Its name comes from the famous moustache which sprouts around its mouth.

The small dam became a choice spot with those members of staff who were adept with the fishing rod. They could also use a fishing net or, as I saw in some places, a mosquito net. The abundance and size of the catfish gave great pleasure to the anglers.

The herbivorous fauna of the area also began to crowd to the channel to quench their thirst, thus attracting the unwelcome presence of big cats. As a result, the camp residents started to be serenaded by the felines, and their presence near the dam always discouraged the fishing aficionados, who from then on always ventured to the dam in a group.

On one late afternoon in 1952, the rushed arrival of an African to the camp attracted our attention. He asked for immediate help to save his son from a very dangerous situation. He explained that he was the owner of a small piece of land, fifty metres to the left of the dam; here the soil had not yet disintegrated and was still fertile. He was growing rice, and since it was nearly ripe, he had placed his son on a platform one and a half metres high. Here he could guard it from birds, as he was in a position to hit them with a piece of wood and shout at them. However, three lions had come to quench their thirst at the dam, and as they had come from behind the dam he had not noticed them; fortunately they had not noticed him either, even though they were only about forty metres away. The situation was then aggravated when the lions decided to hang around; perhaps they were waiting for the appearance of some gazelle.

The boy had thrown a stone in the direction of some pigeons in the adjacent rice field, and emitted his usual scream. This attracted the felines' attention, and they turned their heads in the direction of the noise, replying with a hoarse growl. Their eyes met, and the lions started to near the platform, whilst staying under the cover of the undergrowth. They disappeared from the boy's view; nevertheless he could track their movements by the rustling of the grass. Obviously, he was terrified.

A companion and I set off rapidly towards the dam with a couple of carbines, but without taking any note of the danger that lay ahead of us. Although we had a great juvenile passion for adventure, neither of us had the experience to confront such a situation. With a lot of courage and little good sense we reached the footpath leading to the rice field, with the boy's father leading the way. We did not see any sign of the lions and began to panic, sensing that they were still somewhere in the grass. Our spirit overrode our legs, which felt like running in the opposite direction; in spite of our apprehension, we were past the point of no return. In the immediate vicinity were three hungry lions, hidden by the high grass, perhaps waiting for us. Our ears were stretched, waiting for the faintest rustle in the grass, or perhaps the customary warning growl before their attack, which would maybe give us just enough time to defend ourselves. We were looking, but it was impossible to see, and we were dreading a close-range attack.

We were now nearing the platform, where we saw a space in the grass, and were sure that there was an animal lying there. As I observed more closely, our suppositions were confirmed. The blood drained from my face as my eyes met with those belonging to the king of the jungle who stood two metres in front of me. He was an enormous male, with a dense reddish mane, and was veering towards us from a crouched position, ready to jump, but obviously undecided as to which direction. I was paralysed, and after a moment – which seemed an eternity to us – the beast did the thing we least expected him to: he got up and ran away, in a very smooth movement, all in perhaps a fraction of a second. After having beaten us to the ambush, the lion, maybe believing he was being confronted by a group of men that did not seem afraid of him, had chosen the dishonourable retreat. Whilst doing so, he shattered the air with a roar that made our hair stand on end and, funnily enough, freed me from my temporary paralysis. Instinctively I raised my rifle to my shoulder. The lion had made a narrow escape path through the grass, almost like a topless tunnel; but suddenly he stopped and turned his head, maybe to see what our intentions were. His curiosity was fatal: one shot of my 375 Holland and Holland Magnum nailed him in the middle of the forehead (an easy shot from a few metres), and permanently nullified any future threats from him. That rifle is a very high-velocity weapon and is widely used in Africa for big-game hunting. It has never let me down, and has given me a lot of satisfaction over the many years that I have used it.

As I had expected, the territory was rich with all sorts of animals, a paradise at our disposal, and the adventures could start immediately. With my first salary I bought some new hunting equipment, and a cross-country 4x4, which would allow us to travel almost anywhere during the rainy season.

Today, with the benefit of hindsight, I can see that the two years that I spent on the savannahs of Tanzania were a negative period in my life. I surely took the wrong direction, and soon realised that I had not learnt a lot from my experiences. I was twenty-eight, but I can see now that I needed the guide of a more experienced person to bring me back to my senses, to point out to me that instead of wasting my time and money on profitless hunting, I should remember the reasons why I had come to Africa. Instead of throwing my body and soul into ways of saving money – as most of my friends were – I had given in to my weakness of satisfying my romantic attraction with big-game hunting. At that time it was everything I wanted, and distracted me from pursuing the objectives that would really make a difference to my future.

A year after the new road began to be constructed, the company found it necessary to transfer some of the personnel to other camps along the route, and I was one of them. The company posted me to the workshop at Ubenazamosi, where I was to try to install power at the stone quarry, as it was holding up production. On my arrival, there were five hundred Africans from the Belgian Congo waiting, who had been employed by the company. The quarry's purpose was to supply varying sizes of crushed stone to the road; the workshop's purpose was to provide maintenance for the large motors of the crushers. Our crew consisted of fifteen workers/operators, housed in two barracks, built with the same cheap material as the buildings at the Ubungu camp; in addition, there was a canteen, kitchen, showers and lavatories. A driveway was created which led us from the camp to the workshop and quarry, through a kilometre of dense wood. These twice-a-day trips were an extreme nuisance, and had to always be conducted in a group to lessen the danger from wild animals. When they had to be taken alone, the track seemed very oppressive, I think we could sense the danger; at the same time, we could not avoid asking ourselves: what are we doing here, waiting to be a meal for wild beasts? Nevertheless, we had decided not to use a vehicle for this short walk, considering its distance; after all, if you could ignore the danger, it could be a pleasant stroll. However, sometimes there was urgent work at hand, and one of us would have to stay late, until maybe eight or nine o'clock, and in this case, all the wretched man could do was ask the Eternal Father to see that he returned home unscathed. Many of us naively thought that the light from a torch would be sufficient to discourage any form of feline attack.

Every time someone returned from this walk in the dark, I

considered it a miracle that he had come out alive. It was something that I would never even consider doing: there was plenty of evidence all around us of animals roaming round at night, including the small square in front of our sleeping quarters. It was quite possible to encounter not only lions, but also leopards and other wild beasts. The lavatories were located about fifty metres away from our lodgings, and any excursion in the dark was a nasty experience, although a torch was a little help. The real danger was not treading on a snake, but meeting a lion or leopard that had come to explore our neighbourhood.

One night we were awoken by a great fuss: a beast, maybe a hyena, was running and howling very loudly in the space between our barracks, and judging by the intensity of the screams, it was clear that they were those of panic, perhaps due to the presence of a lion. I came out of my room with my rifle, as I was worried that someone was in danger; but luckily this was not the case.

Another time, one of the workers coming back with the lorry said he had seen some lions, not very far from our houses. This worried us. Lions often have the bad habit of stopping in places that suit them most; they never move too far from these spots, and may be there for a few days or even a week, so you may suddenly find them right in front of you. They love lying down on the middle of the road or at the side, and are almost invisible until somebody treads on them.

In our group there were two workers who were father and son. The father was named Zappata. He was a Caterpillar engineer and worked on the road; the son was the keeper of the spare parts store. Late one afternoon, just before returning to the camp, we suddenly heard lions' roars coming from the direction of the stone quarry. As they were quite close, they were very menacing. That evening the son wanted to stay longer in the store to finish an urgent job and had planned to be home by about eight-thirty; but considering the circumstances he was undecided whether to return with our group or not. In the end he unwisely decided to remain to finish his work. At eight o'clock Zappata came back from work and he himself could now hear the lions' roars. We explained that we had no car to go and fetch his son; we also added that to walk was seriously dangerous, and the best option was for his son to spend the night in the store. Nevertheless, the father boarded his own Land Rover and went to collect his son. On his way to the store, he did not see any beasts along the road; however, when coming back they encountered a group of lions at the beginning of the driveway, right next to the store. There was no doubt in our minds that if the father had not gone to fetch his son, he would have tried to come back home on foot. He would have met the lions that were lying in wait, and would never have made it.

Everyone in the camp was in possession of a paraffin lamp, which we kept alight all night. Its feeble light was sufficient to illuminate the room dimly without hurting the eyes, and helped you to spot potentially dangerous insects, such as scorpions, tarantulas and centipedes. As I had spent many years in Africa, I was convinced that these were the only insects that were a threat. I was wrong.

One night I was awoken from my sleep by a weak noise, like the creaking of a cricket, but more feeble. It was only possible to hear it because of the profound silence in the room at night. Soon I discovered that it was nothing less than a chorus of mandibles, if you can call it that. Looking carefully with my paraffin lamp, I now discovered that my mosquito net had enormous black stains all over, almost completely blocking the light out. The feeble noise was coming from these 'stains', although I could not discover what they were. I prepared to get up from under the mosquito net, which was of course tucked under the mattress to prevent the pests from getting in. Before getting down from the bed, I looked prudently to the floor where I was about to set my feet down, and noticed that the floor had disappeared. It was only then that I realised that I was being assaulted by legions of driver-ants, or safari-ants, as they are called in East African colonies (*safari* means travelling in Kiswahili). These ants have been made famous by a number of Hollywood films, and are renowned for their formidable pincers. The creaking was coming from the opening and closing of these pincers, all apparently in unison. They were now trying to get at me. With two jumps I reached the corner of the room where I kept a container of paraffin, and spilt some onto the ground to stop the little beasts from eating me alive; in the meantime they had climbed up my legs by the hundred, and their continuous pinching compelled me to dance a tarantella. All petroleum products are deadly for any kind of insect; they are killed as soon as they make contact with it, so I scattered the paraffin over the floor with a broom, and I had soon collected a bucketful of dead ants. Some of them escaped the petroleum bath and tried to reach the space under the door; however, I was now enraged, and blocked them off with some more neat broom-work.

Those ants that had climbed on the mosquito net had escaped the massacre so far. For them, I had to use a spray can containing a strong insecticide, like DDT. This operation to render the room habitable again caused me only to lose two hours' sleep, and left a pronounced aroma of paraffin in the air.

I would now like to relate my personal thoughts on the danger that driver-ants represent. They cannot be dangerous to a human in the open, as we can obviously move much quicker than they can, and escape would be easy. I have often stopped to observe them, and stood only half a pace away, and they simply continued about their business. However, when marching in a column of about thirty centimetres wide, they can move much quicker, as sometimes the ants go on top of the slower ones to gain momentum. The real danger would come if a person is rendered immobile or trapped; in this case, death would be certain, slow and horrible. Many insects are not intelligent enough to run, and try to escape the ants by wriggling and twisting on the spot in the hope of shaking them from their backs. This action is useless.

It was near to the time of this encounter that I met a blonde English girl of twenty-two named Sally, who would eventually become my wife. Sally lived near to me in Ubenazamosi: she was with the Public Works Department. The PWD was instructed by the Tanganyika Government to ensure that the work tallied with the contract.

For the first time in my life, I had met a woman who showed different characteristics and emotions from all the rest. On various occasions in Africa, I had met people who had offered their daughters and sisters for marriage; but I had declined every offer. I did not consider it appropriate to involve any woman in my troubles at the time, especially not through an arranged marriage. Sally was different, always so alive and always there, with unlimited energy; surely, I could not miss that opportunity. However, after an unhappy period of work at Ubenazamosi, the company transferred me back to Dar-es-Salaam. This temporarily put an end to my relationship with Sally.

My transfer had a strange effect on me: it modified my character, without me realising it. The years that my soul had spent in solitude started to have a negative effect on my personality, which was becoming more aggressive every day. After some time, I was very dissatisfied: something was amiss inside me. More than once I had been accused of being overly aggressive, and had been involved in court cases for inflicting bodily harm in fist fights. Stirling Astaldi decided that a man of my character was better out of the company, and they gave me the sack. At this sudden loss of my employment, there was only one positive aspect I could think of: from the two years spent in the savannahs, I had gained far more experience than I had done in the preceding five years. Unfortunately with the loss of my job, Sally was even further away, now an unattainable goal; and in the circumstances, the chances of a reprieve with her appeared very remote. I considered her already lost; she had been only a brief gleam in my life.

Two of my companions, my Sardinian friend Salvatore Vacca and the Milanese Pittaluga, were dismissed for the same reason: they were both the same sort as I. All three of us were now together in Dar-es-Salaam, unemployed, and in danger from the authorities unless we found a new job within two months. My complete failure seemed to be beckoning. My car was loaded with Vacca's and my baggage, and we prepared to leave Ubungu camp for good; unknown to us, our former employer had decided to give us one last surprise, the ultimate insult: the Chief Engineer had ordered the Somali gate guard to demand that we open our travelling bag for inspection. Now, that request was out of order: in all the three territories of East Africa it was well known that it was strictly forbidden for any African to carry out an inspection of the property of a European by order of the dictates of the colonial regime; moreover, the English law was very clear on the subject of property inspection, and required that before it was carried out it must be authorised with an order issued by a court of law. Our former superior knew very well that the persons leaving the camp were two characters who would not stand any abuse of their rights; in spite of this, they had chosen to confront us and breach the rules.

When we reached the gate, we asked the Somali guard to open it. The African then turned round to us with a cocky attitude, and with an arrogant manner requested that we open our luggage. The gate of the camp was about eighty metres away from the workshop, which was built without side walls due to the climate, with its roof standing on pillars. Only a waist-high wall separated the two, and from this vantage point the workshop staff had stopped their activities, and now watched the scene with interest. Salvatore immediately suggested ramming the gate down, but I had a better idea: I invited the guard to come and open the bags by himself. He then remained undecided for a moment, looked back briefly towards the office building, and seeing no encouragement, he abandoned his post, obviously fearing for his safety. Now there was nothing left for us to do except find the Chief Engineer, who had given that stupid order, and ask for some sort of explanation.

A military campaign against the Mau Mau revolt was currently in progress in Kenya, and the Colonial Offices of all three East African Territories had warned all possessors of firearms not to leave them unguarded, especially in motor vehicles and at home. So when I went to look for the Chief Engineer I had to leave the car alone, as Salvatore wanted to come with me, and therefore I had to take the carbine; but in an automatic movement from a wartime habit, I swiftly pulled back the breech-block to make sure that it was unloaded. You can imagine the panic of everyone nearby. Everyone obviously thought that I was checking to see if it was loaded, believing that I was about to go and settle the score with my former bosses. All hell broke loose as people scattered from the scene, and it was very amusing to see them running cowering behind the wall, popping their heads up to see if they were being followed. They escaped like scared ducks, provoking the general hilarity of the many that now saw my stupefied face at the scene.

We soon returned to the gate without having been able to contact anyone at the office, and this time I was the one who wanted to run the gate down. However, Salvatore had suddenly become responsible, and went to open it, saying to me that it was not nice for good-mannered people to destroy other people's gates.

Salvatore, albeit with some difficulty, was the first to find a job, with a small navigating company, and he embarked as first officer on a ship of about five thousand tons. The ship carried goods from Mombasa to Dar-es-Salaam, Beria, Madagascar, Durban, Aden and the Seychelles, about a five-month round-trip.

Pittaluga found a job in a large Dar-es-Salaam workshop, which specialised in the construction and repair of machinery for the processing of sisal, convening its fibre into all types and sizes of cable for ships.

Finally I found a job as an electrician with the Ford Motor Company; it was a disaster, definitely a big step backwards, and I still had a big problem to solve: where to find a cheap enough place to stay.

In the meantime, Pittaluga had found lodgings near his place of work, a few kilometres from the centre of town. It was an ancient abandoned house, a pile of tin sheets and bricks, situated under a forest of palm trees, probably planted by the Arabs at the time of the slave trade; it had probably been taken over by successive generations of Africans, and had slowly deteriorated into its present decrepit state. Pittaluga had rented it for a fistful of small change, as he was not one to worry about the state of the dump. There was no drinking water; indeed, there were was no supply plant in the area, and to clean the toilet you had to empty the water with buckets strategically placed nearby. In past times electric light was considered an unnecessary luxury: to be precise, there was not even the wiring for it, so poor Pittaluga was forced to use a paraffin lamp or a dim candle, like Pinocchio in the whale's belly. You could definitely say that the place was very sad.

However, knowing that I was having difficulty in finding suitable accommodation, Pittaluga was generous enough to invite me to share his house, and of course the expenses. I was very grateful to him for his offer, and I soon went to stay with him. I told him that in addition to my share of expenses, I would also share all the heavy chores, like drawing water from the well, and so forth. Nevertheless, after the surprise of the accommodation offer, Pittaluga unfortunately had some more surprises in store for me. Soon I realised how he was living: he had organised his life in an extremely primitive manner, and I was sure that just the sight of the way he was preparing his meals would have caused even the starving troops of Garibaldi to turn pale. Just a few paces from the house stood the well, with its water level at fifteen metres from the top. It was of remote origin, probably also the work of the Arabs, and its water was of a dubious colour; but it was the only nearby supply of water available. We needed this water at our disposal for evening baths, cooking and the toilet; therefore, we had to draw several buckets of water every day, by hand. This was a Herculean operation due to the deepness of the well and the weight of the bucket when full of water. Pittaluga told me that when in the process of pulling up the water, it was sometimes possible to see large rats climbing deftly up the impervious sides of the well; he also assured me that he had seen snakes hunting the rats.

The doors of the house, including the main entrance, were all without locks. This was a dangerous invitation to any shady customers, which the neighbourhood certainly did not lack. We had heard several times in East Africa that there was a type of thief who would enter houses only in the night, always armed with a machete. He was considered much more dangerous than a common thief, as he was prepared to kill if he was discovered and prevented from escaping. The Africans called him *shenzi*, which roughly translates to 'despicable', or 'despised'. He operated only in the dark, completely naked and his whole body anointed with coconut oil, which made any attempt to grab him extremely difficult. He was also very difficult to spot due to the colour of his skin.

Pittaluga had placed an empty tin on the top of his door while sleeping. One night, he told me that the tin had fallen down, and he had been woken up. He got up immediately and rushed towards the door of the room, attempting to intercept the intruder. He did not see him, but he suddenly brushed past him, and was immediately engaged in a struggle. He somehow succeeded in disarming him, but due to his slippery oily skin the *shenzi* managed to reach the door and escape into the night. Pittaluga kept the sharp knife as a souvenir, and showed it to me. It was thirty-five centimetres long.

However, Pittaluga did not lose heart, and despite these experiences battled on whilst trying to save money. He had placed an iron tripod a few metres from the well. It was three metres high, and when it was mounted and ready for use, it was possible to lift up or keep heavy weights suspended in the middle of it by means of a chain. The contraption consisted of three iron pipes, joined at one end by iron rings to form a head that was free to move only a few centimetres; at the other end, the pipes were free to move, and rotate as was needed. With the tripod erected, the three legs at the bottom end were opened, and planted in the ground at an equal distance to form a triangle, the vertical conical form roughly resembling a Native American tepee. This gadget was indispensable in many situations, especially since Pittaluga did not have a kitchen; to avoid setting fire to the house, he must cook out in the open. One of the advantages of the tripod was that it could be moved anywhere; in addition, for those blessed with a large amount of firewood at their disposal, it could be run very cheaply.

Pittaluga had bought an iron cooking pot from the local market, with two robust handles and a twenty-litre capacity. He attached this to the tripod, at a height of about forty or fifty centimetres from the ground, and he could then use this to do the cooking. He explained that as he had no help around the house, he was forced to do it himself; this of course applied to all other domestic chores, including gathering of firewood etc. He said that he found it most arduous to attend to this unavoidable task after a hard day at the factory. But as far as I knew Pittaluga, he was not the type to waste time with the kitchen chores, before or after working hours.

He decided to do the cooking twice a week in a quantity sufficient to last three days, and every night would leave the leftovers of the (disgusting) concoction inside the iron pot until the next cooking day. Anyone can imagine the taste of these leftovers, after three days in a pot in the sweltering African climate, with a mean temperature of at least 30°C. However, Pittaluga maintained that it was useless to quibble about the food if you intended to buy a house in Italy.

He did his foodstuff shopping only once a week. His first visit was to the butcher's where he bought a few kilograms of dog-meat, sold at a give-away price. He said that there was practically no difference between the quality of this meat and that consumed by the average European family; he patiently explained that they were discarded offcuts from premium meat: they contained fat in abundance, and pieces of meaty bones. He added that I did not understand that the dog-meat was free from the bacteria that more expensive meat contained; what was more, the higher fat quantity made it ideal for making broth. As a man with as hard a skin as his, I was more or less convinced by his arguments, and was in agreement with his principles.

Believe you me, it was a privilege to see Pittaluga's cooking. I remember him with affection: a companion of hard, uncertain times. I can picture him near the tripod, be it rain or shine, in his shorts with his powerful muscular torso, mixing that infernal minestrone blend, with a metre-long wooden spoon in his hand, singing his favourite song badly: *Luna Rossa* (*Red Moon*). The preparation of the ingredients for the pot was another brief and concise operation.

Firstly he removed the sand and dirt from the potatoes; he washed them briefly with the water from the well, and threw them into the cauldron without taking the skin off, together with the vegetables and tomatoes; he added some small pieces of margarine, some spices to improve the taste, and to complete the concoction, the dog-meat; then to hasten the cooking process, he brought the contents of the pot to a furious boiling point. The fire was then extremely hot, and compelled Pittaluga to stay a couple of paces away from the flames.

After dinner, to fill the time before going to sleep, we spent an hour or two talking – there was nothing else to do in that place – and in those long hours we recounted episodes of our respective lives. We shared war stories and anything else that came to our minds, separated by an out-of-fashion table, sitting on out-of-date chairs. We went on talking, looking at each other by the paraffin lamp, if he had remembered to buy the paraffin – otherwise the feeble light of a wax candle would do just as well. In the silence of the night, the shrill song of crickets and the croaking of frogs in the semi-dry ponds near the house accompanied our dismal and uniform voices; sometimes, when the night was too oppressive inside the house, we would go outside to look at the sky, always full of stars, and dream of unattainable goals.

One evening, on a tired return from work, I found a great surprise which would change my life for ever. Near the already dark house was a car with an African driver. My Sally was standing near the car, smiling radiantly! She explained that she had come to stay with me from now on, and said that she would like to become my wife.

Whilst waiting for my return she had inspected our abode, our royal palace, in all its splendour. That evening we lit the lamp and sat outside, and she said that she was expecting a baby. No matter how I was living now, she was quite prepared to share my discomforts. However, after about a month her body soon betrayed her will; she found it difficult to digest Pittaluga's minestrone, which was of course boiled using water from the well, and she started having trouble with her stomach which got progressively worse.

However, our salvation was determined by Pittaluga's fate. This is what happened to him:

He was discharged from TOM (the firm that employed him) after a serious incident following a quarrel with an African colleague. I do not know what the quarrel was about, but at the end of it the African attacked him with an iron bar and struck him on the head. Pittaluga began to lose a lot of blood, but instinctively took hold of his ill-fated adversary by the throat in an attempt to strangle him. Luckily, he was prevented from suffocating him completely by the intervention of three other men, who nevertheless could not to get him to release his grip. Finally, his adversary fainted, which induced Pittaluga to eventually let go. Afterwards he showed me his shin, which was badly stained by his own blood. They later took him to court, but he refused to pay the fine, maintaining that he acted in self-defence, as he was attacked from behind, and he was nearly sent to prison. However, perhaps he thought about the life that he would have at the Queen Elizabeth Hotel: the reception that he could expect from the African wardens would not be the most friendly, that was for sure, and the food there would be even worse than what he made at home. Just as the judge was deciding his term of imprisonment, he changed his mind and agreed to pay the fine. He then left Tanzania and went to Nairobi with the intention of joining the police force, which at that time was committed to fighting the Mau Mau. They accepted him, but he refused to wear the uniform as he said it was too tightly fitting on him. After some thought, the police decided that he was more dangerous to them than the Mau Mau were, and discharged him. Without work, he was forced to return to Italy. After a few months, I received a letter from him, begging me to write to the Kenyan Police on his behalf, informing them that he was now disposed to wear the uniform. Obviously, this was not a feasible proposition, and eventually we lost contact with him.

His leaving the country was just what we needed, because we were then free to find alternative accommodation. Sally and I decided to rent a house nearer to the town, with running water and electric lights; finally, we could start to have a decent, normal life.

I had another piece of luck in the Ford workshop. One day I bumped into my previous boss, John Maitland of the electrical company, which in the meantime had changed its name to TANESCO (Tanganyika Electric Supply Company). I had worked under him before I left the company to join Stirling Astaldi, and he had come to have his car repaired. He was surprised to see me in the garage, and asked me if I was happy with my present job. I replied that I was not at all happy, that I could not find any future in this type of work, which I considered dirty, ill-rewarding and tiresome; I was constantly listening to customers' complaints. Then, to my great surprise, he offered me a job. To my knowledge I thought that this was impossible due to the company's very clear rules, which forbade the re-engagement of personnel who had left the company, for any reason. I reminded him of this obstacle, but he assured me that as far as I was concerned, the rules would be different, and that all the European staff would be happy to have me again in their ranks. After this I left the Ford garage in record time: only three days' notice. I was to work again with my old African crew, the same people I knew before I had left the company earlier.

I would like to mention the new conditions of employees to exemplify the way the British Colonial Office conducted themselves; these were the specifications for the employment of European personnel:

The company assigned to me a completely furnished house of four rooms plus services, rent-free; the furnishing included a refrigerator, an electric cooker, and air conditioner in the bedroom; I did not have to pay for the electricity I was using; I had a month a year of local leave; every three years of service, we were obliged to leave the territories of East Africa, where the climate was supposed to be unhealthy, and go anywhere in the world for six months. This six months' leave, according to the Colonial mentality, was necessary to reinvigorate the health of Europeans after working three years in an East African climate. At the start of the long leave (that was what it was called in East Africa) we were given a cheque for the amount equal to six months' salary to be spent as we liked; in addition, the company paid for a return ticket to any place on earth, even as far as New Zealand and Australia; what was more, the company paid for two tickets a year for every child of a staff member to study in Europe: one during the summer vacation, and one during the winter. To complete this list of privileges, I had a car at my disposal, and a company pension (not required by the state).

It is obvious that from then on our life would become much easier. It was also at this time that I discovered how much easier it was to give orders than to receive them.

The company's working hours were from eight o'clock right through to three o'clock. This meant that in the afternoon we were free to go anywhere we wanted, for example to the beach, to practise some water sports. Dar-es-Salaam had a very beautiful sports club, the Gymkhana Club, with many facilities: twelve tennis courts, an extensive golf course, squash courts, and cricket and judo outside. The after-sports amenities were in a large building, where a well-stocked bar provided a large variety of spirits and beers, and, of course, all sorts of non-alcoholic beverages. For the hungry, a variety of sandwiches were available, all at reasonable prices. The club was the ideal place to meet with friends for a cold beer, and to spend a carefree afternoon until sundown.

Chapter 6

The rocky coasts of Tanzania are very rich in crustaceans. Unfortunately for the Africans their culture forbids them to consume these choice dishes, such as lobster, langouste, crabs, oysters etc. I never understood their reluctance, and thought that maybe the strange and menacing appearance of these creatures had scared the fishermen in past times; perhaps they thought that they could be venomous, or maybe harm them in some way. They were also forbidden to eat pork, but it is unbelievable that these people led a life of hardship (as do most Africans) without tasting this meat. However, this state of affairs put the Europeans at an advantage as it was simple for us to go down to the beach and buy some fresh shellfish at a low price, as no African would touch them. The only thing to make sure of was that the crustaceans were still alive and fresh; otherwise you would be poisoned. Lobsters can remain alive for several hours out of the water, staying immobile. To find out if they were still alive, the African fishermen used a simple experiment: they grabbed one of the two eyes that was protruding from the head between the thumb and the index finger, and squeezed. If the wretched lobster was still alive, it would emit a shrill cry of pain. When I heard that cry, I always remembered that they too felt pain, and wondered what a human's cry would be like if he had one of his eyes squeezed. However, the torment for the lobster did not end there: after finding that it was still breathing, it would be thrown into a pot of boiling water to be cooked. After this kind of performance, we have the brass face to claim shamelessly that we are the superior species of animal! After processing this through my mind, I was convinced that if the crustacean had a choice, it would prefer to be eaten by a more congenial octopus.

The local anglers were very lucky, as the waters of the Indian Ocean were not yet polluted and industrial fishing was non-existent. Therefore the then abundant sea fauna were at the disposal of the low numbers of European inhabitants in Tanganyika. We could go fishing every day after working hours, and on weekends we could go deep-sea fishing, hooking prize fish such as sailfish, which everyone could afford.

In 1953 we decided to spend our Christmas holiday in Mombasa with my brother Vittorio, and Salvatore Vacca asked to come with us. Mombasa is in Kenya on the shores of the Indian Ocean, about three hundred kilometres from Dar-es-Salaam, and we used a Vanguard to get there: an old English car that had the bad habit of losing the rear left wheel from time to time – perhaps too often for my liking. The man who had sold me the car was a mechanic by the name of Poltronerieri, and he had told me about the problem. He said it would be all right if I tightened the bolts every now and then, and I had to stop the car twice to do exactly this when I felt the car wobbling; luckily, there were no serious incidents. I realised how naive I had been to buy a car with this kind of defect, but as I did not know how to fix it, I did not remedy the situation.

We started the trip at lunchtime during the rainy season, and after a while torrential rain started to pour down on us. After the town of Morogoro we left the tarmac road; Salvatore suggested he drove for a while so that Sally and I could have a short sleep in the back before resuming the driving. As we travelled on the muddy dirt track our nerves were as unstable as the car was; what were also precarious were the one-litre bottles of beer that we had carelessly placed on the ledge behind the rear seats before departing. The continuous tinkling of these bottles had now become quite noticeable, and added to our already highly-strung nerves. At about 11 p.m. it was raining hard. We were on a stretch of road full of red mud, and with the visibility reduced to eighty metres Vacca found it hard to clearly distinguish the roadside. I think we were driving at about eighty kilometres an hour when the left rear wheel departed from its axle. Vacca lost control of the vehicle, which then skidded sideways on the thick mud, went off the road into the bush and collided head-on with a large tree. Due to the abrupt stop the beer bottles came forward and smashed on our heads, covering us with broken glass. Sally and I came out of the car pouring blood – Sally from her head, me from my neck. The sheer abundance of blood mixed with the rain gave the impression that we would soon bleed to death: its flow had not relented for a moment. Vacca only had a small wound on the bridge of his nose;

he had avoided the main force of the impact by holding the steering wheel at arm's length.

At that late hour we did not expect assistance from any passing cars: our only option was to pick out the pieces of glass in our heads, bind our wounds with a handkerchief and pass the night in the car. However, as if by a miracle we saw the headlights of another car after half an hour. The driver was an Indian, and realising the seriousness of the accident, he was persuaded to help us. We arrived at the small Morogoro hospital just after midnight and they had no choice but to call a doctor by phone, who arrived immediately. He was an Englishman, and first he inspected Sally's head wound to make sure there were no more pieces of glass left inside. Luckily there were not, and he closed it with four stitches and put her in one of the wards. My wound was much more serious, and I required a general anaesthetic in the form of a morphine injection; later the doctor informed me that the point of a piece of glass had missed my aorta by a centimetre. This was my first experience of morphine, and it put me into such a deep sleep that no noise could wake me. I felt as though I was floating in limbo, a peaceful dream devoid of any emotions or worries, wishing it would last for ever. I slept continuously for fifteen hours, waking up the next afternoon with Sally and the doctor at my bedside; they had been worried by my unbroken sleep. The doctor asked me if I would like something to eat, but I refused – I wished only to return to sleep again and the world that I had just exited.

To Sally's great relief I woke up of my own accord the morning after, and was ready to go back to Dar-es-Salaam. Luckily Morogoro had a railway connection, and we aborted the planned visit to Mombasa without any more trouble.

Around the middle of 1954, the Stirling Astaldi Company had finished the roadwork, and was leaving Tanganyika temporarily. For Sally and me, this meant the loss of some of our friends, and only the Fiat agents remained in the country to represent Italy. The Italian community then numbered about four hundred, all high-class artisans and technicians. However, due to the professional superiority of our compatriots, it was quite easy to find a job. Activity in the industrial, manufacturing and commercial sectors of the country was stagnant; with the exception of sisal production, the export figures had fallen to new lows. In this uncertain climate, the numbers were continuously changing: some were arriving; others were departing, only to return again, all in a continuous effort to find new work prospects. It was only after a few years that a more permanent community was established and it became possible for us to start more permanent friendships.

In the meantime, Sally decided to get a job, and as she was a British national, she did not have much difficulty in finding one. With two salaries, our standard of living improved dramatically, and with my new contract, many new horizons were opening. In addition to a life free of worry, and the opportunity of enjoying the long holidays that were at our disposal, we could now concentrate on something more important: it was our dream to own a house in Italy, and there was now a real chance that it could become a reality.

Shortly after the Italian community had begun to flourish, it decided to build an 'Italian Club'. The design and supervision of the club's construction was entrusted to Dr Galliussi, former teacher in the Faculty of Architecture at the University of Rome. There was abundant space in Tanganyika, and we did not find it difficult to find a beautiful piece of land adjacent to the sea. When the Italian Club was completed it was a masterpiece of modern art, and received the admiration of the Europeans; of course, every one of us was very proud.

From the club, the view to the horizon over the open sea was dotted by a few small islands, which nevertheless fitted well with the marvellous scenery. At high tide, sea water impetuously invaded a dry narrow estuary, running alongside the club for two kilometres, transforming it into a small river; at low tide, when the water left the estuary, it became swampy, and resulted in a luxurious growth of mangroves, the exposed roots of these trees providing an environment that ensured the proliferation of all that was amphibious. We could observe large colonies of undisturbed crabs, which would grow to large sizes; when the tide rose again, the estuary lapped against the side of the wall, and on some occasions would reach a level higher than the base of the building; therefore a one-metre-high wall was constructed, and from this we could have an excellent view of the movement of crabs and the vast extent of the mangroves.

Many of the English became members of the club. Our relations with them had improved over the years since the war, and at that time we got on with them very well. Nevertheless, sometimes there was still a slight uneasiness, due to the fact that the hostile ashes of the war were still not entirely doused in people's hearts; but they soon were completely dormant. An English friend of mine also pointed out that the Italian community appeared to be reluctant to mix with other communities, and I had to agree with him.

On 9th June 1954, Sally gave birth to Lucia, and this event made us very happy. To continue our financial success, Sally decided not to leave her job, and we employed a nanny to take care of the baby during working hours. One of the nanny's tasks was to take Lucia to Sally's office every four hours for feeding. This task was easier than it sounds, as the nanny sat in the park right opposite from the office, with the baby in the pram. Luckily for Sally, her superiors did not object to this unorthodox procedure and actually found it quite original.

Soon we had our own favourite sports: for me, tennis, judo and hunting; for Sally, tennis, squash and occasionally hunting. In addition, we became members of the KAR (King's African Rifle) Club, where we trained to shoot with the official Army rifle (.303 calibre) every other Saturday. The club was managed by a division of the KAR, whose quarters were a few kilometres out of Dar-es-Salaam. One of the advantages of being a member of the club was that the Army supplied free ammunition for our training.

I never had a better life than I had then: I did not have any financial troubles, I was in excellent health, and my work went on smoothly; the only daily problem that I faced was working out how to spend my free time.

The cultural affinity between the Europeans, and the unconscious desire to congregate in a minority of similar race, had created a very open fraternity; you could rely on most other Europeans, no matter what their national origin. The wives would meet daily in the town, and end up in a café on the main street to exchange pleasantries and the latest news. There were many private or public festivities and national celebrations, which most were invited to. These festivities all had one thing in common: they consisted mainly of a large numbers of toasts and libations, which always ensured a very uninhibited and casual attitude from the men, and sometimes from the women.

When all of our friends from Stirling Astaldi moved back to Italy, we found the need to find new ones, and we befriended Franco Galliussi, the son of Dr Galliussi, the designer of the Italian Club. Franco at that time was only seventeen, but soon emerged as a very bright young boy, just like his father. After a brief consultation with Piero Mannini, we decided to go hunting to our preferred area, also taking along my new friend Franco Galliussi.

The area was called Mikumi, and was about two hundred and fifty kilometres from Dar-es-Salaam. It was the best hunting ground in Tanganyika, a mixture of flatland and rough scrub, with small perennial watercourses that kept the animals in the area, and also hosted a large population of hippopotami. Here you could encounter a diverse range of game, including elephants. There were no rhinoceroses, as poachers had exterminated them, probably because their horns were supposed to be aphrodisiacs. However, this was definitely an area where you had to have your wits about you at all times.

This is how Mikumi translates in the Kiswahili language: *mi* (adjective-prefix); *kumi* (ten). Many years ago it may have referred to the number of houses (or, more precisely, huts) that were in that area, so perhaps Mikumi meant: The Ten Houses, although this is just a guess. After having met one of the occupants of one of the huts and the elder of the group, we chose our tracker, who was called Ramadhani and was an African of the Islamic religion. A good tracker is an indispensable assistant when hunting in dense woods or the savannah, as very often the life of the hunter depends on his competence and ruthlessness. 'Tracker' roughly means a man who can follow the imprints left by game on the ground, and can recognise which animal left them, and how long ago they have been there. He must also have eyesight capable of locating a feline hidden among bushes, and detect small traces of blood left on the ground by a wounded animal. Last, but not least, he must be able to retrace the way back home, or to the car abandoned in the wood, at sundown, after having led the hunter around the bush since the early morning. Very few Europeans, if any, can boast of that amount of experience.

That was a short list of what is required from a tracker, but to list the capabilities of Ramadhani would take quite a few pages.

It is difficult to guess the age of an African accurately. To us, Ramadhani appeared to be about twenty-five, but that was only a very rough guess: it could easily have been double that. He was a man of small stature, as are most Africans who come with a family stricken with poverty Like bonsai trees, a life of constrained misery condemns them to limited growth. Nevertheless, Ramadhani had a lean, well-proportioned body, and later displayed great stamina and endurance. It was amazing how the people of Mikumi managed to survive, and only by looking round the four remaining huts did we discover their secret. Their only possible resource was the cassava, which was the only plant that would yield a reliable crop in that inhospitable terrain. The roots and fruits of the cassava ripen underground, and there they are safe from the herbivorous fauna. The plant only has one enemy: the warthog, which is very fond of it. Ramadhani's small cassava field (which was not any bigger than forty square metres) was adjacent to his hut, so he could hear whenever an invasion of warthogs occurred; the noise from the beasts greedily munching on the plants was enough to wake him and other occupants of the hut, and they would come out to defend their precious crop. However, the warthogs also had their own family, and they would bring them along to have another try.

Ramadhani remained our loyal hunting companion for eighteen years, and during this time we had quite a number of adventures together. When I think of Ramadhani (I must admit, with infinite sadness and remorse), I realise that I did not do enough for him: I could have helped my friend more with little effort on my part. I could have given him financial help without any loss to my family and me: the amount of money that I normally spent on an afternoon drinking at the club with friends would have meant a month-long Christmas for him. This would have been over five times the amount I paid him for a full day's hunting, not including the confidence that he inspired in me whilst we were tracking in the dense bush, and the feeling of safety that he provided, as he could sense any oncoming danger before well before it had the chance to surprise us.

However, I did not help enough, and I deeply regret it. My failure to provide relief was perhaps not due to egotism or greed, but an immature nature and a lack of understanding of the important things in life. This ignorance has unfortunately sometimes prevented me from understanding an important situation, and in this case I neglected to change misery into joyous relief. Over the course of the years I often did not go to Mikumi for two or three months at a time, and the last time I returned I found the people in a pitiful condition. Ramadhani explained that the cassava had failed, and there had been a famine in the entire region. There had been no rain for months, and the dry flatlands around Mikumi had burnt under an implacable sun. Some of the inhabitants had died, and this was of no significance to the flourishing European community.

After a few months of famine, Ramadhani's physical appearance had undergone a radical transformation. His neck was extremely thin, supporting a head that now appeared largely out of proportion, his hollow cheeks made his bones protrude grotesquely, his skin, normally a smooth opaque dark brown, had become ash-grey, and the empty expressions of his eyes, now looking constantly into the distance, indicated the severe prolonged suffering he had endured. All the members of his family were surely in the same condition as he was. On his tired face, I detected the desperation of a father who foresees the prospect of slowly losing his family, without being able to do anything about it. Ramadhani, in his modesty, never asked for anything. Had he asked for some help from me, I would have sensed his desperation, and surely would have intervened financially.

It was with gratitude that Ramadhani accepted the pay of ten miserable shillings per day for his precious services. I must add, however, that the forty shillings he received from us for four days was then reasonable standard pay for the services of an African living in the Tanganyika hinterland; therefore, we were not abusing him, nor trying to take advantage of him, as some hunters of other nationalities were doing. That amount of money would enable him to buy several kilograms of cornflour, and scrape along for some time. The killing of an antelope for his family's consumption would have provided a few more days of essential nourishment; unfortunately, this was impossible, for he and his family would not eat the meat of an animal that was not butchered in accordance with the Koran. Those that are faithful to Allah will only eat the meat of animals (except pigs) if they have been slaughtered in the fashion that I mentioned earlier.

Our preparations with Ramadhani usually started in the late afternoon, and left us with one hour of light to organise the bivouac. From that moment on, our hunting for the next two days would depend entirely on Ramadhani's knowledge and expertise: he would decide in which part of the savannah it would be best to hunt; he would decide where to erect the tent. Nearly always this would be near the first dry tree along the way, which had normally been struck by lightning or semi-burnt by the seasonal conflagration of the grass: this never failed to take some trees with it. I have always had the impression that Ramadhani derived some pride and satisfaction from seeing the Europeans depending on his expertise.

At night, Ramadhani would sleep on the hard ground in the open, near the fire, with a blanket covering his body and his head. He did not worry about any beasts, and slept peacefully. The fire was always extinguished: Ramadhani maintained that this was likely to encourage a lion attack, as the light attracts them from afar, contrary to what people believe. And with the silence in the camp, they may even decide to stop for a meal.

There is a set of rules for all big-game hunters that came from the colonial territories of East Africa and other British territories around the world. The most important of these is that any hunter who wounds a dangerous wild animal, such as an elephant, lion or buffalo, MUST track down the beast until he kills it. For no reason whatsoever must one of these animals be left to survive after it has been wounded, as it will become ferocious and vindictive, lose its fear of man, and attack any human with ferocious determination, until one of them is dead.

In a situation where you happen to wound a big-game animal in a non-vital area, it will normally run away to hide in the densest bush it can find, take a rest, and lick its wound. This is when the help of a tracker is indispensable, to follow the trail and spoor of the bleeding animal up to a few metres from its hiding point. The tracker will also have to share the danger with the hunter in this situation, and there are many stories told by old hunters about the animal pretending to be dead, but suddenly springing up to attack whoever has had the imprudence to go near it. Therefore it is wise to throw a stone at the animal first; or better still, take a shot at the beast from a safe distance.

During the rainy season, the flatlands of Mikumi became full of obstacles. In some places, the grass reached a height of over three metres, rendering it impossible to see more than one metre ahead. To be able to hunt, it is necessary to reach clear surroundings. However, to cross a small brook with only a few centimetres of water (which was often encountered) sometimes became a major undertaking. Its muddy banks did not offer any grip to car tyres, and the car must be pushed by hand up the other bank. Nevertheless, these obstacles were very exciting for us youngsters who were hungry for adventure, and the roughness of the trip always improved the flavour of the hunt. We would return home on Sunday evening, very often splattered from head to toe in mud, always tired and ready for bed, but always satisfied by the days that we had spent in the beautiful wilderness.

When wet after days of torrential rain, the high grass of the savannah gave life to millions of bovine tzetze fly, and as there was an absence of better fodder, they were only too happy to suck our blood. It is impossible to defend yourself from this scourge, as their number goes far beyond anything that you can imagine. They also seem to be intelligent, as they understand that it is better to land on top of animals where they are out of the reach of their tail. A man takes notice of them only when he feels a painful puncture on his back, and the only way to get rid of them is to have another person squash them with a slap of their hand; otherwise it is necessary to take off your shirt and remove the unwanted beast, which will not hesitate to fly to another part of the body.

The species of the tzetze fly we found at Mikumi apparently did not infect man with sleeping sickness. All my friends and I have received innumerable punctures from the insect without any consequence except the burning pain of the sting. The carrier of sleeping sickness is a different species to that found in the Mikumi area; however, I do not know the details of that species, or its effects. In all my years in Africa, I have met only one or two Africans who have contracted the disease, and I noted their devastated appearance. I have been told that the disease is incurable and that it eventually leads to death.

The areas that are infested by the bovine fly are not suitable pastures for cows, as they will also die if they are bitten. Only the buffalo is immune from infection, and a few small villages made up of two or three huts inhabit the vast spaces that are dominated by this insect.

One day, when Franco and I were walking along the bank of a river, we heard a strange humming emanating from about fifty metres away from the valley. As we got closer, the buzzing grew louder, and when we reached the edge of the incline we stopped, amazed by the sight that confronted us. Over a hundred buffalo were herded towards the riverbank, and above them were millions of hovering tzetze fly, swarming around them and landing on their backs.

The savannahs of Mikumi were host to a family of lions (up to fifteen) which we encountered occasionally in random places. They usually observed us peacefully, whilst lying under the shade of a tree, and were not afraid of us. These encounters sometimes occurred when we were in the car, and sometimes on foot; but we were always lucky enough to spot them early and modify our route, as we did not want a confrontation with a large pride. When we passed on foot only sixty or so metres away from them, they never showed any interest in us, and did not move from their spot; maybe they sensed that we were not afraid of them either, and were happy enough to follow us with their attentive eyes; we were also calm, and we got the impression that they had no urge to attack us whatsoever. However, they later recanted this imaginary benevolence.

During his school years, Franco Galliussi had heard mention of another fabulous area to hunt on the same road as Mikumi, only much further away. It was called the Kilombero Valley, and was home to the Kilombero River. Franco had decided to visit this place, and he came back full of exciting stories, which he told with great enthusiasm. At that time he was only eighteen, and he did not have enough experience to embark on that dangerous adventure on his own. However, luck was on his side: along the banks of the Kilombero he met Pretorius, a well-known South African hunter, who was camping with his wife in a tent, and Franco joined them.

Pretorius, like many of his compatriots, was an expert hunter, as only South Africans can be: they are the best hunters in all respects. Many of them live inland in their country, as tropical agricultural workers or farmers, and have a deep knowledge of animals. They are the only hunters who can shoot a rifle with reasonable precision whilst riding a galloping horse. The British paid dearly during the war against the Boers, and when they discuss those events nowadays, they still remark how efficient the Boers were with their rifles.

Sometime before meeting with Franco, Pretorius and his wife had just survived a serious incident. A hippopotamus had attacked both of them during a pirogue excursion in the low waters of the Kilombero River. By a miracle, the hippo did not take Pretorius' wife's head off with one of its infamous bites. According to Pretorius' version of the incident, the hippopotamus had attacked the canoe without any provocation; to tell the truth, I have heard hippos have a nasty habit of doing this, and Pretorius must have known of the danger, so maybe he was taken by surprise. They frequently attack pirogues, and it is this beast that accounts for the highest number of anglers' deaths. When you spot this animal it is best to be extremely prudent, have your rifle ready, and expect the worst. Even Pretorius' quick response (which killed the beast) was not enough to stop his wife's lower jaw being seriously damaged, putting her in hospital for a long time and scarring her face severely. From then on, you could only tell she was crying by her eyes, as the wound gave the impression that she was always laughing: a sick reminder of the hippo's deadliness.

Pretorius was an elderly man, and when he saw Franco so young and so full of enthusiasm he immediately took a liking to him, and promised that he would help him kill an elephant, for which Franco happened to have acquired a hunting permit. After a few days' hunting, they managed to make contact with a herd of elephants; among the herd, an old patriarch stood out, with huge tusks. Pretorius pointed out the old beast to Franco, suggesting to him that it was the target to go for. However, it was Franco's first experience, and he was rather scared. He counted on Pretorius to accompany him to at least a few metres from the right distance to shoot, but Pretorius had other intentions. He wanted to teach his young pupil not to be scared, and gestured Franco to go ahead on his own. So with much trepidation, Franco crept up to within ten metres of the herd, and managed to bring the old elephant down with the first shot to the animal's brain, giving him the great pleasure of having done it all by himself.

However, then something strange happened. Instead of running away as expected, the rest of the herd stayed put, looking at their dead companion on the ground and nervously moving around the carcass; maybe they had not heard the thunder of a rifle before and could not understand what had happened. Franco remained in the same spot, and did not know what to do. He intermittently looked at the elephants and Pretorius, needing instruction, but the South African was a hundred metres away. Pretorius did not intervene, but made a hand signal to Franco for him to withdraw slowly. If the elephants had attacked Franco, then Pretorius would have opened fire with his rifle; there was also no doubt that none of his shots would have missed the target. Luckily, Franco retreated unharmed.

Pretorius was good company, and around a fire at night he would tell interesting stories from his life. He also gave advice, and he suggested to Franco that he should try and shoot a young hippopotamus; if possible, one that was only a few days old, as it would be delicious to cook on the spit. According to him, it was the best meat in Africa, even superior to that of the eland, a wild bovine renowned for the beauty of its horns and its tasty and tender meat.

The tusks of the elephant killed by Franco reached the notable weight of fifty kilos each. This meant that they automatically acquired the title of trophy and they could be sold to a museum or a private collector. Tusks in this category were not sold according to their weight; in view of their rarity, they had a far greater value than any lighter tusks. They were much sought after, and their value could reach several million liras. After this hunting experience, Franco convinced me to help him organise the first of what was eventually four hunts in the Kilombero region.

In 1956, another large Italian company came to Tanganyika to build a petroleum refinery in Dar-es-Salaam. This project was subsidised by Agip, and was in partnership with the Tanzanian Government.

Mr Palazzi, whom we had met in the Italian Club, was an engineer from Agip of Milan. He had heard of our imminent hunting expedition, and fervently begged me to take him along with us. Franco did not like the idea, but I did not have the heart to turn him down, so I insisted to Franco that he come along with us: I understood his desire to be able to recount his African adventures to his friends upon his return to Italy. A passionate hunter friend of ours also wanted to join us, a Venetian named Tassan, who enjoyed his reputation for killing a few elephants. Later I found out that he improvised his hunting techniques in a manner that I did not like.

When we reached Mikumi, we stopped briefly to find out whether Ramadhani wanted to come with us. As usual, he did not say a word, but went back into his hut, picked up his small blanket and inseparable machete, and jumped into the car.

The road from Mikumi up to the Kilombero highland is not particularly attractive, and all of the vegetation particularly uniform, which is typical of that area. The road climbs tortuously, and the terrain is dusty and full of hard stones, which prevented us from travelling quickly, as it would have damaged the car: if a suspension spring had broken in that isolated area, it would have compromised the whole expedition.

The safari was well organised, and the equipment I had very adequate, including a tent to comfortably host four people. It was made with very robust material, impervious to rain, and was fitted with a very strong zip, which would easily stop any snake or insect from getting in. Its plastic bottom was sewn to the canvas sides and incorporated a waterproof joint, and the mosquito nets on the two windows ensured good ventilation. Another useful item that we took was a five-litre thermos flask with a large mouth, capable of keeping a reserve of ice cubes for more than a week; it could also allow us the pleasure of ice-cold beer on a few evenings. A light-canvas camp shower provided the luxury of a daily wash upon return from the various expeditions, and prevented the need to immerse ourselves in a river full of crocodiles.

Some hundred metres away from the Kilombero River was a small village of maybe twenty huts. At the side of it was the ever-present *duka walla*, or Indian grocer's shop. It sold the usual merchandise: maize flour, rice, dried fish and, much more importantly to us, one-litre bottles of ice-cold beer, kept inside the paraffin refrigerator, which had its familiar smell.

We had everything we needed, and the hunt could begin. Franco, who knew the place well from his preceding visit, did not waste any time, and engaged two guides, each with their own pirogue.

Due to a drought over the past month, the river was very low, and we could not use the oars; therefore we had to propel the pirogue by pushing long poles. In some spots the water was so low that the pirogue touched the bottom of the river, and we had to get out and push them along by hand. The water level was rising and falling, but there was a steady flow, even at the lowest points. The depth was very unpredictable, and at some points the poles would not even reach the bottom. In these places we just simply drifted along with the current; but it was dangerous not to be in control of the vessels as there was a strong chance that we could run into hippos. After navigating for several hours, we reached a point where the river became wider and formed a small lake. Sure enough, two hippos immediately surfaced a short distance from our crafts. They appeared to be very irritated, and expressed their dislike of our arrival very clearly. One of them in particular seemed to be on the point of attacking us, but Tassan did not waste any time and killed him instantly. The other disappeared under the water.

The episode was then over, and I did not give it much thought. However, it had alerted something deep in my subconscious: I felt as if someone was telling me to remember the death of the hippopotamus.

Every now and then the screams of the white eagles perched on the branches of the highest trees broke the silence of the flatlands, and accompanied us on our trip. The sound of these birds, heard in the immensity of those deserted spaces, is the part of Africa that I love. With the comforting warmth, and the happy feeling of my healthy youth, I did not yearn for anything else except maybe one day to die in one of those places.

After going upstream for another few hours, we decided to camp in a suitable place near the riverbank. When we had finished putting up the tent, we noted a wild fig tree about twenty-five metres away. At a height of maybe five metres, at a branch bifurcation, the carcass of a gazelle hung down. We all knew that a leopard had put it there. Having killed and eaten part of it, being a thief himself, he was ensuring that jackals and hyenas would not rob him of what was left of the gazelle. He frequently visited that spot, day and night, not at all troubled by our presence. He would climb up the tree, and from this vantage point observe all of our movements. One evening we heard him arrive as he scattered up the vertical tree trunk, and I was sure that the inveterate robber had come to observe us for a different reason. A comical situation then ensued.

We spent all night constantly observing one another: the feline watched us sitting around our bivouac, and we watched him sit in the tree, just visible from the dull light of our fire. However, so poor was the light that we felt the need to use the electric torch just to keep an eye on him. He had obviously smelt the evening roast that the Africans had prepared, or spotted the carcass of another gazelle, which we had killed in the morning, hanging from a tree branch near to our tent. However, he just remained there motionless, calculating, observing. He had obviously noted that we were absent from the camp for several hours in the morning – this was a good time for hunting ducks and suchlike – and the silence would suggest to him that this was the best time to conduct a foray on the camp and abduct the remains of the gazelle. Sure enough, one day he was unable to resist temptation any longer, and came down from the tree onto the short track leading to our camp. The plan was very clever, but he had ignored one very important factor: the youngest of the Africans: Ramadhani. We had decided to use local trackers and leave him in the camp every day to carry out minor chores like washing the dishes, providing water for the evening baths and guarding the tent; as it happened, he was just on his way to the river with two empty buckets. The unexpected encounter was a fearful shock for both of them. Ramadhani threw his buckets and ran off into the distance, scaring the hell out of the leopard and provoking a similar reaction: the feline turned around and fled into the opposite direction as quickly as possible.

I had noted that Tassan, when hunting, did not carry his rifle on the shoulder as every hunter normally does, and I asked him the reason for this. He replied that his rifle, a precious twin-barrel carbine with a calibre of more than ten millimetres, was too heavy to be carried on the shoulder for a long time, and if he did so, he would be too tired to shoot precisely. This weapon, due to the high cost of the ammunition, is exclusively reserved for hunting the more dangerous animals; indeed, the rifle itself is far more expensive than normal rifles, and weighs nearly twice as much. Therefore he always employed an African to carry it, and only took it when he needed it. I pointed out that the first reaction of an African arms-bearer when confronted with an imminent attack from a dangerous beast is to run away, leaving the person to face the danger disarmed. To this Tassan simply smiled and added that he was ready for every emergency; to which I realised that in light of this superior attitude it was useless to continue talking to him.

A few days later he decided to go hunting with just his African tracker. He crossed the river, and we lost sight of him on the flatland in front of our tent. I was sure that he was thinking of killing a large herbivore, such as a zebra or gnu. After a couple of hours, we heard the noise of a weapon of large calibre. Both Franco and I immediately recognised that it was coming from Tassan's rifle, and after another few seconds there was another shot. But the sequence of the shots was unusual, and I said to Franco that I thought something had happened.

To our relief, we saw Tassan and the tracker return in the pirogue. Tassan told us that they had encountered a small herd of buffalo, and they had all fled except for one, which charged them. The tracker moved to avoid the buffalo, and was separated from Tassan, taking the rifle with him; however, Tassan's luck was in: this tracker was perhaps one in a million that knew how to use a rifle, probably from watching other hunters, and with his second shot the buffalo fell less than a metre from Tassan's feet.

Two or three days before the end of our hunting expedition, we were returning to our camp after a tiring day, and as we were convinced that there was not a European within a radius of one hundred kilometres, we were very surprised to find a German missionary waiting for us in front of our tent; there was also a brand new motorboat, ten metres long, anchored to the bank on our side of the river. The missionary was an old acquaintance of Franco's whom he had met during the time he was with Pretorius, and he introduced me to him with a sardonic smile. His name was Father Gallus, also known as 'Father Cock'. I now understood the reason for Franco's smug smile: he looked very energetic, very sure of himself, with his shoulders back and his chest pushed forward. He was not alone in the mission: according to Franco, five young nuns helped him, and he was 'exactly like a cock in a hen-house'.

However, Father Gallus had come to ask a favour. He asked if we would very kindly kill a buffalo to provide meat for the mission (I believe his mission was a leprosy hospital). A buffalo can weigh up to eight hundred kilograms. It was late in the afternoon, and the prospect of having to walk for another few hours without a revitalising shower made me refuse Father Gallus. I explained to him that hunting a buffalo requires several hours, and was certainly something that you could not rush, particularly after a tiring day. However, Father Gallus insisted, so I went on to say that not only was it too late to go hunting for buffalo, but I also did not have a licence to kill them. To obtain this licence you needed to pay a sum of ten pounds at the government office, and that was far from where we were. However, Father Cock would not give up: he said that for me, a Christian, it was more opportune to follow the Gospel, which clearly states that you must appease the hunger of the famished, and he put it exactly that way. It now became my responsibility to appease the hunger of all the starving people of Africa (in particular those of Father Gallus's mission), and the Father, a connoisseur of handling human souls, was looking intently at my face to watch the progress he was making in convincing me.

He continued with his sermon, and said that to pay for the licence to kill a buffalo was not opportune: as I knew very well, that money would not have helped anyone, except the capacious pockets of some corrupt official. Then, suddenly, in the midst of the argument, one of the excited Africans told us all to look at the river. What I saw was incredible! On the opposite riverbank, about seventy metres away, two enormous buffalo had just entered the river; and Father Gallus, with a sparkle in his eyes and a large smile on his face, cried out at the miracle, and explained that this was with no doubt the intervention of Jesus Christ. Tassan and I could now not refuse to appease the hunger of the famished, even if we were not completely convinced by the intervention theory.

From previous experience we knew that the buffalo were going to stay in the water for some time yet, and our approach would be easy, or so we thought. At first the two beasts observed our manoeuvres without a single sign of apprehension; however, when they saw the pirogue coming in their direction, they started to show signs of nervousness. We were only forty metres from them, and their fate was decided; to be honest, they could not have been in a more vulnerable position. They now understood the danger, and started to head for the opposite riverbank. I told Tassan to not kill them when they were in the water, as this would have created serious problems when recovering the carcass: it was better to wait until they were at least five or six metres away from the bank. By this point we were only about twenty metres from the buffalo: an easy shot, and after Tassan fired, one of the beasts fell a few metres from the river. Our mission was completed, and Father Gallus did not waste any time; in less than half-an-hour he had cut the buffalo into pieces and loaded it into his motorboat. Before he disappeared into the distance, I saw Father Gallus raise his arm for a blessing, and I guess he was showing his gratitude. Three days later, our safari came to an end.

We decided to dismantle the camp at one o'clock on our last night. Luckily, the sky was clear and a full moon was out; the light that reflected off the river was enough not to need torches. To dismantle the camp and load the canoe took at least one hour; we also had to follow the custom of all hunters and clean the camping area, making sure that no rubbish was left behind.

At the end of an expedition, when you leave areas frequented by dangerous animals, you must never let your guard down, even when you believe yourself to be safe. Complacency can cost you your life, as is proved by the following episode.

After loading the pirogue, Franco and Tassan considered the hunt to be terminated. They were thinking of being home soon, and did not give much thought to the dangers of the river, even though they knew it was crocodile-infested. They made sure that their rifles were unloaded before they put them into their cases, and placed them at the bottom of the canoe. I was the last person to board the boat, but after I had done so, I realised that I had forgotten to unload my rifle. Suddenly, I was revisited by the presentiment that something was going to happen, as it had two weeks ago after Tassan had killed the hippo. Although it had since been buried deep in my subconscious, it was now more persistent, and every time I have had premonitions in the past, they have always been to my advantage. Now this one was definite and persistent, and I decided to keep the loaded rifle with me. I climbed into the canoe, but did not tell any of my companions of my worrying thoughts: perhaps I was a little embarrassed to reveal that I believed in premonitions. I sat down with my rifle between my knees, a round in the barrel chamber, the safety on. There were six people in the canoe, and all of the cargo. With the full moon out, the visibility on the water ahead was about one hundred metres: the ideal conditions for a pleasant return journey.

Pushed along by the poles, we made slow progress. In the silence and the fresh air of the night, the thought that we would be home in a few hours was on everyone's mind. After several hours, we reached the small lake where we had killed the hippopotamus. I was probably the only one that had the feeling that something was going to happen, and I automatically became very tense. Just before we reached the other side of the lake, we crossed a point were the water was deep and the poles could not reach the bottom. We let the canoe drift, free to follow the current; but it had almost come to a halt. At that moment we saw the shape of a hippo appear about fifteen metres away and, with the moon behind it, it was like a stain of black ink, a sketch on a child's book cover. I think he hesitated to attack us right away, as he was unsure what he was up against; maybe he thought that his companion had returned, but having realised that this was not the case, he hurled himself ferociously at the canoe, which was now almost motionless.

The hippopotamus can attack a canoe successfully in two ways. The first is to swim underwater, come right up underneath the boat, and capsize it. The second is a direct attack from the flank, when the canoe is turned on its side by the weight and momentum of the beast. In both cases, the hippo will bite right and left at anything in the water that moves after the vessel has been overturned. This attack was from the side, as the water was not deep enough for him to swim under us, and we watched him coming towards us with wide eyes, our hairs as stiff as a hedgehog's. The animal was infuriated because of the depth of the water, and he moved in a series of bounds. Every time he bunched up his body, half of him came out of the water, like a horse rearing in front of us. When he was five metres from us I shot him: if he had reached the deeper part then he could have disappeared underwater and out of sight. It was dark, and I remember the one-metre-long flame coming out of the barrel, and the red-hot trace of the bullet before it entered the beast's neck. If I had put the rifle away like Tassan and Franco, it would have been certain death for at least a few of us.

I consider the neck shot to be the most deadly to inflict on any beast. Death is always immediate, especially from a Magnum rifle like the one I used, which fires ammunition at a very high velocity; in some instances, it can even kill without hitting a vital organ. Anyway, after everyone had congratulated me, we all laughed hysterically with relief. The trip back home was without further incident.

Following this expedition, Franco became a good friend of the family. After a long absence from hunting in Mikumi, he asked me if I would like to return with his fiancée, Veronica, and another couple of youngsters, Roger and Liz. He said he not only wanted to have the pleasure of my company, but as the fathers of the young girls had refused to give them permission to participate in this adventure, it was only when Franco suggested my name as a possible guardian that Veronica's father gave his consent. He came to see me, and said that he trusted me completely, nominating me chaperone to the two young girls. I must say that I was surprised: I did not know that I had acquired such a reputation!

We soon arrived in Mikumi, ready to go hunting. I was driving my DKW, and with five people already in the car, I regretted that we would not be able to take Ramadhani along. Without him, I decided that it would be a good plan not to stray far from the track; the idea was to have a secure and easy point of reference at all times.

It was not long before I had to intervene drastically, probably saving Veronica's life. Franco, having used one of my two rifles, had shot and wounded a guinea fowl. Having automatically reloaded the weapon, he handed it over to Veronica (a girl just fifteen years old) and had the intention of capturing the still fluttering bird with his hands. The gun was a .22 calibre, and shot devastating high-velocity soft-nosed bullets, which expanded at the moment of impact. The makers had rightly named them 'Hornet': although small, it was capable of killing a medium-sized animal from one hundred metres. The guinea fowl was sadly wounded, and was fluttering around on the ground with a broken wing; but was still managing to evade Franco's hands. Veronica, in her attempts to assist Franco, was now trying to hit the bird with the butt of the rifle. You cannot imagine the feeling that took grip of my heart. I shrank every time she hit the ground, with the gun to her chest, and fully expected the thing to go off; surely only a miracle could stop the thing from firing, and I was terrified. In those few instants, I envisaged the consequences of a fatal accident: a dead girl, and my shame for having betrayed the confidence of the father, which he had given to me with a smile on his face. With two jumps I was on her, stopping her arm rather brutally before she could bring the rifle down for another blow, which could well have proved to be her last action. She looked at me, surprised and scared at my violent intervention, which she obviously did not understand. I was furious at the scare I had to endure, and now ordered Franco with regrettably strong language never to hand the weapon to Veronica ever again, or I would terminate the safari. It was only by sheer luck that the breech-block had not released the shot, and on the way back to the camp I explained to Veronica what could have happened. I had now regained normal composure, and felt sorry for my violent behaviour a little earlier, as Veronica was not really to blame for her actions; after all, it was up to the head of the safari to be responsible for all the other members of the party.

We returned to the camp as the sun went down, and after having put up the tent and had dinner, we sat around the small table near the fire, discussing the day's events. Nothing could have made us foresee what happened next: all of a sudden, a strong wind started to blow, carrying with it a whole mass of black clouds. They were very low, and very menacing; after a short while it seemed that torrents of water were coming down from the sky, accompanied by loud thunderbolts. The view had changed from a serene clear sky to a tremendous cyclone, in a matter of half an hour. The tent started to give signs of collapsing, compelling all five of us to go inside, in an attempt to keep the two poles that held it up upright; however, our efforts were in vain, and we soon had to come out, as the weight of the collapsing tent rendered it impossible to remain inside it. In all this confusion, Franco and I somehow had the good sense not to neglect the weapons, and after we came out of the tent, we took care to keep the barrels of the rifles facing the ground, in order not to get them wet; for the same reason, we bent our arms, with our elbows tightly over the breech-block. A blinding flash of a thunderbolt then fell onto a small ebony tree about three or four metres away from where we were standing. This was the last breath of the cyclone, which stopped as rapidly as it had started; within half-an-hour the sky turned as clear as it had been before the storm. However, the rain had left the plains flooded with about ten centimetres of water.

The rain had of course extinguished the fire, and it proved rather difficult to start again; nevertheless, with the help of a bottle of spirit and some small branches, we managed to get a small blaze going on top of a low anthill. At that moment a lion's roar from about thirty metres away brought us back to reality. Our position was as follows: the only place where we could get protection, the car, was more than thirty metres away in the opposite direction to the lion's roar. To reach the car, it was necessary to go past the fire. This was not an advisable action: a common lions' trick is to induce their prey into going in the opposite direction to the roars, where they would find two or three lionesses waiting for them. To confirm our suspicions, we heard movement in the water behind us. Fearing an attack, I told the girls to wait by the fire in a group, whilst Franco and I loaded our rifles, ready to fire at first sight. Franco tried to make contact with their eyes with the torch, which in the night would reflect like lighted carbon and make an easy target. We could hear the beasts moving in the water; but they did not attack, probably because they suspected that we would not be easy prey. Only on two occasions did I see their paws moving in the water, just for a split second. Another few hours passed, and by then we were convinced that the lions would not attack us that day; they were hoping that we would do as the monkeys do: resort to a panicked escape, when the lions would be waiting, with their sharp claws. We waited until first light, and saw that they had disappeared; however, it was not very clear where they had gone, and we could only see for several hundred metres. At only about sixty metres from where the tent had been, there was an area as large as two football grounds, covered by grass one metre high.

The light of day and the apparent disappearance of the danger had raised our spirits, and we now laughed and joked about the previous night. A little while afterwards, Roger had to leave the group to satisfy bodily needs, and he thought there was no better place than the long grass. After a few minutes, we saw him quickly emerge from the wall of grass with his trousers lowered half-mast. He then told us in broken words that he had heard a low roar from inside the grass; obviously he was only a few metres from the group of lions of the previous night, and he had only been saved by his prompt retreat. When reflecting on that night's occurrences, we concluded that if Ramadhani had been with us, he would not have allowed Roger to go into the grass: if the lions had gone anywhere, it was likely to be there, as was the case.

Two or three years after this event, a consortium of hotel owners built a hotel not far from Ramadhani's village. It was built on a promontory, and on the side where the land fell away they had built a large sheltered veranda, providing the tourists with a very attractive view of the lower flatland, where a brook passed through. The owners tried to entice the largest number of animals possible to frequent this area, and they scattered salt granules among the green grass of the plain, which is well liked by all types of gazelle and monkey. As time went by (although it was not yet as famous as Serengeti, Masai Mara or Ngoro Ngoro Crater), it attracted an ever-increasing amount of clients. There were also a number of mini-buses that could hold eight passengers, which were used to take the visitors around the tracks of the Mikumi area to view the beautiful wildlife. The hotel management had given strict orders to the African mini-bus drivers that if the bus broke down, no one must abandon the vehicle; if any bus was not back at the hotel by six o'clock, then another one would be sent out to look for it.

One day this exact thing happened. The bus was about one and a half kilometres from the hotel, but although it was dark and already past six o'clock, no one turned up with assistance. In the dark and silence of the night, it was possible to see the hotel's inviting lights and hear the faint music. At nine o'clock the African driver was tired of waiting, and decided to walk to the hotel to get help. At eleven o'clock he had still not returned, and one of the German tourists proposed that they should all walk to the hotel together. This proposal began a bitter discussion, and no one else agreed, so he decided to go alone; unfortunately, he also did not return. At this point, all of the other passengers were in agreement not to put even their noses out of the bus; however, it was only in the morning that another mini-bus arrived to rescue the stranded people. The driver told them that he had seen the remains of two human bodies along the way. The horror of the tourists upon hearing the news cannot be imagined. Whilst walking under the stars, the driver and the German man must have suddenly found themselves encircled by a group of lions, and in the moment just before they were torn to pieces, they would have scarcely had time to realise their folly.

In 1957, after three years of service with the company, I was entitled to six months' leave. We bought a new Fiat 1100, and decided not to go to Europe, but instead to visit South Africa, via Northern and Southern Rhodesia (now Zambia and Zimbabwe). Earlier we had become friends with an English couple, Maureen and Frank, and their two children, whom we had met in Dar-es-Salaam. They were from Southern Rhodesia and were returning there shortly, so we suggested that we travel with them. Both families had cars, and we agreed that we would follow them until we reached Bulawayo.

I do not remember why we left Dar-es-Salaam in the late afternoon, but it turned out to be a decision that would endanger the life of my daughter Lucia. Our first stop was at Morogoro, about two hundred kilometres away. We arrived there well into the night, and found the only hotel closed, so we had to pass the night in the car. Because of the heat, we had to leave the windows partially open, and we did not realise that by doing so we were giving access to the malarial mosquitoes, which bit us while we were sleeping. It was only in the morning that we noticed that the place we had chosen for our stop was near a swamp. After a frugal breakfast, we proceeded to Mbeya, another small town situated on the highland that borders Northern Rhodesia; I remember that to get there we had to cross vast uninhabited territory. We drove for hours over a road of red soil, typical of those regions, swept by a cold wind saturating the air with impenetrable clouds of red dust raised by the wheels of our motorcars. The temperature kept dropping as we continued to climb up towards Mbeya. At about four o'clock in the afternoon we stopped to stretch our legs, and had another economic meal on the car's bonnet. The sky was of a grey colour to the right of the horizon; the flatland, whichever way you looked, was cold and deserted, generating a sense of solitude and making you feel a desire to leave that sad, inhospitable place.

We drove until sundown, and were about forty kilometres from the border with Northern Rhodesia when we decided to stop for the night and cross it the next morning. We chose to enter the woods as a precautionary measure, and hopefully avoid any encounters with any ill-intentioned characters who could be attracted by the sight of two stopped motorcars. We found a spot two hundred metres from the road. These woods were not very dense but could supply an ample quantity of dry firewood. We lit a large fire to keep the wild beasts at bay, and after a simple dinner, we went to sleep in the cars. Ignoring the danger of some errant lion, we left the car doors open, in order to have more space for our legs.

In the light of sun-up after a cold and uncomfortable night, we did not waste any time and started along the way to the main road. Some one hundred metres from where we had stayed, we encountered a lioness, who watched us with interest as we drove by. Having crossed the border of Northern Rhodesia, we expected a country with a completely different landscape to the one that we had seen in the past few days, but were sadly disappointed: from the car, all we could see on both sides of the road were interminable flat planes. There were no animals, only a little dry grass, and the soil had the appearance of the sort you might find in a desert. There were no rivers, not even a hill in sight to interrupt the monotony of the journey. Every now and then we would encounter a welcome service-post, which offered the opportunity to have a short break and refill the petrol tank. Around these posts was evidence of the great lack of water; only a few jacaranda trees, with their marvellous violet-coloured flowers and multi-coloured bougainvillea managed to cheer up these dull areas, as they had adapted to living in these incredibly dry conditions.

The Victoria Falls are on the Zambezi River near the border between Zambia and Zimbabwe, and were named by the English explorer David Livingstone, who discovered them in 1885. Here the Zambezi drops from a height of 900 metres above sea level down a 122-metre step. The width of the falls is 1,700 metres, and at the bottom the water is channelled into a gorge that is only 75 metres wide. The spectacular view of these falls far exceeded all of our expectations: we never imagined that such beauty could exist. At that time there were no railings on the opposite riverbank, which preserves the natural beauty of the place. When viewed from the front, the huge mass of water appears as though it is moving through a slow-motion camera; however, if your eyes follow it down to the bottom, a well-known magnetic phenomenon is created, and quite a few people have been fatally attracted by this image: it tends to draw the watcher towards the precipice, and unaware of the spell, they move forward and fall into the whirlpools in the turbulent water. I have heard of a few episodes where some lucky people who on falling into the water have been saved by branches growing on the edge of the bank. Apparently records do exist of these incredibly fortunate circumstances.

A short way from the main falls is another great attraction: the Devil's Cataract. This takes its threatening name from the shape of its formation. Imagine two great granite slabs, their edges one in front of the other, separated by a distance of about six metres, and in a manner to restrict the passage of the waters of the Zambezi. The concentrated volume of water rushes through, reaching ten centimetres from the top of the slabs, and exits from the other side with an enormous squirt forwards and downwards for about one hundred metres. It is possible to walk right onto one of the two slabs and up to the brink of the water; to look at the water rushing through at that speed is overawing, and it came to my mind that only one step forward would be enough to be swept away by the jet of water and become part of the falls for ever. According to local stories, the Devil's Cataract is a preferred place for suicides. Most people, before taking the last step into the water, undress and leave their clothes on the platform as evidence of their gesture. Sally and I decided to climb onto the platform, and walked up to a few centimetres from the brink. I must confess that this was an experience I never wish to repeat.

We eventually left Victoria Falls, and decided to go and visit one of the National Parks, namely the Wanke National Reserve. We arrived at the Park Lodge in the evening, which was typically Colonial British. There was a well-stocked bar, with nice cold beer: the preferred drink in British territory. In the bar, we heard that a pack of lions had killed a buffalo not far from the lodge, and they were still in the area, so in the morning we decided to drive to the place where the lions had been spotted and take a look at the scene of the killing. When we reached the spot, we saw a small group of lions around a buffalo carcass, which was lying in a muddy puddle with its belly inflated. However, although the buffalo had been killed the day before, the lions had not yet touched it; puzzled, we tried to find an explanation for the lions' strange behaviour, and we could only conclude that they had left it because it was covered in mud.

However, we returned four days later and found only one male lion with a thick black mane. He was lying down, apparently uninterested in what was going on around him, and the carcass of the buffalo was still lying there untouched, with its belly even more inflated. We arrived behind the lion, and Sally stopped about forty metres away, a few metres behind Frank's car. Frank, reassured by the lazy attitude of the lion, thought that this was a good chance to get a few good pictures, and he got out of the car and started to snap away; however, not satisfied by this, he had the impudence to walk around the car and go up to about thirty metres away from the lion, which I considered open provocation. The lion had never acknowledged our presence, nor moved its head a fraction of a centimetre, and we thought it was still was unaware of Frank's movements. Then, to our great surprise, it suddenly rotated on its back, jumped up and started running in Frank's direction. In a few seconds, he had gained half of the distance that separated him and Frank, and it appeared that Frank was not going to have time to make it to the car and shut himself inside. I quickly told Sally to try to intercept the feline and cut him off, but she had already anticipated this and had never switched off the engine; she promptly sprinted past Frank's car and came to a stop between the lion and our friend. The lion saw the car was blocking his way, and stopped, disconcerted; meanwhile Frank, with one final effort, made it to his car and closed the door. I gently told him that he had taken a hell of a chance by going so near to that lion. He agreed and apologised to me, and thanked Sally for saving his life. Back at the bar, we all had a few well-needed drinks, and soon went to bed. However, that was not the only incident during our stay at the Wanke Reserve.

The next day was our last in the park, and we wanted to re-visit all of it before leaving. Near to the exit, as if to say goodbye to us, a small herd of elephants was about to cross the road. Frank and Maureen did not seem to be in a hurry, and as a measure of caution stopped about eighty metres away from the pachyderms. The animals also did not seem to be in a hurry, and gave us time to observe them at our leisure. The last adult elephant, which was following the main group at some distance away, arrived at the middle of the road and stopped, turned its head towards us, and lifted its proboscis to smell our scent. Its signals were clear enough; they told us that we were not his friends, and our presence was making him angry, which in turn made us feel very uneasy. The beast now started to trumpet in order to scare us away; but we did not move, and after a few seconds he started a furious charge towards us. At this point, there was no time to lose; Sally, who had not liked the signals from the elephant, was prepared for the worst, and had left the engine idling. Her reaction to the charge was instant: she put the car in reverse and drove backwards as quickly as possible, allowing Frank to do the same, probably saving his life for the second time in twenty-four hours. The pachyderm, satisfied by our flight, stopped fifty metres from Frank's car, hesitated briefly, turned around, and went to join his companions.

We left the reserve, and having crossed the Northern Rhodesian frontier, we resumed our trip towards the Southern Rhodesian capital, Salisbury (now Harare). The road that we were on attracted our attention, as it was constructed very strangely. It had two bitumen strips in the centre. When two cars going in the opposite direction approached one another, they would go on either side, with the offside front and rear wheels on one of the strips.

This kind of construction is a peculiarity typical of the British mentality: a good example are the bridges that were built during the World Wars in all three East African territories. In order to save money, they had been built only one lane wide, and the vehicle at one end would have to wait their turn while the other passed through. We all thought that this was ridiculous, and they certainly could not say that they had run out of money, as the reaches of Northern Rhodesia were rich with Virginia tobacco (the best in the world). The Italians were great sceptics, as they had carried out a grandiose road project during their five-year occupation in Ethiopia.

A more natural peculiarity in those countries was the intensity of the thunderstorms, which I have never seen the likes of before. Shortly before reaching the capital of Northern Rhodesia, we encountered one. It started like regular rain, but as we went along, the tempo increased and in no time at all it became a deluge. Up to then it was nothing extraordinary, but suddenly thunderbolts began to come down amongst the water. They came down with the same frequency and intensity as the rain: I cannot tell whether they were coming in the tens or in the hundreds. They were hitting the ground all around the car, some a few metres away, others a little more distant. It was like a concentrated attack of artillery, minus the noise.

Inside the car we did not dare speak; Lucia, thank God, was sleeping. To reassure Sally, I told her I had read that if lightning hit a car, the people inside it were not in danger, as according to Faraday, when the electricity hits metal it will glide over it, and find the shortest route to discharge on the ground.

As quickly as it had started, the rain and lightning were over. Lucia was still sleeping, as if nothing had happened; Sally, I noted, appeared a little more relaxed. She did not say a word. That experience remained a mystery to me: I was never able to understand how it could have been possible with lightning of that intensity, that none had struck the car. The storm brought back memories of the stories I had heard as a prisoner of war, from prisoners returning from the camps of the Transvaal who had had similar experiences.

In our initial programme we had planned a visit to South Africa; however, when we arrived at the border, Sally and I changed our minds. We had had enough after Northern and Southern Rhodesia, and began to feel homesick. Maureen's father had a farm in Northern Rhodesia, not far from the border with Botswana; when we reached Bulawayo, which was also near the Botswana border, Maureen and Frank announced that their trip was at an end. So with sorrow, we separated from our friends after three thousand kilometres of good company. After their departure, we felt a strong desire to go back to Dar-es-Salaam, and travel on our own.

We kept up a sporadic correspondence with Maureen for some years, which was interrupted by the dangerous political changes in those countries. For us, it was one of the many short friendships that you happen to make during the course of your life: so long as you see your friends regularly, their company seems essential; but as time goes by without contact, and the uncertainty of ever seeing them again, the relationship gets weaker. After a while it is completely severed, and the only thing left is a memory. We never met each other again, and the memory of those days is condensed into an old photograph which sometimes resurfaces when you are browsing through a photograph album. We look at it with a breath of nostalgia, and that is all, until the photo pops up again in the future.

We decided we would do the return trip in two stops, at about one thousand kilometres a day; hopefully we would reach Arusha in Tanzania with only a one-night stop in Rhodesia. We were not daunted by the formidable number of kilometres that faced us, and looked forward to this part of our holidays Sally and I are an ideal couple for covering long distances by car: she had and still does have an insatiable appetite for driving, whilst I prefer to observe what passes in front of my eyes in detail, and daydream the journey away.

Lucia was unusually quiet in the back seat. She seemed to be suffering; but I thought it was just a bout of tiredness. When we arrived in Lusaka, the capital of Northern Rhodesia, she was considerably worse, and Sally decided to take her temperature. I saw her scrutinise the thermometer, and was worried at her perplexed expression. I asked her what was wrong, and she said that she could not see where the mercury column had stopped, and she said that she thought that the thermometer was faulty. However, after we had both made a closer inspection, we realised with horror that the column had disappeared because it had gone right off the scale; Lucia's temperature was above 42.5°C, and I knew that she could die at any moment in our hands. I felt panic spread inside me and I made an effort to remain calm. We got her to the hospital just outside Lusaka which was for Europeans only, so it was not very crowded; in fact, to our good fortune, it was practically empty, and staff were available immediately. It was a small white building,

My Father - Giovanni - 1st World War 1918

My Mother - Colomba - circa 1920

Black Mamba - shot by me with Holland & Holland .375 rifle - Tanganyika, 1964

Involuntary dive when hunting by canoe in Kilombero river, nearly lost my rifle overboard, 1966

Hunting in Kilombero river area, Tanganyika. Ramadhani, my tracker, last man on right, 1976

Man-eating crocodile shot by Vittorio to help village people in Tana River area, Kenya, 1967

Ruvu river, Tanganyika, 1959

My family - Tanganyika, 1960

Hunting in Tana River area, Kenya, with Gela the Tracker, 1949

Vittorio - Mau Mau war, Mount Kenya siege, 1952

Sally and Lamberto hunting in Ubenazamozi, Tanganyika, 1952

Lion which attacked Maccagnini (2nd right) shot by Vittorio in Tsavo, Kenya, 1955

set amongst the ever-present jacaranda trees Soon two or three nurses were taking care of Lucia. After a thorough examination, the doctor said that Lucia was having a very strong attack of malaria and it was necessary to act now to have any chance of saving her, and he proceeded to inject her with the first of numerous quinine injections. However, the doctor's tone then changed. He told us that if she survived, then we could not visit her for the next fortnight; he also added with an irate voice that he knew very well the common behaviour of travellers who neglect the health of their children rather than interrupt their vacations and he warned that on more than one occasion he had been a witness to deaths for this very reason.

Early on the morning of the fifteenth day, Sally and I were outside the hospital at the main entrance, waiting for the doctor, who arrived shortly after afterwards. Lucia was in the arms of a nurse, and when she saw us she began to call repeatedly, 'Mummy, Mummy'. When she was near enough, she clasped Sally's neck, and buried her head in her mother's shoulder, as if to say 'never leave me again'. She had recovered, and we could continue our journey.

Things started to change from the moment we stopped at a petrol station to refuel. Here we asked a coloured man which road we should take, and as soon as he knew that we were going to Arusha he went and sat in the passenger seat of the car. I told him that I did not like this at all, and that he had to get out immediately. I was about to throw him out when he started to plead with me to be good, for the love of Jesus Christ, and that he badly needed help, and so on... He was obviously desperate. He was a Cape Coloured; in other words, a South African of mixed race. Two people were observing the scene with interest: one looked wealthy, dressed in a sporty suit, with a high-powered luxury car; the other, a white man, was the petrol station owner. While I was paying him, he told me that picking up hitchhikers in that part of the world was dangerous; he also added that he would not be surprised if I ended up with my throat cut. However, I had decided by then to help the man, and thanked him for his advice, telling him that I was prepared to take the risk.

We started our journey; Sally was driving, I sat next to her, and the man sat in the front next to me. In the meantime, he tried to be friendly, and attempted to make Lucia laugh; but she was not in the right mood for it. Soon we concluded we had given a lift to some poor devil who was actually respectable, and quite shy. As we drove on, he told his story.

He had left the vast territory of South Africa with the intention of crossing the Tanzanian border and reaching Arusha, where he could rejoin his family, who had a small property in the suburbs. He did not have much money, but was confident that he could travel in special African buses, which were very low priced; he also counted on hitching a lift from some vehicles that were travelling in his direction. Soon he realised that he was being too optimistic. He discovered at a crossroads that the bus was not going in his direction, and he got off; but by now it was too late. However, instead of waiting for another motor vehicle, he started to walk along the road to the border. His thoughtlessness could have cost him his life. Many kilometres afterwards, he realised that white people would never stop to give a lift to a Coloured man, and the few cars that passed his way drove on. These zones are almost deserted, and It is impossible to find water anywhere. After a few days of walking, and nights of sleeping on the bare ground (luckily for him, there were no ferocious beasts around) he was in serious danger of dying of thirst. He continued to drag himself along as well as he could, until he eventually fell at the roadside, more dead than alive. Luckily someone stopped to investigate this body that lay at the side of the road, and they took pity, gave him some food and drink, and brought him to the petrol station, where he had met us.

In the evening, around nine o'clock, we reached our first stop: a lodge where we could have dinner, spend the night, and refuel the car. Unfortunately, our guest was not allowed to enter the premises, as they were reserved for Europeans only. He understood the situation, and said that he hoped that we would continue to help him; he also went on to say, with some embarrassment, that he had forgotten to tell us that he had spent all of his money. I agreed with Sally that we would help him as long as he was with us; therefore that evening Botha (that was his name) was provided with an abundant dinner of sandwiches. Like most South Africans of his social class, Botha was a tough man. He did not require any special treatment, and he was used to accepting the eccentric attitude of the white man without resentment. That night he slept on the ground outside the lodge.

The morning after, before resuming our trip, we again met the smartly dressed tourist whom we had encountered the day before at the petrol station; he had also stopped for the night at the same lodge. Upon seeing us, the dandy came over, told us that he had noted the scene at the petrol station, and said that we were very kind people. He also said that he would like to help us by transferring Botha to his car, thus alleviating the weight in our car; however, Botha did not like the idea: he said that he felt fine with us, and did not care to arrive in Tanzania in a luxury motorcar. So we departed a short time afterwards, with Botha in our car. A day later we crossed the Tanzanian border, and as we went towards the centre of the town of Mbeya, with the intention of putting Botha on the first bus for Arusha, he again reminded us that he did not have a penny for the bus ticket, or food for the next two days. We gave him seven and a half pounds, which was enough to buy the bus ticket and provisions; however, he did not thank us warmly, as we could clearly see from the expression on his face that he thought that he had been wrongly thrown out. His was a well-known attitude that we had observed from previous experiences with other Africans. If you give them a meal and a place to stay for the night because you feel sorry for them, they automatically think it is for ever.

After stopping for a much-desired glass of beer in one of the comfortable hotels of Mbeya, we were again on the road for Arusha, which is not far from Mount Kilimanjaro, the highest mountain (5,895 metres) on the African continent. It is in Tanzania, just near the Kenyan border. It has two peaks: Kibo and Mawenzi (both above 5,000m) and the first is permanently covered in snow. Covered by dense woods between 1,500m and 3,000m, it is intensely cultivated at the lower altitudes (coffee, bananas, cotton and sisal).

The road descended slightly at first, but an unexpected surprise was waiting for us; it began to get steeper, and we found ourselves running along the escarpment edge on an elbow-bend, which were very common in Africa (one is described in an earlier chapter). I was driving at a speed of about sixty kilometres an hour, far too fast to negotiate that road safely. The right hand side of the ledge had no barrier, and faced a frightful rocky ravine several hundreds of metres deep. It was necessary to brake and engage a lower gear to reduce speed, but to my surprise and terror I felt the brake hitting the floorboard without any resistance at all. I felt fear gripping my heart as I realised the full gravity of the situation on that critical point in the road; I repeatedly pumped the brake pedal, but without success. I could see there was only one thing left to do: bring the car to the left, chafe gradually against the inner rock wall, and attempt to slow and finally stop the car. I did not have any illusions about the outcome of this manoeuvre: it was my last resort, and there was a thousand-to-one chance of it succeeding. An instant before initiating my plan, I turned briefly towards Sally, who had been dozing, to give her the bad news. I told her to be ready for a hard collision; we were without brakes, and I was about to try and barge into the wall. Sally, as always, understood the situation fully. Without a word, her reply was to grab the handbrake lever firmly, which I had completely forgotten about in my panic, and pull it up with a sharp movement. The rear wheel stopped turning and began to screech, with clouds of smoke; the wretched Fiat, shaking all over with the effort, finally stopped. I then remember Sally looking at me for a few seconds, but she refrained from making any comment.

After that scary experience, we had no alternative but to continue our journey very slowly down the escarpment in low gear with continuous use of the handbrake until we reached the bottom, and then on to Arusha in a similar manner.

The stretch of road from Mbeya to Arusha runs in the middle of completely deserted territory. During the entire journey, we did not see a single native hut, or one person. However, on the otherwise deserted road, there was a great abundance of birds of all species, more numerous than any other place we had seen before. In the middle of the track (which was in need of a lot of maintenance), we encountered flocks of hundreds of guinea fowl. This is a bird that has a great lack of intelligence, as it has a tendency to stay in the middle of the road when facing oncoming vehicles; therefore, it would have been very easy to run over several of them. There was also an abundance of African partridges and wood pigeons. However, we found the region far too remote and empty, and consequently not interesting enough to justify further delay. Upon arriving at Arusha, we stopped at the local Fiat garage and had the brake problem sorted out.

Having satisfied every desire we had during the holiday, nothing else remained for us but to return to Dar-es-Salaam. Our absence from work had been six months long. The visits to the territories in the southern part of Africa had been marvellous, even though we had renounced our visit to South Africa. This was mainly due to fatigue and a shortage of money. True, there had been some unpleasant events, like Lucia's malaria, but otherwise our visit had been very educational, and unforgettable in every respect. Sally and I returned from this vacation greatly enriched with many new experiences, some strange, but none repeatable. These are now a precious part of the memories of our youth.

In July 1958, about a year after our return from our memorable holiday, our second daughter, Linda, was born. An English nurse told me of the joyful news in Dar-es-Salaam hospital. She was full of happiness, and told me in a funnily formal tone that she 'had the pleasure to announce the birth of another small Italian "spaghetti" girl, weighing nearly four kilos, and in full health'. Linda, to our great joy, was born with blue eyes; however, as is commonplace, they changed to a beautiful brown after about ten months.

The years from 1950 up to the end of 1965 were the best years we had in Africa. We did not desire anything more than what we had: we were young, with an established family, the security of a job, and that marvellous territory at our disposal. During that period, we went to Europe three times in a luxury Italian ship run by the Lloyd Triestino shipping line, each being a voyage of fourteen days; however, Sally disliked travelling by sea, so subsequently we flew to Europe.

The Italian ship began its journey at Durban in South Africa, docked at Dar-es-Salaam and then continued to the port of Trieste.

The cabins were small but well equipped, sufficient for four people. The shower/bath was shared between two cabins, and could be locked from the inside, so the occupants of the other cabin would know when it was being used. Most of the passengers were either South Africans or Germans from South-West Africa (Namibia). The Italian Maritime Company had also agreed to allow passengers on from their ports – as long as they were European.

Our girls were fascinated by the novelties of the first trip, but Sally and I did not like travelling by sea. Both of us occasionally suffered from seasickness – even when it was calm – and after a while the slow up-and-down movement of the ship made us vomit and want to die.

The ships did not have a fixed course, and would often stop by request at different ports in South Africa on the journey home. When she called at Dar-es-Salaam – considered an important port – she would dock for half a day, and stock up on water, vegetables and fruits. In Tanzania, there is a large quantity of tomatoes, oranges, limes, papayas, bananas, mangoes and other oriental fruits, all then little known in Europe. After this stop the ship would continue on her voyage, ignoring some ports if there was no demand for them; but it always stopped at Mogadishu. I was surprised to find that I was not too pleased by this news, as I was not keen to see one of the places where I had spent my unhappy infancy. It was about thirty-two years since I had seen that town. However, during the first trip, when we got to Mogadishu we were informed that we could not get off the boat, and the ship cast anchor out in the bay, opposite the Consolata Mission. I looked through my binoculars from the ship's bridge, and pointed out the different areas of the mission to Sally. I showed her the tower with the black and white stripes, which lay high to the right, unchanged after three decades. I also pointed out my favourite place in the middle of the terrace, where I would sit on my own for hours, watching the sea, fascinated, listening to its monotonous undertow – it never failed to take me away from the real world. Near the stretch of rocky beach lay the small cemetery where my mother was buried, and in that moment all my memories came back to me. The mission had not changed one bit, and now some of the names of the long-since dead fathers and nuns came back to me. I was fascinated, rooted to the spot. I had never appreciated my years in the mission, because they had been too near to the time of my parents' death.

After a few hours the ship set sail for Aden. This stop was important for many of the passengers, as there were many little curio shops which sold their goods at duty-free prices. We planned to buy a German camera and projector for ourselves, and visited several shops to compare prices, which differed from one place to the next. After two hours we had not found exactly what we wanted, so we gave up and resumed to the ship. However, returning on board was not to be as easy as we thought...

In Aden there were many Arabs who were notorious for harassing tourists. One of them had been tailing us for some time, trying to convince us to go and visit the crater of a dormant volcano about ten kilometres from the town. One of the last things we wanted to do was to visit the crater of a volcano, especially in the searing heat of Aden; besides, the ship's crew had been very explicit in warning us about going there, as it was located in a deserted place at the edge of the urban area. One sailor recounted the misadventure of some tourists who had been conned by the taxi driver, who asked for a substantial extra fee upon reaching the crater. The tourists were shocked, and at first refused to pay; however, the driver was ready for this, and knew exactly how to convince them to abide by his request: he got into his car and started his engine, demonstrating that he was fully capable of leaving them for dead in the middle of nowhere. The wretched tourists had no option but to pay.

Anyway, the persistent Arab continued to talk constantly, and now started to annoy Sally, who was walking a few steps behind me. He even had the impudence to grab her arm, with the intention of getting her to change direction. She was clearly alarmed, and asked me to stop him. Without hesitating I fumed and landed a punch in the face of the Arab, and in a flash the previously deserted road was full of about fifteen Arabs, each one trying to get me. They closed around me like grapes on a stalk, one on top of the other, trying to land punches on my head. This did not overly worry me, as there was too much commotion for the throng to inflict any serious damage. I defended myself, throwing punches to my left and right, at whoever was nearest; in the meantime Sally was observing the fray from the outside, worried that sooner or later someone would produce a knife, as was often the case in these brawls. She was hoping for the arrival of the police. Finally a Somali police officer appeared, and naturally he was on the side of the crowd. He threw himself amongst them with verve, made directly for me, grabbed me by the shirt collar, tearing it, and instructed me to stop being so aggressive, As the first Arab was asking for a monetary payment, which I obviously refused to pay, I was arrested and taken to the nearest police station.

Half an hour later I had still not budged, and they had no choice but to release me, so we returned to the ship. On the way back several Hebrew shopkeepers who had heard of the incident advised us to hasten on our way – they said there was a good chance that we would be attacked again; but luckily nothing happened. At the wharf we met two sailors who were about to cast off. They told us that they had been informed of the incident by the police, and that we had been very lucky that the ship had not set sail without us; they also told us that Aden had a firmly established reputation for the ill treatment of tourists – especially young women. They must always stay alert if they wanted to avoid unpleasant surprises, especially if they were not accompanied by a man.

In the years just after the end of the last war, the Australian Government agreed with the German authorities to accept a large number of young German women who were willing to immigrate to Australia. The idea was to balance the ratio of men and women, which was a result of the death of millions of German males in the war. At the same time, this would benefit Australia, where there was a shortage of women.

Our ship, the *Africa*, and its sister, the *Europa*, had been chosen to transport thousands of these women – five hundred on every voyage from Trieste to Sydney. Before embarking, the women would be counted, and given a travel document to be presented upon their arrival at Sydney, where their number would again be verified. But each time the ship landed at Sydney it was discovered that three or four of the young women were missing. They had only been authorised to leave the ship at the port of Aden. After an investigation, the authorities arrived at the rather obvious conclusion that they must have been abducted at this stop. According to the rumour circulating among the ship's crew, this was how they were abducted:

The women chosen usually had blonde hair and blue eyes, and they were oblivious to the danger that awaited them among the many small shops. If the girls had the required physical requisites, then they were considered to be ideal white slaves, who could still be found in some countries. The girls that were in most danger were the ones that were alone, or with just one friend. The Arabs would insist that they entered one of the strange shops with unusual smells and the goods piled confusingly. Once inside, if they showed interest in a particular object then they would be invited with courteous insistence into another room at the back of the shop, where the shopkeeper guaranteed to have a vast variety of the specific object. If the curious girls decided to enter that room then their fate would be sealed, as they would instantly find themselves locked in, and no sound – no matter how loud – could be heard from outside. At this point everything was easy for the kidnappers: the ship would depart without having any knowledge that someone was missing, until they got to Sydney. The girls were then subject to brutal treatment, and could consider themselves the property of their master. After dark, the kidnappers would take the girls out of the shop and out of the city, where they would disappear without trace, for ever.

The incident at Aden had left me furious and wanting revenge. I understood that it would not be easy to find the right opportunity, and I should be careful to avoid losing my temper again – it is necessary to control yourself when you are out of your territory, as you will always be the enemy to the authorities. However, there were only two more stops along the Suez Canal, and my desire seemed destined to remain unsatisfied.

After leaving Aden we passed the Tropic of Cancer, and were subjected to the pathetic and boring ceremony that was conducted by the ship's crew every time they arrived at the canal. The usual King Neptune was waiting in the swimming pool armed with a trident, and gave orders to his soldiers to tear apart some complacent young girls. Two willing sailors obliged, and by the girls' screams it appeared as though they were too busy fondling them underwater to tear them apart. The charade ended when Neptune's soldiers proudly displayed a large animal bone with meat still attached to it, allegedly torn from a girl's body. The sailors then rushed to cover the swimming pool with a large net after the bathers had left, once the ceremony got out of control.

At Suez the ship had to stop and wait for other traffic to pass. The town's merchants were already waiting for our arrival with their merchandise, and started immediately to try and board the ship. They tried to hook it with ropes at several points on the stern, but on this occasion they were not permitted to board – there had been an epidemic of cholera at Massawa in Eritrea, and the ship had declared a state of quarantine. The merchants were furious, and exchanged insults with the crew members, who stood with hydrants at the ready. The atmosphere was decidedly tense.

There was only one exception to the quarantine rule, and this was a magician-cum-comedian from Egypt. He was called the Galli Galli man, and was considered indispensable by the ship's captain, as he broke the monotony of the voyage. The Galli Galli man was a well-known figure with the tourists of that period, a first-rate magician and comedian who provided people of all ages with much amusement.

We had been offered the opportunity to go on a bus trip to Cairo and the Pyramids. There you could do some shopping in the colourful markets, and then continue on to Port Said, where the ship would be waiting. However, Sally and I were not museum types, and decided to stay in the comfort of the ship.

My daughters began to pull at my sleeves, and insisted on going below deck to see the performance of the Galli Galli man. However, I could sense that violence was imminent, and did not want to miss it – the merchants had the same attitude as the inhabitants of Aden, and I did not want to pass up on this chance of revenge. But Sally joined forces with the girls, and I had to give in. She convinced me that there would be plenty of time to watch the Galli Galli man, and fight the merchants.

When we returned on deck it looked as though it had been hit by a hurricane. The relics of deck chairs were scattered everywhere, and the deck was covered with water. The captain of arms – a Sicilian – was excitedly explaining the details of the fight that had only happened a few minutes before (he still had a knife in his hand). He was proudly saying that he had single-handedly repulsed all of the merchants on his side of the rail. It appeared that the merchants had overcome the sailors on the rest of the ship, though, and it was only the intervention of the South African tourists that had saved the day.

It had all started when the merchants succeeded in climbing on board, and somehow managed to get a powerful hose from one of the sailors. One of them directed it into the face of the crewman, and it was only because a South African smashed a chair on the head of the merchant that the crewman did not die from drowning. The battle must have had a funny side, as the South Africans are notorious for swinging chairs left and right, as is depicted in many American films. On this occasion, they added a suitable finale by throwing the merchants overboard. At this point, the amusing situation was at its acme. The sailors were trying to fill the little boats with water, and the merchants were frantically trying to get as far away as possible. The tourists were now applauding from the ship's deck, and many of them thought that they would not succeed in getting away; however, the merchants did get out of range, and started muttering insults in their language, which were met with equal enthusiasm by the sailors and tourists. The whole thing looked like scene from a Charlie Chaplin film.

We disembarked at Brindisi. Lucy and I went to Rome by train, and Sally and Linda went by train to Munich to collect a new DKW car; they then drove down to Rome to join us. Later we all went by car to England for a month as guests of Sally's parents in London. For them it was four unforgettable weeks, and I was quite moved to see that they did everything that they could to make our stay as pleasant as possible.

The food was excellent: we often went for lunch in one of their two favourite pubs, for Scottish salmon and pints of beer, and every morning Sally's father prepared breakfast for everyone. Sally claimed that he was the world's best cook of bacon and eggs, and I had to agree with her.

We also visited some famous tourist attractions. For example: the National Portrait Gallery and the Tower of London, with all its bloody history, where we had the opportunity to admire the Queen's crown, and the largest diamond in the world, which originated from the mines of South Africa. However, it all ended too soon – one month seemed like one week – and the time came to say goodbye. Before we left, Sally's father brusquely closed the door of the bedroom that we had used for a month. I was a little perplexed, as I did not understand the significance of that gesture. It was only a few years after that it dawned on me: he could not stand the sight of that empty room, a harsh reminder of the departure of his little girl. When I think back to that separation even today, my heart misses a beat, and I find it difficult to keep a tear in check.

The return voyage was rather monotonous, especially when you think of the incidents of the outgoing voyage. We had already seen all of these places, and were just anxious to get home.

Only one worry started to change the atmosphere for the European residents in Tanganyika. There were some cases of public disorder in Dar-es-Salaam, started by the sectors of the local population who advocated Tanganyika's independence from Great Britain. However, the action that was controlled by the humanitarian Julius Nyerere was never violent. In a few months, thanks to the clever diplomatic policy of Nyerere, Britain granted independence to Tanganyika, which under his leadership changed its name to 'The United Republic of Tanzania'.

Britain had chosen to grant independence to Tanganyika before

Kenya because it had personal stakes in the Kenyan economy. Firstly, there were a large number of European landowners, tea and coffee cultivators, and livestock breeders. They were also the uncontested owners of farms of thousand of hectares of land, producing very large amounts of export products, and they all maintained highly profitable export and import relations with the UK. As a whole, Kenya was a territory far richer, albeit smaller, than Tanganyika.

If I remember correctly, Great Britain granted independence to Tanganyika in 1961 (and a Republic in 1962). Less than a month later, the soldiers of the Permanent Detachment of the Tanganyika British Army revolted against their British officers. This coup d'état aimed to take command of the now independent Tanganyika, and the Prime Minister, Julius Nyerere, was compelled to go into hiding. For several weeks, the African Army looked for Nyerere everywhere; but he could not be found: he seemed to have disappeared from the face of the Earth.

Nyerere was a fervent Catholic. He had completed his studies at the Catholic Mission of Kingolwira, near Dar-es-Salaam; in this crisis, there could not have been a better hiding place. The African Army may have considered this possibility, but they did not imagine that a religious order would have taken the risk of giving him asylum.

Those were ugly days for Tanganyika, especially on the island of Zanzibar, which became part of the nation of Tanzania in 1964. It is separated by a sea corridor fifty kilometres wide, and is a little north of Dar-es-Salaam. The Arabs (who subdued the native African population) occupied Zanzibar in the eleventh century; however, in 1503 the island was conquered by the Portuguese, who controlled it until the end of the seventeenth century, and it became the principal ivory and slave market of Africa. It was then taken over by the Iman of Mascat, before becoming a protectorate and eventually a colony of Great Britain in 1913; this lasted up to 1962, when it became an internal self-governing state.

Many years had passed since Zanzibar had been the major centre of the African slave market. After having being taken away by force from their own families in the remote interior of Africa, slaves arrived in Zanzibar to be sold by auction to the highest bidder. The square where they were taken in chains is still there, in the centre of Zanzibar town. Those who bought them, usually rich Arabs, became the undisputed owners of their life or death. The slave trade was gradually abolished around the year 1890.

At the time of Independence, the population of Zanzibar consisted mostly of African Bantu and Kiswahili. There were also about thirteen thousand Indians, about thirty-two thousand Arabs and few more than two hundred and sixty Europeans.

Together with the island of Pemba, it made up the Sultanate of Zanzibar and Pemba, a protectorate of Great Britain since 1st July 1890. It had a small Legislative Council presided over by the Sultan, with whom the English Government also resided.

In Zanzibar, the Arabs had assumed the same attitude towards the African population as the Europeans had assumed earlier towards the Africans in mainland Tanganyika, and during the coup d'état in the 1960s an armed band of Africans had accounted for the deaths of several hundred Arabs.

Luckily for us, the violence had not reached the same proportions in our area as it had in Zanzibar. However, it was rumoured that one Arab shopkeeper had been killed in the town. It appeared that this man had to defend himself from a group of rebel soldiers; hidden behind an empty two-hundred-litre petrol keg, he had killed seven soldiers with his rifle before he himself was shot. They also shot his wife, but spared his two-year-old son.

We lived in a building with four apartments, sharing with three other European families. They were the Kenny family, the Devine family and the Evans family. Right opposite us was a former police station that was now occupied by the rebel army, and full of excited African soldiers. It goes without saying that we were all very apprehensive about the position of the rebels, especially knowing how similar situations in Africa had ended. We were all certain that eventually we would attract the attention of the soldiers, particularly with the presence of our young wives. We also imagined the probable consequences, but were reluctant to think too much about them.

However, the four families held a meeting, and as a precaution decided to fill all of our bathtubs with water, as we thought that this was a commodity that would soon run out. If we had to leave our homes to seek water elsewhere, the situation would be severely complicated. We also agreed that we would defend any violent attack with all of the guns and rifles at our disposal; in this case, our only hope would be to fire a few rounds in the air to show our determination: it was clear that if we got into a gunfight then our chances of survival were zero. Our arsenal consisted of three guns, with some forty rounds for the two carbines and about twenty cartridges for Evans's shotgun. Nevertheless, we decided that if the worst came to the worst, we would defend our families at all costs.

Before the coup d'état, the troops were under the command of a British colonel, who was most probably warned in advance by some loyal soldier, and was able to avoid being captured; in fact, some soldiers refused to rebel and disappeared. The colonel had managed to take refuge in the British High Commission, which was situated in a solid modern building along the Dar-es-Salaam sea front. The BHC, like most embassies, was equipped with a powerful short-wave radio transmitter. After a few days, English warships appeared on the horizon, about twenty kilometres away from the Dar-es-Salaam harbour and the BHC.

The next day, one of the warships, under the charge of a man who had spent some time in Africa and knew its people like the back of his hand, arranged for a clever diversion by way of the ship's guns. The ship fired several salvos into the air, so the African Army focused their attention on the bursts exploding in the air, and in the meantime the marines landed on the coast in rubber boats. By the time the Africans realised, it was too late: the marines had taken the colonel from the BHC and were well on their way back to the ship. The operation was completed without a single shot being fired.

After having seen these manoeuvres, the rebels began to fear an assault from ground troops, and deployed a battalion of soldiers to some strategically chosen spots along the coast. However, they could not cover everywhere. According to the information received from European sources on the telephone, the colonel had taken over the command. His knowledge of locations was not the only advantage he had: he also knew personally several soldiers who were now commanding the rebel troops, and hoped to appeal and convince them to surrender without hostility.

The marines landed easily, as there was hardly any opposition, and carried out an attack during the night. After the first shots, the rebel troops took advantage of the dark, and lay in the high grass of the flatland, hoping to hide themselves. The colonel, after his first success, decided to turn his attention to the military base, where most of the troops were lodged. He arrived at the camp without any opposition at all, and secured the immediate surrender of a group of soldiers, with the exception of a few who had taken refuge in the guards' barrack. He then appealed to the sergeant, calling him by name and telling him to come out without fear, as everything would be 'settled in a pacific manner'. The sergeant did not answer his old commander: he was probably too afraid to trust him. In the end, the colonel lost his patience and gave the order to open fire with a small piece of field artillery. One shot destroyed the entire building and killed all of the soldiers who had taken refuge inside it.

The next morning the chase began for the soldiers who were hidden in the grass. It was in this operation that helicopters were employed for the first time. We Europeans had not even seen these flying monsters before, so you can imagine the terror of the African soldiers, hidden in the grass, with these things flying two metres above their heads. The wind generated by their rotors was used to flatten the grass, thereby exposing the rebel soldiers, who were then captured by the marines on foot. In just one day, the marines had achieved all of their objectives.

The British troops remained in Tanzania for a couple of months to stabilise the country, re-establish the legitimate government, and ensure the citizens' security. President Nyerere returned to the command of the country, and did not order any reprisal against the guilty soldiers: something of a rarity for an African president. They were simply dismissed from the army, and sent back to their own villages. The President had ensured the re-establishment of peace in the territory. In 1965, after three years of independence, the country had completely recovered. The Government launched a programme that would create a new managerial and ruling class of Tanzanian personnel within ten years. They would be trained in high schools and universities, and would eventually take over from the European staff, who then dominated all positions of power and importance. The collective term for this plan was Africanisation. As far as we were concerned, we would be dismissed within this ten-year period.

After the return of political security, the Italian community had become more compact, like a fellowship. In the same year, the Italian Club was lucky enough to acquire a very esteemed person in its ranks: Dr Ugo Fornari. He graduated in Medicine and

Obstetrics from the University of Rome, and later obtained a diploma in public health from the University of Edinburgh. He had come to Africa to join, as a doctor, the established White Father Mission on the Island of Ukerewe, near Mwanza. There he gained a lot of experience dealing with patients and diseases different from those found in Europe. He specialised in treating tropical diseases, including malaria, elephantiasis, bilharziasis and other parasitic infestations such as the lethal intestine and blood parasite hookworm, which causes anaemia and a quick loss of weight, bringing rapid death. He had also become well known for having performed several successful operations for the reconstruction of the lips of those who were affected by harelip. He had gained great esteem and recognition from all Africans who had met him. His ability as a medical man became so prestigious that the Town Mayor dedicated a street to his name: Fornari Avenue.

After he had been working with the mission for three years, the Tanzanian Government offered him a job as Overseas Civil Service Senior Medical Officer, which he accepted, and he was posted at the Muhimbili Hospital of Dar-es-Salaam.

The Africans are very superstitious, and it is a side of their character that, although very interesting, is very difficult to penetrate. In the twenty-two years that I worked in Dar-es-Salaam, I never once discussed this topic with my co-workers. I knew that they were too embarrassed to tell a European about their ridiculous means of treatment, of which we saw the results every now and then. Their doctors, or witch doctors as we call them, adopted absurd methods to counter the effects of their superstitions.

One day, I noted that Ali Mohammed, one of my workers, had lost a lot of weight within a very short time. In the space of a month, he had reached such a poor physical condition that it prevented him from working. I learnt from his friends that he had been bewitched by an unknown source that wanted him dead. This led him to suspect everybody around him, including the members of his family. I was unable to convince him that he had fallen ill naturally, and all that he needed was a good doctor. After an inner battle with himself, he decided to look for therapy in Bagamoyo, a village about twenty kilometres from Dar-es-Salaam. All of the Africans in the surroundings knew this village as the only place where one could be exorcised, and I asked Mohammed's friends for more information about Bagamoyo. I was told that when a person was prey to these symptoms, as Mohammed was, and decided to go to Bagamoyo to consult with a witch doctor, they would die for sure.

As was expected, Mohammed's visit to the witch doctor had been a failure. On the Monday, he presented himself at work for the last time. He had some small cuts on his head and forehead, and signs of burns on the temples. Having seen his attempt fail, Mohammed abandoned his job after a week, saying that he wished to die in his village on the banks of the Rufiji River, two hundred kilometres from Dar-es-Salaam.

For nine months, there was no news of him; I did not know whether he was dead or alive. Finally I asked some of his companions from the same village, and they told me that he was still alive, although in a very bad shape, close to death. Through his companions, I sent Mohammed a message, telling him to come back to Dar-es-Salaam, and there I would have him reintegrated into work with sick leave and full salary until fully recovered; in addition, I would take him to a European doctor to be cured.

A week later, Mohammed turned up for work. He was like the walking dead: a bunch of skin and bones, with enormous eyes. I took him to the Muhimbili Hospital to see Dr Fornari, whom I had already informed about Mohammed's details, including the story of the witch doctor. Fornari said that the first thing to do was to perform a faeces analysis. Now the entire European community knew of the uselessness of the analyses performed by the African staff of this hospital, and I told Fornari this. But Fornari was a born idealist, and said that my opinion was merely the stale colonial attitude of the old Europeans. I countered this by saying that all the private European doctors of the town performed their own analyses, but the doctor was not convinced, and told us to come back after three days.

When I returned with Mohammed, the doctor welcomed us with a peculiar smile that I could not understand. He told us that the test had been negative, but he was sure that Mohammed was infested with hookworm. I immediately thought of his earlier smile: how did he know that Mohammed had hookworm if the tests had been negative? I preferred not to comment. He gave Mohammed a pill the size of a grain of corn, at which Mohammed stared with an incredulous expression. The doctor smiled again, and said that one pill would take care of his illness, giving him a second one in case he wanted to make sure. There was now nothing left to do, so we went away, sceptical but hopeful.

Mohammed soon regained his appetite, and within a month his health and his former good humour returned. I am glad to say that he remained part of my team of workers for many years until, finally, I had to leave the territory.

I know of another example of African superstition, which occurred a few years later. However, since we are on the subject, I will tell you of this other case now. Ali Saidi was the foreman of my squad of African workers. Unlike Ali Mohammed, who was always outgoing and cheerful, Ali Saidi was always taciturn and serious, and hardly ever smiled. He was also without doubt the best of the Africans who worked under me. He had attended school for several years, and could read and write in English; in addition, his professional capabilities were far superior to those of all his companions. Ali had precious natural gifts that were appreciated by everyone: he was reliable, punctual, and very well suited to his role of intermediary between his companions and me. As he had the respect of all the members of the squad, his role was invaluable when settling their problems.

One day, Ali started to feel unwell: a dry cough was irritating him at all hours of the day. As time went by, the cough became so persistent that it was almost intolerable to everyone around him. It reminded me of the year 1930, and my childhood, when the fear of tuberculosis was widespread in Europe. The resultant cough from this disease is easy to differentiate from other types of common coughs, as it is highly unique.

Before the arrival of the Europeans and the Indians, tuberculosis was unknown in Africa, but in the 1960s had spread through the indigenous population. Hearing Ali Saidi coughing now, I had no doubt that it was a dangerous sign. After a month, Ali's condition had deteriorated greatly. He had lost a lot of weight, and his face had turned grey, as most Africans' faces do when they are ill. I soon learned from his companions that he had decided to go to Bagamoyo to consult a witch doctor. I was pained to hear this news, as I knew all too well of the inevitable outcome of this decision, and I decided to have a serious talk with him. I considered him to be more intelligent than the majority of the other Africans, and probably less superstitious too; for this reason I hoped that I could persuade him not to go and see the witch doctor. As I expected, he listened to me; to tell the truth, I did not even have to say much: I only repeated the same arguments that I had used to convince Ali Mohammed. Since Ali held the Europeans in great esteem, I was trying to make him understand the reasons why they did not have superstitions of any kind. I kept insisting that he was sick, and to get well again, he needed a real doctor. I was pleased to see that (unlike Ali Mohammed) he was attentively following my argument with interest; naturally, he knew of the extraordinary healing of Ali Mohammed a few years earlier.

At this point I have to go back a few years. When she was five, Linda began to get a strange cough, which only stopped after taking antibiotics. However, the cough resumed after a month or so, and again only disappeared after another course of antibiotics; of course, Sally and I were worried by this strange phenomenon.

During one of our periodic visits to Italy, we took Linda to Dr Pieraccini, a lung specialist. After an X-ray on Linda's chest, he was still unsure, and began to treat her for tuberculosis. Together with some advice, he gave me some tablets, which were to be taken daily; he explained that they were not antibiotics but were very efficacious in this sort of case, and together with a course of streptomycin would help rid Linda of her trouble.

When we got back to Tanzania, the cough had not troubled her again, and I went to see our family doctor, an Irishman. I told of the Italian doctor's diagnosis and of his treatment, also mentioning that the X-ray did not show anything untoward. He examined the X-rays that I had brought along, and confirmed that they were clear; however, just to make sure, he said that he would consult one of his colleagues, an X-ray specialist. In the meantime, he suggested suspending treatment until he had carried out tests on Linda's arm which, he assured me, would be more credible than the X-rays. To our great relief, the tests were negative and the specialist confirmed that my daughter had never contracted tuberculosis. For good measure, he vaccinated her against the disease. During the 1960s, vaccination became a very successful means to combat tuberculosis, and was probably the reason why it was defeated so quickly in Europe.

At the end of all this I was left with three of the pills that the Italian doctor had given me, and I remembered that I had kept them in a drawer in the medicine cabinet. As I suspected that I knew what Ali Saidi's illness was, I thought I could try and convince him to swallow the pills, and see what happened. The next day I told him the story of the pills and asked him to take them, as it was very likely that they were for tuberculosis. Luckily the disease was in the early stages, and was therefore easier to cure. Even if they were unsuccessful, they were still harmless, and he agreed to take them. Incredible! After having taken all three pills in three days, Ali Saidi's cough suddenly stopped, as if by a miracle. After a month, the cough had not reappeared, confirming that he had completely recovered from the terrible disease. I can say with pleasure that Ali Saidi also remained in my team for many years, again up until I left the territory.

There were no private schools for European children in Dar-es-Salaam, and when each of my daughters reached the age of seven, they had leave town to go to the only private European school in Tanganyika. It was situated on the eastern side of the country, at Lushoto in the Uluguro Mountains, about three hundred kilometres from Dar-es-Salaam. This area had been chosen for its cool and healthy climate: there were no mosquitoes, and therefore no malaria.

The mountains were studded with numerous waterfalls, and it was an ideal area for having picnics with the family at weekend visiting days. From these vantage points it was also possible to admire the spectacular scenery. The long journey there was unexpectedly enjoyable. It was always nice to meet the other parents whom we had not seen for a while; many of them had even further to go than us. We were in the same boat, and on Saturday evenings the children and parents had a cheerful party in the hotel dining room. The children had also made friends, and they were glad to meet up again in Dar-es-Salaam after school had ended.

Considering the brevity of the visit and length of the drive, the trip from Lushoto to Dar-es-Salaam was still rather demanding. If I remember rightly, it took about five or six hours to cover the distance. We would leave our children at five o'clock, and return to Dar-es-Salaam well into the night, after a long and solitary run on the deserted road. About two hundred and forty kilometres from Lushoto, the all-weather dirt road ended as we arrived at the junction with the tarmac road that connected Dar-es-Salaam with Morogoro. For various reasons, we tackled the dirt road with some apprehension; there were only a few huts along the roadside, perhaps one every ten kilometres, and the traffic would gradually disappear with the light of day. In the four years of visiting my daughters, I encountered only a handful of motor vehicles along that road at night. I believe that a vague sensation of dread prevented people from trying it; a breakdown in that isolated area would have been extremely dangerous. Due to the abundant rainfall, the vegetation was luxuriant, and the grass at the edge of the road reached up to chest-high on an adult. The region also hosted an abundant number of lions, and in the absence of more regular food, they would not hesitate to take human flesh as a substitute.

By the end of the 1960s, a large number of Europeans had left Tanzania; most of them were redundant British Government personnel. Unfortunately, the first substituted were the Europeans on the Police, with the exception of a few officers, whose authority was considerably reduced. The consequences of these changes were soon evident. Public order became slack, and crime rapidly increased; the general respect enjoyed by Europeans up until then was disappearing.

There was now a new class of Europeans emerging, made up mostly of Peace Corps and tourists, who had new ideas of how to handle relations with the indigenous population; they were far more liberal and idealistic. In cases of aggression and hostility, they would always adopt a paternal attitude, and would search for a reason to justify the Africans' actions. I thought this approach was the wrong one, and in the long run would lead to disorder and injustice. However, I do not wish to dwell on this subject, and prefer not to offer any more comments.

Our homes had become the principal target of thieves, who were often armed. There were also rumours of attacks on motorcars on the Dar-es-Salaam – Lushoto road that were carried out at night by gangs of criminals. There were many methods to stop the cars; one was to place a tree-trunk across the road, while the robbers hid in the high grass, waiting for a car to stop. Alternatively, a bandit would lie in the middle of the road when he saw a car's headlights approaching, feigning to be dead. When the Samaritan stopped and got out of the car, the men that were waiting at the side of the road would attack. This second method could be risky, as some car drivers were fully aware of this trick and would drive right over the body. On one occasion, I was on my own, driving home, and saw the shape of a body in the road a few hundred metres away. It appeared to be dead, but I was well aware of the possible danger, and decided to drive right over it; given the late hour and the lack of traffic, I was certain that it was a trap. Sure enough, when I got about a hundred metres away, the 'body' got smartly up and disappeared into the grass on the roadside. It is hard to imagine the consequences of being caught out by one of these ambushes, especially if you were with your family. As there was no moral, cultural or ethical affinity with the perpetrators of such crimes, one lost all hope when appealing to them: the victim belonged to them up to their death, and age was of no consequence to them. I would rather die than go through such an experience, which could last up to several hours.

I remember another occasion when Sally and I were returning from Lushoto after our usual visit to see the girls. It was eleven o'clock at night, and we were on the all-weather road, about halfway to Dar-es-Salaam. Our car was a small Citroën with a Panard 2 cylinder engine; a good little car with a bad defect: the tyres were inclined to puncture a little too frequently, especially on that type of road. It had happened before, but always during daytime; this time it happened in the middle of nowhere, in the dead of night, and changing a tyre in these circumstances was an operation to be performed with caution. Although it would only take twenty minutes, danger was represented by the possible presence of lions: there was little chance of encountering a band of criminals in such an isolated place; in any case, I always travelled armed, and had loaded five rounds into the magazine of my rifle. In order to change the wheel, it was necessary to keep the car headlights on. Sally stood with the rifle in front of the headlights, in order not to be surprised by a beast. As I was working, the headlights of a car appeared about a kilometre away; I noted that it was slowly coming in our direction, and I did not like it. The fact that the vehicle was moving so slowly could indicate that the car did not really have a precise destination. When it was about twenty metres away it stopped, as I had suspected. I took the rifle from Sally and told her to get inside the car. I then placed myself right in front of the car, with the intention of showing that I was armed. Now I could see that it was a run-down motorcar. Fortunately, in those first years of independence, firearms had not yet fallen into the hands of the indigenous population, and more importantly, those of the criminals. If they were bandits, I was expecting that they would only be armed with machetes, and I would not have been too afraid: the presence of the rifle would have been enough to frighten them. There were about five people in the car; I was now convinced that it was one of those bands that I had heard of and I needed to keep a minimum distance of twenty metres to avoid a close-range attack. I knew all too well that a mistake on my part could be fatal. In a menacing voice I asked them what they wanted. One of them told me that they wanted to know if we needed help. In the same tone of voice, I told them that their help was not necessary, and that they could go on their way. They had no choice but to follow my command.

I completed the change of tyres and as I drove away, I saw from my rear view mirror that they had turned the truck round and gone back the way they had come from. I have no doubt that if I had been unarmed, that night would have ended in tragedy. This episode has stuck in my memory so clearly that I have included it among these happenings which represent the changing atmosphere in my last days in Africa.

Sometime after this, on the same stretch of road, I was returning from Kenya, driving a van loaded with new furniture for my house, which I had bought in Nairobi. I had also brought Ali Mohammed with me as a companion. It was about nine hundred kilometres from Nairobi to Dar-es-Salaam, and with the loaded van, took about twelve hours to cover. Sally and I had done this mostly pleasant trip several times already, and we always completed it without stopping, except for refuelling. It was still in the dark early hours of the morning, and we arrived at roughly the same spot where I had met the bandits. At a wide bend in the road, about a hundred metres away, our headlights reflected off two pairs of eyes. From our previous experience of hunting at night with torches, I recognised these beasts as lions. When we got closer, I realised that they were lying in ambush about three metres away from the door of a roadside hut, clearly waiting for it to be opened. It was quite possible that the inhabitants of this isolated hut could come out to relieve themselves at any time, especially if they had drunk a lot of beer the night before. Some of the intelligent lions had probably witnessed this necessity, and now waited patiently for someone to show themselves; on some occasions they had probably been successful. Who knows? For a lion, there is nothing more enticing than an easy ambush. Ali Mohammed turned to me and exclaimed excitedly: '*Simba, Simba*' (lions, lions), and without waiting for my reaction steered the vehicle towards the felines with the intention of scaring them off. The two lions, seeing the van driving towards them at full speed, got up to take flight, but Mohammed managed to touch the lioness's posterior with a final burst of acceleration. With a grimace, she turned her head towards the van and made a frightening show of her teeth before disappearing out of view into the high grass with her mate: she did not appreciate that impertinent piece of human machinery making contact with her behind. We then tried to warn the people in the hut of the danger, but they were probably scared of the strange voices, and refused to open the door. Frustrated, I decided to continue our journey.

After another two kilometres we encountered a very long bridge; I'm afraid I cannot remember the name of the river that runs underneath. The light from the stars and the reflection on the water provided satisfactory visibility, and we were surprised to see a solitary soldier halfway across the bridge, armed with a rifle. He was obviously a guard, and was only too happy to exchange a few words and enjoy our company for a while. We chatted for about a quarter of an hour, and he said that we were the only people who had passed over the bridge that night. I noted that he wisely stayed in the middle, and I understood why: an attack from lions was far more worrying than a sabotage attempt (the reason why he was guarding the bridge). We told him about the man-eating lions we had just seen, and described their ambush attempt. He showed an immediate interest and concern at the same time, and asked how far from the bridge it had happened; he also added that he knew that the area was dangerous and lions had already devoured several people. After a handshake and a few words of encouragement we bade him goodbye, and carried on our way. We arrived back in Dar-es-Salaam without any more stops or incidents.

Towards the end of the 1960s, we started to see around another kind of tourist, never seen before in the country: Backpackers. To avoid hotel expenses, to follow the latest fashion, or maybe to be more independent, they chose to travel with a rucksack on their shoulders. This sack contained the necessary essentials of everyday life: a change of clothing, toiletries, something to sleep on etc. This was often an ultra-light rubber mattress with a small blanket, which could be used for sleeping almost anywhere. The more luxurious alternative was the sleeping bag, of which there must be hundreds of varieties.

The more fortunate would have the financial support of their parents, but those who were self-sufficient would often find themselves in absurd and dangerous situations because of their inexperience and naivety, and it is these people that I intend to talk about.

A few months after my voyage to Nairobi, my company sent me to Iringa, a small town some hundreds of kilometres from the capital. Here I was to test the electrics for a new company, and certify that it was safe to use. As always on these occasions, I was looking forward to the interesting job that lay ahead. I was familiar with the road, as it passed through Mikumi and then continued on up to Iringa. For this trip I drove an old military-type Volkswagen, which was quite sporty, with no roof, and had a windscreen that could be folded forward. On the driver's side, between the two front seats, I had fitted a rack for my trusty Holland & Holland .375 Magnum Carbine, which I always took with me when going on a trip. It was about six-thirty, and I was coming up to halfway to Iringa, when I reached the village of Mikumi. I began to slow down as it was starting to get dark and I was finding it more and more difficult to distinguish the more distant objects; however, I knew exactly where I was: it was the spot where some time before a family of lions had besieged Franco and me for a whole night. Suddenly, out of the dark, I saw the figures of a boy and a girl appear in the car headlights. They were standing at the roadside, between two trees, and were frantically signalling for me to stop; I thought that they must be wary of the approaching darkness and were eager for a lift: my car would have almost certainly been the last vehicle on that road until morning. Upon seeing two youngsters in that place, unarmed, I was stunned: I could not believe what I was seeing. When I stopped the car, they asked me if they could hitch a lift to Iringa.

I remember that moment with pleasure; for the first time, I felt a paternal sentiment towards strangers. Maybe it was because they were so young and vulnerable that I wanted to protect them as if they were my own son and daughter. The girl was in her twenties and was called Linda; the boy was a year older, and seemed like a pleasant and well-mannered person. Both were American, and surely not used to wandering around the African savannah at night. I asked them what they were doing, and it appeared that someone had told them the best place to stop would have been a petrol station; if this had not been possible, it would have been safe to go a hundred metres into the woods and spend the night there. To this, I told them that there were more lions and hyenas around than there were drops of rain in a summer downpour, and they would be all searching for a meal of tender flesh. I told them of the night with Franco and his friends, when we had to endure the siege of the lions, which had only happened a short distance from where we were standing at that moment; I also recounted the tragic story of the tourist and the African bus driver at the nearby hotel, who had both been devoured alive, probably by the same group of lions. It was obviously a very naive person that had given that advice, especially to two people who were so unfamiliar with the country. They would be safe from bandits in the bush, but not from carnivorous felines which swarmed around places like Mikumi.

We began to drive again. I counted on arriving in Iringa at nine-thirty that evening. The tarmac road ended a few kilometres past Mikumi, and we reached the dirt track on which vehicles had created deep furrows that were now full of dust. Driving on this road was more difficult, and I had to reduce my speed considerably to cope with it. I was not worried about arriving in Iringa later than expected; in fact I thought it would be a good experience for my American friends, who were searching for adventure. It is not easy to avoid any surprises when driving on this sort of road in the dark, and the road deteriorated without me being aware of it. The dust on that track was as fine as baby's talcum powder, and was so dense as to prevent visibility of more than a couple of metres; the dust lifted by the wheels also caused us to cough violently. I decided not to slow down any further in order to cover that diabolical section of road as quickly as possible; however, it returned to normal after only about three hundred metres. I then stopped the car, and turned round to find my friends looking as if they had been in a dust-bath; in spite of their stunned faces, I could not suppress a loud burst of laughter. However, the expression on Linda's face suggested that I had arranged the dust as a joke!

After driving for a short while, we saw the lights of Iringa in the distance. Here I helped the youngsters to find the Indian Sikh temple, which was not very difficult, as the town was very small. I followed them inside to see what kind of hospitality the Sikh was offering to travellers. We had to call the guardian of the temple, who was an old man, which was not unusual for this kind of job. He directed us to a large room which was probably used for social services in the daytime and was nearly completely empty. A solitary paraffin lamp suspended by a chain in the corner of the room provided a very dim light, just enough to see where you placed your feet; in another corner, wooden beds were amassed in a disorderly heap, ready to be used by travellers. The place was a depressing spectacle of poverty, which was enhanced by the gloomy lamp. The Sikh's assistance ended in that small room: the use of a washroom or the provision of meal was too onerous for the small Sikh community of Iringa.

Considering the long dusty day and the drudgery of their journey, the situation of my two young friends was rather depressing. I gathered from their discouraged attitude that they would rather have been sleeping in their own bedrooms in their houses in America, and I decided to invite them to my hotel to use my bathroom. I also asked them if they would join me at the hotel bar for a cold beer, and after that perhaps give me the pleasure of dining with them. With a large smile, they said they were happy to accept my invitation.

My hotel was typically colonial, and was again for Europeans only. I waited in the pleasant but empty bar until my friends finished in the bathroom. We then had a beer before sitting down in the dining room, and chatted whilst we waited for our meals. The dinner was very pleasant, and we continued to talk over a good bottle of red wine. We got round to talking about Italy, where I had just recently visited. I brought the place alive like a good tourist guide with my descriptions of Rome and its history: the view of the Colosseum – my favourite monument – and the marvellous paintings of the Uffizi Gallery in Florence. They listened to me enchanted, and said they were looking forward to seeing these wonders with their own eyes.

At the end of the dinner I accompanied them to the temple: the time had come to say goodbye. I must confess, when I left them I felt very apprehensive about their future travels; however, as is the case with casual meetings, I bid them adieu and never heard from them again.

When I returned to Dar-es-Salaam, I heard at the Italian Club that Tassan intended to dedicate all his free time to hunting elephants. I also heard that he had bought all the necessary equipment, including a cine camera. For a long time, I had wanted to dedicate myself to this branch of big-game hunting also; but had always postponed it, as I considered it too time-consuming and also rather expensive. However, in the last few years the elephants had increased in number, and now were creating many problems for the natives who had the misfortune to live near large herds of them. The Government now offered elephant licences at a reduced cost, and I therefore considered this to be a favourable time to engage in this pastime. The offer was open to all hunters in the possession of a rifle with a minimum calibre of .375 Magnum, and allowed you to kill five elephants at a price of fifty pounds sterling. Having the prerequisites to obtain the licence, I decided to upgrade my sport and join the other fans of serious big-game hunting.

The first expedition was made together with my friends Mannini and Tassan. We chose an area about seventy kilometres from Dar-es-Salaam; however, we soon realised that the place did not live up to our expectations: there was too much woodland, and the elephants that live in the woods are generally smaller, and consequently have lighter tusks. It is also far more dangerous to hunt in these surroundings; it is well known that elephants living in the woods eventually become very aggressive: they have a tendency to appear from nowhere, and charge without warning, at the first sign of human presence. Another drawback is the wind, as it constantly changes direction with the trees, and it is very hard for humans to avoid being smelt by the pachyderms. The scent also remains in the air for longer in enclosed areas, and the elephants do not even need to smell the ground to detect human presence. The final encumbrance is the dim light, a major problem when spotting the animals and aiming the rifle. In open areas it is possible to see them in the distance, and they are always marked by the presence of birds, which hover above them persistently, waiting to feed on the seeds in their faeces. Smaller birds will search their leg joints, bellies and ears for ticks, which are much larger than those found on cows.

Persistent rain accompanied us along the track that day, and the rifles were turned upside-down so that the water did not enter their barrels. I had my Holland & Holland .375 Magnum rifle, Tassan had his double-barrelled .404 Winchester, and Piero had recently purchased the famous American Weatherby .300 (7.62mm) Magnum. This was the only rifle under .375 (9.52mm) that was authorised for hunting big game. Tassan's Winchester had two drawbacks: it was very expensive and very heavy.

Since before the First World War, the bibles of big-game hunting had instructed that no gun must be smaller then .375 of an inch. The majority of big-game hunters followed this advice, even if it did sacrifice speed and trajectory and was often heavier. Not all of them, though: the renowned elephant hunter, Bell of Africa, killed over two hundred elephants with an ordinary 7mm calibre rifle.

Piero's Weatherby used high-speed magnum cartridges that were nearly twice the size of mine, and the bullet could reach the speed of 1,097 metres per second. Its manufacture was based on experiments that ensured that the bullet travelling at that speed would kill an animal instantly from two hundred metres. This rate of velocity had a tremendous impact on the animal's internal fibres, and could even kill if it did not hit a vital organ.

Walking under a moderate rainstorm in Africa is not very unpleasant, as it has a cooling effect in the hot air. After half a day of marching we had only encountered one elephant, and it did not have particularly big tusks. In the absence of anything better, we decided to put it down. It turned its head towards us, and appeared to be nervous, probably due to the unfamiliar noises; however, it was very suspicious, and turned around as if he was going to retreat, but then turned back with his ears fully extended – a sign of extreme irritation – and gave us the impression that it was going to charge. I whispered to Tassan to shoot while it was not moving: if it started to charge then the shot could have been impaired. Tassan had a larger rifle than us, and was more experienced, so I thought that it would be better for him to shoot. It was about sixty metres away: a fairly easy target, but perhaps a little too far. Under the impact of Tassan's powerful shot he collapsed to the ground, but was not finished. After a few seconds he got up and started a furious charge, but Piero was anxious to try out his new rifle and did not waste any time: he killed it instantly with a shot to the head.

The two trackers were experts at removing the tusks with hatchet and machete, and this took three or four hours. These are not the only financially rewarding parts of the elephant. The front legs are a little bigger than the hind ones, and are cut at a height of about fifty centimetres. You then remove the bones, muscles and the three centimetres of grease present on the lower part of the foot, which helps the elephant to walk. This operation requires another two or three hours of work. The most difficult part is to remove all the remaining grease, as the foot may putrefy if even a small quantity is left behind. This grease is as hard as the leather sole of a shoe, and requires strong fingers and a good deal of patience. The knife must be no longer than ten centimetres, and must be sharpened at regular intervals (a short knife is more manoeuvrable, and permits close-quarter work). When all of the flesh is removed, the legs can be salted and a piece of wood inserted to keep the leg erect. After being exposed to the sun for a few days, the hide becomes rigid, and can now stand up on its own. The nails are then filed and polished until they turn a grey, marble-like colour. Finally, the hide is oiled so that it has a black polished finish. Elephant's legs can be fairly profitable, even if they are only used as umbrella holders, small tabletops or vases: not a very dignified end for the mightiest of all beasts.

From the ears it is possible to obtain pieces of hide a little smaller than one square metre that are similar to the colour of ground black peppercorns. This hide is suitable for making ladies' handbags, men's briefcases, wallets, belts and many other similar articles, all much appreciated by tourists. The tail hairs are not perfectly round: each has a different diameter between one and two millimetres, and is plaited to make bracelets and talismans, which were sold in Indian shops.

When we had finished removing the tusks (which we found to be just over the minimum weight on the licence), we decided to return home, and set off in the rain to the car, which was hidden under the trees a few kilometres away. We marched in an orderly line, with one tracker at the front and one at the back. After some time, the tracker at the rear calmly told us that he could see a large snake. As he had said the words 'large snake' we all assumed that he meant a python, and considering that we had virtually no experience of any snakes, we were quite alarmed.

The reptile was in a tree about thirty metres away, and was proceeding quickly, employing full use of its elongated body to glide across the branches. I had never seen a snake move in that manner across a tree, and I then realised that it was a black mamba, a member of the cobra family, the most dangerous snake in Africa. I have heard many stories about it. Unlike most others, it is an aggressive reptile that will never give right of way to another animal; it is very quick and is confident it will win any confrontation, and injects its potent venom in several different places to make sure that its adversary is completely finished.

It had now stopped moving, and was watching us from high up in the trees. If we had seen him earlier it would have been better to deviate slightly and avoid him completely. He was quite an easy target, but the head was partially hidden, apart from the eyes. I do not know why, but I decided to try and hit him in the middle, believing I could divide him in two and put him out of action. It was a reckless decision that could have had very severe consequences; however powerful my rifle was, it was loaded with hard-nosed bullets. If my shot was good, the best I could have hoped for was the bullet to pass right through the body. If I had soft-nosed bullets, they would have exploded upon impact with the dorsal spine; however, you do not use this ammunition for hunting elephants. The rain did not make aiming any easier, but the serpent was immobile, and I pulled the trigger. To my surprise, I realised that the bullet had hit right where I had aimed; but instead of dividing the beast into two, the projectile indeed had gone right through the body. The mamba was still capable of moving, and started to drop onto another branch, albeit with some difficulty. Luckily he stopped about five metres away, at about head-height. I noted that he was looking at me intently, testing the air with his bifurcated tongue. I am sure he was about to attack, and I just had time to shoot. The bullet missed the head, but went through the neck, fracturing the spine and killing him instantly. He remained hanging motionless on the tree branch, and at first I thought I had missed him altogether. Upon examination, we confirmed that it was indeed a black mamba.

It is not easy to encounter two large serpents on the same day, even in Africa. However, on that day, our business with snakes was not over. On the way back, Piero was driving the Jeep and had just left the track. He was gathering speed on the new tarmac road, when suddenly we saw a large cobra, over two metres long: he was scurrying across the road to avoid being run over by the car.

Large spiders and reptiles are the two creatures that only a very few people like or will tolerate; they are feared and hated by almost everyone in every place I know. In my thirty-three years in Africa I have never seen any native handling a snake – their religion does not respect them, and they fear them like the plague. The great majority of Europeans also feel the same way about them, especially women. When they are encountered, the usual reaction is to run away or try to kill them, although the majority of the time they mind their own business. On this occasion Piero accelerated and managed to run it over (after our encouragement). However, on looking behind we realised that it was unharmed and had now stopped on the tarmac with his head erect and his hood raised in defiance. As far as reptiles were concerned, Piero and I had the same ideas; without wasting any time he took out a 9mm long-barrel Luger Parabellum, a weapon he loved to carry for hunting emergencies. He was a good shot with the pistol as well as the rifle, and nailed the cobra in the head, killing it instantly, its body collapsing on the ground in a heap twenty centimetres high. It looked like a thick coil of rope, and was a magnificent example of its species, with very beautiful skin. At first we wanted to keep it as a trophy, but to have it tanned was difficult, and in the end we decided that it would be best left alone.

Chapter 7

During one of our trips to Mombasa to visit Vittorio, in the middle of the colonial era, a friend invited us to have lunch with him, and we left our elder daughter Lucia with her African nanny. On our return home, a couple of hours after the nanny's departure, we heard Lucia crying, and she was obviously not well. When we picked her up, we noticed a strong smell of paraffin on her breath. The nanny had mentioned nothing of this, as she was afraid of the consequences, and the smell had passed temporarily when we returned; but now it had come back, and Lucia was obviously in some discomfort. We pressed the nanny later and she admitted that Lucia had drunk an unknown quantity of paraffin from a bottle which was on the kitchen floor, when her back had been turned. Both Sally and I were obviously alarmed, and we rushed Lucia to the hospital, where we explained what had happened. The European doctor on duty told us not to worry, as she was not in any serious danger and would be all right after a gastric ravage, so we left her there overnight, and went back the next morning to collect her.

The next morning we collected a smiling Lucia who did not show any signs of her unpleasant experience. Of course we were very pleased with the excellent job performed by a responsible person.

As the years went by after Independence, the tone and standard of life for European residents gradually got worse; by the end of the sixties a considerable number of specialised workers in all fields had left the country for good, and their successors did not have the same education or training, which led to a decline in public organisation. Up to then the tarmac roads had been kept in a reasonably good condition; now they no longer received adequate maintenance. Sporadic and temporary repairs were carried out by incompetent, indolent personnel who lacked proper instruction and direction; in some parts of the city the asphalt had completely disintegrated, and the resultant potholes became a real menace to the vehicles. However, the deterioration of the roads was only one aspect of the worsening general situation. It was very dangerous to walk in the environs of the town late at night, as the European police force was being dissolved (the streets were now also very dark, as many street lights had been destroyed by vandals throwing stones). You could now only travel around at night by car; even during daytime it was no longer possible to stop on the beach without being attacked. In particular the women who used to spend days on the beach with their children suffered. They could now only go there if they had a man to look after them.

Another severe and demoralising blow to the European community was the departure of most of their doctors. The remaining Indian doctors had obtained their degrees from their own country, and did not inspire much confidence in the Europeans. I also believe that in most cases this scepticism was justified, as some examples prove.

There was now a stark contrast appearing between colonial times and the present. Public services were once highly efficient and well organised, with highly motivated personnel that ranked with some of the best in Europe. Now corruption was unopposed in the high echelons of the government; there was also no sense of duty, which I consider an absolutely essential characteristic for the heads of any organisation, and was one of the principal causes of the comparatively rapid decline. This did not only happen in the East African territories, but also all other African countries that removed their colonial governments too quickly, thirsty for individual power, without any sense of loyalty towards the nation and its citizens. This general decline can be demonstrated by a very unpleasant occurrence following the death of a friend of mine – Ferrari.

It was six o'clock in the morning when I was walking along the deserted Acacia Avenue, one of the main roads in Dar-es-Salaam. I was on my way to work, and had got into the habit of stopping at a café every morning to have a cup of espresso and chat to Mr Luciano, the owner. As soon as I entered, he asked me if I knew what had happened to Bruno Ferrari, who had died the day before, not far from the café. I told him I had not, and he proceeded to explain. While Bruno was having his brew he was boasting about his robustness and his impeccable health, even though he was fifty-four. A short while after leaving the café he had died suddenly. In Italy there is a superstition amongst the working class that suggests you should never boast of being in good health; also, you should never remark to someone that they look well if you have not seen them for a while. Mr Luciano added that both actions could be taken as an ill omen, and could tempt fate. The poor Ferrari, bless his soul, was a non-believer and a man full of vices. He had ignored this superstition, and provoked the evil forces that surely – insisted Mr Luciano – were monitoring him closely. In the end they had had enough of him, and pulled him out of this world.

I had met Ferrari in Rome, and we became friends when we both emigrated to Africa, travelling on the same flight. He did not have any family or friends, and I was the only one willing to help him take care of his financial interests – to tell the truth, he was not particularly popular around town. Anyway, I went to the hospital to identify the body, and I was told to speak to the mortuary worker. Unable to find him, I asked someone else, who told me that the worker preferred to pass his time actually in the mortuary room. It struck me as quite odd that anyone would prefer to stay in the company of the dead rather than the living. However, I opened the noisy door and went inside, awakening a man, who had been sleeping on a stretcher normally reserved for dead bodies. He jumped down from the pallet, and brought his joined arms high over his head to stretch the tendons of his arms and shoulder, smiling a satisfied smile. He preferred to rest in the air-conditioned room with his dead companions to avoid the summer heat, which was at times unbearable outside. There were ten or so cadavers covered with bed sheets; but I could not find the body of Ferrari lying amongst them. The man said that there was a corpse outside in a cold storage cubicle: those who had died a sudden death were kept in there in case an autopsy was required, as it was in the case of Ferrari. I was fascinated by the indifference with which he pulled Ferrari's frozen body from the cubicle – as casually opening a piece of furniture.

A week after the autopsy, the funeral took place, and I was one of the four coffin-bearers. We removed it from the car, put it on our shoulders, and made our way along the aisle. The benches at each side were full of people from the community – they never failed to pay their respects at such sad events; I also noticed that they were distracted by something on the floor behind us, but we could not turn round due to the weight of the coffin. Only after we reached the altar did we realise what had happened. My right shoulder and arm were soaking wet, and from touching it I guessed that it must be the blood of Ferrari, which I now realised was oozing copiously from the side of the coffin. There was also a red trail from the church entrance to the altar, and a small pool was gathering under our feet. Having got used to seeing blood during the war years, and from hunting in the forests and woods in Africa, I was not too squeamish; however, it was most unpleasant to have part of my body drenched with the blood of a dead person.

More important than all this is the point that most of the replacements for the Europeans did not know how to do their job; equally irresponsible were those in the higher ranks of the Government who entrusted these people with the jobs that they did not deserve – from the Ferrari incident alone, you can outline the incompetence of a number of employees.

Firstly there is the doctor who performed the autopsy. One would have assumed he was a reasonably intelligent person; but he failed to remove all of the blood from the corpse, and knew that his stitching would not prevent the blood from escaping. Secondly there is the manufacturer of the coffin. He is supposed to supply a casket made from sound wood, with properly matching joints; in addition to this, by law he must equip the coffin with an airtight lining of galvanised steel. There is also a cover of the same material that must be soldered on top to ensure that no air escapes. Lastly there are the morgue workers, who shamefully stole all of Ferrari's clothes, leaving his stark-naked corpse lying in the coffin.

In 1962 Vera and Piero Mannini, to their great delight, had a son, whom they named Alessandro, and they asked us to be his godparents, which we accepted with much pleasure. He grew up with our girls and, indeed, they used to call him their 'brother'!

At the age of eleven the girls had to leave Lushoto School and we sent them to the UK to finish their education and subsequently qualify at the London School of Secretaries. They used to come out twice a year to spend the school holidays with us, always exciting times as they brought us up to date with life in the UK and the latest pop music!

After almost ten years of independence in Tanzania came the

deadline for replacing all of the Europeans still working in state organisations. I learnt of my impending redundancy in an unorthodox fashion, typical of the general atmosphere in all large companies at that time. An African worker cheerfully asked me one day if I wanted to sell my car; I told him that I had no intention to do so, as I needed it. He replied: 'Not for long', and told me that I would soon be discharged, clearly surprised that I was unaware of this. Up to then, I did not even have an inkling that my job was in danger, and felt quite secure; however, in that environment even the most confidential news could not be kept secret for long. I was certain that the man's information was accurate, and told Sally. Sure enough, after a short time I received an official letter terminating my contract and explaining the terms of my redundancy. I was given four months to vacate our apartment, and our property would be transferred to wherever we wanted, at the company's expense.

There is a saying that every cloud has a silver lining. However, this seemed to be a disaster without a solution, as it would be almost impossible to find a job as good as my current one. It was just as well that we were to find out that luck was on our side.

With the start of inflation all round the world, including the Anglo-Saxon area, permanent employment in an African country did not appear an ideal proposition. The East African governments then decided that it was illegal to transfer money abroad. This was a serious handicap to us as we wanted to deposit money in England in order to pay for the children's education. Anyone breaking this law would be arrested and sent to prison, especially in Tanzania, where the Government was acquiring a left-wing position. However, we had no choice but to resolve it in an illegal manner, and it was necessary to find a third person in East Africa with the following requisites:

Firstly, they must require cash in East African currency. Secondly, they must have an account in an English bank, from which they could transfer the equivalent amount to the account of one of our family members. Finally, they must agree to the unofficial fee of 22%. This was the only way to by-pass the East African banks.

As a matter of curiosity, I tried to estimate the cost of this exercise over a period of seven years, and I calculated that I lost about ten thousand pounds sterling (based on 1970s' equivalent) – enough to buy two beautiful apartments. I mention this fact as an illustration of the difficulties that confronted any person who wanted to live in Tanzania/Kenya. Now Sally and I were very keen on this idea, but a resident's permit cost seven thousand shillings, and the same to renew every five years.

Luckily my gratuity from TANESCO was enough to cover all these expenses, and twenty-two years of work had paid off: we bought a nice apartment on the outskirts of Nairobi. This was a much safer investment than renting, but we still had to manage our financial resources carefully, and Sally worked in Dar-es-Salaam for another four months.

At the beginning of 1972 I left Dar-es-Salaam, and was very sorry – it was a place full of happy memories. After saying goodbye to everyone at the Italian Club, we agreed to meet up with Piero and Vera Mannini at the end of every year and spend the Christmas holiday together. We kept our promise for a few years – even though we had to drive two thousand kilometres from Nairobi to Dar-es-Salaam and back – but this had to stop due to security reasons. This journey was possible by two routes: both roads ran for three hundred kilometres in the same direction, and then diverged. One was via Tanga, the small harbour town north of Dar-es-Salaam, and followed the coast towards Kenya and the important town of Mombasa. The first part up to Tanga was not very interesting, as the vast numbers of palm trees and the thick scrub hid all the wildlife. From Mombasa the road climbed slowly up the plateau towards the Tsavo Park until arriving in Nairobi. The alternative fork rose slowly towards the mountains – including Kilimanjaro and Kibo – and was quite spectacular. You then reached the Kenyan border through the town of Arusha. As you have probably guessed, this way was a lot more interesting; however, I had chosen the first route in order to pay a visit to Franco Galliussi in Tanga, where he was supervising the construction of a bridge.

Franco was very happy to see me, and persuaded me to stay for two days. He told me the town had nothing to offer, and to go there on vacation would be a definite waste of time – there was no decent hotel, very few shops. The only thing worth visiting was the Grotto of Amboni, and Franco said he would take me there.

He had the privilege of being one of the only two Europeans left in town; the other, a Greek owner of a small restaurant, was offering extravagantly large meals as there was a shortage of customers – large plates heaped full of crabs, lobsters, prawns and cuttlefish, bought from fishermen for a fistful of coins and then sold to the lucky customers for ludicrous prices.

Tanga is in a volcanic region, and occasionally small tremors are felt on the surrounding mountains. There were also some sulphur springs nearby; but unfortunately they were badly equipped and unhygienic – the rough cement the bathtubs were made from rendered them impossible to use properly, and the only people who frequented them were local Indians who needed to treat their skin.

When we arrived at the Amboni Grotto we found police on the scene, and Franco explained that there had been a tragedy there some time before. An amateur German explorer, his dog and his house servant had gone there to explore, but never returned home. After about ten days, only the dog reappeared – certainly not a good omen. The family members organised a search, and did not find it difficult to locate the tracks of two humans and a dog at the end of a passage covered by the faeces of thousands of bats. These led to a long narrow crevice in the rock some ten metres deep. Two dangling ropes showed where they had descended, and simply disappeared into nothing. The bodies were never found, but it was evident that they had been unable to get back up that fearful hole; maybe they had got lost in the labyrinths of the grotto, and exhausted the batteries of their torches. The dog, which most probably did not go down with them, had found an exit from the subterranean maze and returned home. It is possible to imagine the last hours of these people, and the terror that would have slowly engulfed their souls. As their search went on, their torches would have become dimmer and dimmer, until they faded completely. As the torches died, their last hopes would have vanished also, as they knew from the way they had organised the excursion that they could not expect any outside help. Nobody had even tried to look for their corpses, and the African police were under the impression that a monster had devoured them both. I found their worried faces ludicrous as they scrutinised the dark depths of the grotto, as if they expected a *shitani* (devil) to appear. They forbade us to go near the entrance, and only after bribing them would they escort us three hundred metres into the cave. The ancient underground river had changed its course several times and had created several outlets that formed a vast labyrinth of tunnels; to find your way back on your own from even a few hundred metres would be extremely confusing. Franco told me he had heard that the underground river originated from somewhere on the lower slopes of Mount Kilimanjaro, three hundred kilometres to the east. The grotto had never been seriously explored.

My visit came to an end the next day, and I thanked him and said goodbye, with the promise to meet him again in Kenya, where he hoped to find a new occupation.

On the way back I took the alternative route, as it commanded a distant view of the Usambara Mountains. This area has almost constant rainfall, and is rich with vegetation. It is also home to colobus monkeys, whose black and white fur was once in high demand to make exotic living-room carpets. To hunt this animal nowadays is strictly forbidden, and rightly so.

The village of Lushoto, where my daughters' school used to be, is not visible from the road. I had heard that it had closed down because of dwindling numbers, and the place had deteriorated and reverted back to a small indigenous village; what was more, the departure of the stubborn German residents – who had been there through both wars – had further aggravated the situation.

There was uninhabited savannah in this part of the country for hundreds of kilometres, probably because of the absence of water, and only low shrubs with a few bits of grass – an indication of the poor fertility of the terrain. To make up for the lack of people, there was an abundance of animals.

Driving along for hours and hours on this long deserted road could make the traveller very nervous, especially if he was alone. This made the trip interesting in a way, as did the many animals that you spotted along the way. Anyone tempted to rest or stretch their legs outside the car had to be very careful where they put their feet – it was easy to tread on the tail of an invisible lion asleep under a tree; or you could have an abrupt encounter with the claws of a leopard who had mistaken you for a monkey. I have heard real-life accounts of these types of incidents.

When you were in Moshi or Arusha, and when there were no clouds on the folds of Kilimanjaro, it was possible to enjoy the spectacular view of the tip of the mountain, with its perennial snow-cover. These areas were a remarkable contrast to the surrounding countryside, and the terrain around the lower part of the mountain was very fertile – maybe the richest region of Tanzania – ensuring their inhabitants a fair degree of prosperity. As I mentioned earlier, there was a vast demand for coffee, and a small market for tea –

both very important export products. There was also vast cultivation of vegetables, cereals and fruit. Not far from there were the beautiful national parks: one was inside the crater of the long inactive Ngoro Ngoro Volcano, while Momela was home to the unique giant Tanzanian warthog. The mountain terrain was full of rivers, and here it was possible to catch very large trout.

I had no trouble when crossing the Tanzanian/Kenyan border. However, I could detect a tension between the two nations from the demeanour of the border police. They were once very friendly, but Tanzania's independence had prompted them to adopt a more leftist policy, similar to communist regimes. Kenya obtained its independence shortly afterwards, and remained rooted in the British-style democracy. The frontier between the two countries was soon closed.

I arrived in Nairobi after a twenty-one-year absence, and it had changed for the worse. The next day, I found my brother Vittorio waiting for me in front of the New Stanley Hotel. The greeting was limited to a brief handshake – clearly the distance between us had separated us in more ways than one. As Vittorio had experience in Kenya, he reckoned he could help me obtain the various permits that I needed, and temporarily put me up in his house in Embakasi. It was about ten kilometres from Nairobi, two from the airport, and barely three hundred metres from the Nairobi National Park. This house had its own story.

Immediately after Independence, the space near the airport had attracted the interest of Africans who were looking for a place to sleep, and an agglomeration of shabby houses made from petrol-drum sheets and empty boxes of every sort had slowly emerged; of course, these hovels were devoid of running water and hygienic services. Soon there were complaints about the view presented to the tourists arriving by air in Nairobi, and the President – Jomo Kenyatta – gave orders to remove all of the shacks and burn them. When they had finished, there were only three brick houses left standing, and the Indian owners had managed to bribe the authorities not to destroy them. Vittorio had then rented one, and his property included a few hectares of land and a small building of iron sheeting with four cubicles, where the African labourers stayed.

Our contrasting views were exemplified on the first day I entered the house. On a table next to the bed, with ogling eyes, thirty centimetres from my head, sat a human skull, albeit cleaned and refined with a splash of whitewash. I asked Vittorio to remove it, adding that if he really liked it he could put it near his bed. I brought it to his attention that I was not Saint Louis, who had been known to keep a human skull in his bedroom to remind him of the brevity of life. He got the wrong end of the stick, and suggested that I should not be scared: it would not bite me after all, it was just a piece of bone. I brought to his attention that it could be dangerous. It would be difficult to convince an African policeman if, by chance, he was in search of a man to arrest, that it was all a joke and he had not killed the owner of the head. However, it stared at me for the next two months until Sally arrived, when I could then change house.

I did not like Vittorio's eccentric aspect. He told me that when he was living in Mombasa he was staying in an isolated house, on the edge of the town. There he had the idea of sharing his lodgings with a poisonous snake, which was left free to move around the house at its leisure. The serpent was a nasicorne viper, and could grow to be as thick as a man's arm. Luckily these snakes are relatively slow and cannot climb, so they can only move by crawling across the ground, and with a little care it may be possible to avoid them (but for how long?). I have no doubt that my brother was one of those types who liked people to talk about their strange behaviour.

He told me another story about when he was still living in that house, regarding some African labourers who were working nearby and always came home about one o'clock in the morning. They used to go home in a group, and always took a trail about fifty metres from Vittorio's house. Now they were a noisy bunch, and constantly woke Vittorio up with their joking and singing. My brother had asked them several times to keep the noise down; but that had not worked, so he decided to teach them a lesson they would remember for the rest of their life.

Vittorio was in the possession of a rubber mask that resembled a human skull, which he had bought for a party. Personally, I thought that among friends, this mask would have been grossly inappropriate, and in bad taste. Anyway, one night, after having covered his body with a bed sheet, he put the mask on, and went to hide behind a bush along the trail, half an hour before the labourers would pass to go home. The place he had chosen to hide was next to a dimly lit street lamp. Soon he heard them coming from the distance, and emerged from his hiding place, his arms wide open so he looked like a giant white bat. At the same time he emitted a howl that resembled an infuriated chimpanzee. The mask completed the fantastic image. The group did not know where to run, and with leaps and bounds they scrambled on top of one another, desperate to get away from that horrible apparition.

The workers never disturbed him again. A few days later, they went to advise him to leave the house, as there was a devil going around in the neighbourhood.

The Embakasi house was located only three hundred metres from the National Park, and after the removal of all the ramshackle tin houses, it seemed isolated from the world. Although comparatively near to Nairobi, the place had the air of a frontier post. With the absence of people, and the return of silence at night during the rainy season, I had the occasional visit of some lions around the house; more than once in the early morning I had seen the imprints of a feline on the wet terrain.

Vittorio told me that his stay in Nairobi was ending soon, and if I wished, I could take possession of the house, thus avoiding its destruction. He said that he had decided to move near to the mouth of the Tana River, a place seven hundred kilometres from Nairobi where there were no administrative centres, only cabins, few and far apart. He said that his final wish was to live the rest of his life in a savage place called Tarasaa. It was a hundred and twenty kilometres north of the fishing village of Malindi, a place well known to many Italian tourists. He explained that to convert his dream into reality, he had saved his pay from his five years of working at Pepsi-Cola, and now he had enough to set up a fish filleting plant; all it needed was to be made operative, and to do this he required my electrical skills. He wished to establish it on the Tana River and produce fillets of tilapia fish, which had been introduced to the Tana by the British in order to control the numbers of mosquitoes, although I do not know if it was successful; as far as I knew, there were still millions of mosquitoes around the Tana.

The tilapia is a voracious fish, capable of eliminating a high number of larvae every day; however, the fish also has the misfortune of being very tasty and very easy to catch, and these attributes attracted the attention of the African angler, who by fishing them ruthlessly defied the primary purpose for why they were put in the river in the first place. An attempt to fish the tilapia on an industrial scale was attempted three years earlier by an Italian company on Lake Naivasha; but the experiment failed. Lake Naivasha was not fed by any river, and although it was comparatively large, there was not enough stock to sustain a daily catch of at least three tons, the minimum to render the investment worthwhile. Theoretically, the advantageous position next to a large city like Nairobi would mean a ready market for the fish; but after fishing with nets for some time, the Italian company suffered a severe loss due to decreasing numbers of the fish, and was forced to abort the operation. The damage to life in the lake took a long time to repair, during which time it was not possible to fish.

I had decided to try to set up my own business as an electrical contractor, and Vittorio was very helpful. He advised me well on how to form the nucleus of seven workers, and suggested I should choose only workers from the Kikuyu tribe (they had a tendency to steal, but if this did not bother you then it did not matter). He also suggested that I engage the younger ones who had probably just left the missionary schools and were not yet influenced by corrupt cultures, of which there were plenty around. I followed his advice, and to my great satisfaction the staff were always excellent. They called me '*Mzee*' (Old Man), which in their culture is a show of respect; they did it timidly at first, but later it became a habit, and eventually they would address me in this fashion any time they wanted my attention.

Two months after my arrival I had finished buying the material to complete the work at my brother's enterprise, and I drove with Vittorio and my best worker (the only one I had engaged in Tanzania) towards the River Tana. The trip from Nairobi took about ten hours. After crossing the Tsavo National Park and driving for another few hours we arrived at the port of Mombasa. We then went north along the partially asphalt road on the coast, which led to the Somaliland border. Along this stretch we came to the picturesque ferry at Kilifi (now replaced by a normal stone bridge), which was basically a group of Africans pulling a pontoon across a stretch of sea water. This would be accompanied by a tribal dance, the men beating their feet to keep the pulling in time, twisting their bodies, and exhaling noisily. All this created an exotic atmosphere that never failed to entertain the few passengers, who were always grateful for the exhibition, and when disembarking never forgot to reward them with some money.

After the ferry we encountered the last relatively important town: the fishing village of Malindi. Between here and Tarasaa lay a hundred and twenty kilometres of bad road, so we refuelled the car and got going. The stretch did not disappoint us; it was badly damaged during the wet season, and some parts were badly grooved and extremely hard to negotiate. The Somaliland border was about a hundred kilometres away, if we could stand the punishment of driving that distance over that murderous terrain. I know Vittorio was a man with a vivid imagination, therefore I am not sure if he was serious when he told me that he once had to swim across a road to get to Tarasaa. He seemed to find this very amusing.

The industrial complex had been built two hundred metres away from the river, and by the look of things it was evident that the effort and organisation of a single person had paid off: it looked very impressive. My brother had thought of everything.

The premises were to be equipped with two electrical generators. The large 50kw one, to be used during the daytime, supplied energy to the deep-freeze room, where the fresh fish were kept; if required, this room could be kept at $-25°C$. It also supplied energy to the electric welding machine and the water purification area, essential for filleting the fish; obviously this water was also essential for human use. The smaller generator was in use mainly after working hours, supplying the power for the house and the lights on the perimeter.

The house was made of seasoned wood, and had been built a short distance from the factory. It consisted of an ample kitchen and two large bedrooms with beds, mosquito nets and all of the usual accessories, ready to accommodate guests. The longest side of the building that faced the factory had an ample veranda, and was an ideal place to rest after work, waiting for the cool of the night, and perhaps have a couple of beers with friends. However, there was no bathroom or toilet; these facilities were built outside, a short distance from the building, which was not very pleasant as they were near a dense wood, a potential refuge for wild animals. Other indispensable equipment was a refrigerator truck, sufficient to carry a load of up to one and a half tons, and a four-metre super-light aluminium boat, easy to carry by hand when it was needed on the river. However, it was rather dangerous, as it could very easily be turned over by a hippo.

Judging by the effort Vittorio had devoted to the construction of his plant, it was a pity that he did not bother to investigate with equal thoroughness the factors upon which the success or failure of his enterprise depended. The way I saw it, it would not survive for long. His desire was so strong to live in that place that he had neglected the most important factor: demand. He had convinced himself that so long as he could produce the fish fillets, then all other problems would be solved automatically. I was not really surprised by his blasé approach; it was all part of his eccentric persona. Firstly he had to pay his maintenance expenses, which included the salaries of the six workers who filleted the fish, and the cost of transporting the fillets to where they would be sold. However, his most important target was to maintain a daily production of about one ton of fish fillets. This he definitely could not do.

To sell the fish to the nearest populated place, say Malindi, the truck had to travel a hundred and twenty kilometres. As I have said, Malindi is a fishing town, rich with all kinds of fish; certainly, the few hotels would not buy river fish – it is well known that they could often have a muddy taste (depending on which part of the river they are caught in). The cost of the trip would also have taken a chunk out of the profits. The second possibility was Mombasa, which was much further away, and had the same problems as Malindi. A last resort would be Nairobi, which meant a voyage of six hundred kilometres in a comparatively slow vehicle; as far as I know, only once did Vittorio attempt to sell fish in Nairobi. On that occasion he did not even succeed in selling one kilogram, and got rid of the load by burying it in the surroundings of the house in Embakasi, which at that time was already in my possession.

Anyway, the tilapia in the Tana River were only sufficient to satisfy the demands of the local population; if there had have been a large industrial demand, then it never would have been met.

After I put the plant in working order, I was able to witness the first few days of production before I returned to Nairobi. I am not sure that the twenty fishermen who supplied him with fish were directly dependent on Vittorio; they had organised themselves into a small co-operative, and were openly selling their freshly produced goods.

I also had the opportunity to observe the technique of the native fishermen. They fished with water up to their navel, launching their net by hand. This method clearly was not very efficient; but it was compelling to watch them remain immersed in water for half a day, struggling to meet the quota. The nets frequently got entangled in debris from the river, and to free them was a long, laborious process. The fishermen were also risking their life every day, as the river was host to a large population of hippos and crocodiles.

The relationship between crocodiles and fishermen aroused my curiosity. I could not understand the reason why the crocodiles refrained from attacking them; they were certainly not afraid of them. Fishermen were easy prey in the water, yet incidents were rare; perhaps they preferred to eat fish, although I doubt that. It seemed as though their relationship was the same as between the crocodiles and the gulls, who mingled together freely.

After the fish were filleted, there were a couple of hundred kilos of residue left over, and this was taken care of in a hygienic and efficient manner – it was placed on the open ground about a hundred metres away from the factory. In a matter of minutes a large number of marabou, vultures, pelicans and sea gulls would flock to the feast, an appointment that they always kept. It was great fun to watch their scuffles, and in half an hour not a morsel of fishbone was left.

Due to the constant territorial struggles in Somaliland, Tarasaa became a dangerous place to live. Some years later the *Shifta* (Somali bandits) killed four missionaries (three men and a woman) only some three hundred metres from Vittorio's house. The mission was very isolated, far away from any authority. Its purpose was to try and alleviate the suffering of the local population, who were incredibly poor and lacked a school, doctors and food. It is difficult to understand how people from so far away, who knew nothing about the place and had no motivation whatsoever, could be so cruel as to kill good, innocent people. The four missionaries (a teacher, a doctor and two nurses) had arrived in Africa not long before they were killed. The mission assisted everybody free of charge, including Somalis, but principally the members of the Ghiriama tribe, who were lucky enough to live nearby.

After the work was completed, I returned to Nairobi to take care of my own affairs.

Five months later, I heard that my brother had gone bankrupt and closed his business. He then had to move to Malindi, the nearest town to Tarasaa. Difficult times lay ahead; at that moment his only way of making money was by helping Italian immigrants obtain the required permits, so they could work in the then expanding town of Malindi, and this was just enough to survive on. He was hoping to make a comeback under a different guise, as the house and the land in Tarasaa were still in his possession, and relatively near. For the time being he was thinking of becoming a professional hunter – an extremely lucrative activity. However, there were numerous difficulties to be considered; for instance, it was very difficult to obtain the special hunting licence; the applicant must prove that he had taken part in big-game hunting as a 'second gun' to a licensed professional hunter for a substantial period. Assuming that he did this, he would then have to establish contact with an overseas agent to provide rich clientele, and then set up an office in an accessible locality. And last, but not least, he would have to buy all of the necessary equipment: at least one modified four-wheel-drive vehicle, tents, guns, ammunition etc.

The obstacles to his dream were great, and to overcome them he would require money, and plenty of it. This was the most serious problem, as my brother had none.

Vittorio did not want to move from that part of Kenya, and this had interested me, as I could live with him if I had a job in Malindi town; there was also the possibility that I could hunt elephants in the Tarasaa area, known to host concentrations of up to twenty thousand during the dry season.

Just before Sally arrived in Nairobi, a friend of Vittorio contacted me. He had bought a new house on the periphery of the city, with considerable land, covering ten hectares. However, he was going to Italy on business and would be away for twenty days, leaving his twenty-three-year-old daughter Franca behind. He did not want to leave her alone, as he thought it would be too dangerous, and asked me whether I would move into the house to protect her during his absence. I agreed.

The house was not too far from a famous place, called Karen. Here, being transformed into a museum, was a house that once belonged to the well-known Danish writer Karen Blixen, author of the book *Out of Africa*.

In the house I found a companion, a very nice alsatian named Rex. Rex was a beast of large proportions – he was even big for his breed – and inspired fear just by looking at you. During the night he was kept indoors, to give an extra sense of security.

A few days after the departure of Franca's father, Sally arrived. A couple of days later we were woken in the middle of the night by furious barking. Rex was throwing himself against the door, and somebody was obviously trying to open it from the outside. In his attempts to get out, Rex knocked down several copper ornaments that had been hanging by the side of the door. Coupled with the barking, their clatter had startled us, and I grabbed the rifle and rushed outside; but the would-be intruders had quickly vanished into the dark.

After the return of Franca's father, Sally and I went to our new home situated in an area called Westlands. The windows of the apartment had iron grilles and, as we will see later on, they proved to be an extremely useful precaution.

My company was starting to develop, and Sally got a job in Nairobi through Colin Hood, for whom she used to work in Tanganyika. Colin and Marjorie became close friends of ours in later years. Sally decided to continue her shooting and made an application to join the Rifle Club. Everyone said Douglas Walker, who ran the Nairobi Firearms Bureau, had very strict rules regarding the acquisition of firearms and they doubted he would give her a licence; however, they were proved wrong and she later became the happy owner of a Walther .22/.32 conversion pistol and shot regularly in competitions at the club. We had a safe at home in which to keep the pistol and being armed made us feel much more secure. Kathy and Duggie also became close friends of ours.

In 1974, two years after our arrival in Nairobi, Sally and I were about to set off to Dar-es-Salaam for the usual visit to Piero and Vera. However, on that occasion, two events made us decide to suspend any future visits.

We arrived at their home on the evening of 31st December, and found them both very disturbed. Piero was employed with the Italian Embassy in Dar-es-Salaam, and at about one o'clock that morning he had been awoken by a call from the Italian ambassador. He told him that he had just heard some terrible news concerning one of their compatriots, who was said to have been assassinated, and the ambassador wanted Piero to travel twenty-five kilometres out of town to the scene of the crime, which was down a small dirt track in the forest. The man's name was Lino, a friend of ours, and Piero was to confirm that it was actually him. Naturally, Piero was a bit reluctant to obey this unusual order from his boss;

given the late hour and that he had to go alone, it was not a very pleasant prospective. However, he had had to go, and he expected to find police on the spot; but this was not the case.

In the middle of the track he saw Lino's car, illuminated by his own headlights. And about twenty metres further on, in front of the car, he could see the decapitated head of his friend. His headless body was still in the driving seat of the car, leaning on the car door bathed in blood. In the balmy night, the stench was almost unbearable.

I am reluctant to describe the details of this brutal episode, as I believe it might be in bad taste. However, Sally and both my daughters remember it well, and insist that I include it in my story.

It appears that the car was parked outside a small hotel, called The Inn by the Sea, which was about forty metres from the beach, and had certainly known better days when the Colonial Government was in power. At night this area was very isolated; there were very few cars parked outside – there were very few clients. The murderer must have been aware of Lino's nightly visit to the hotel for a couple of beers, and after Lino went inside he would have climbed in the back seat of the car and waited for him to return. He then would have waited until the car was about a kilometre away from the hotel, when it was easy to carry out the gruesome crime unseen and undisturbed.

Piero was not sure what was used for the murder. I suggested that it was probably piano wire or a guitar string, and he agreed. However, he pointed out that the autopsy would probably provide the answer.

It is common knowledge that the heart continues to beat for a few seconds after a violent death. This phenomenon is amply explained in military manuals; it was often referred to by the British during the campaign against the Mau Mau in Kenya, and we also knew of it from our hunting experiences.

In his last spasms he had kicked the car windscreen, and there was blood and hair found on the bonnet, so it appeared that the head had been taken through the windscreen and first placed on the bonnet. Later it was found twenty metres away.

This type of murder was very uncommon in East Africa, and the authorities were perplexed. Shortly afterwards, a Somalian was stupidly boasting he had cut off the head of an Italian man, and he was doing this openly around the indigenous hotels. A member of the Special Police Squad happened to be in one of the hotels, and upon hearing his bragging promptly arrested him. The penalty for this crime was execution, but the man escaped from custody a few days before this sentence was to be carried out, and was never found again.

After the holiday was over, we set off to return to Nairobi; however, it was not to be an easy trip. We passed the town of Arusha and drove through the vast lowlands, but before reaching the Kenyan border, we were stopped five times by armed soldiers who seemed to appear from nowhere. They asked us for our documents and let us go; still, we were very worried: it was very difficult to know what they were looking for in that isolated area, a place without a single house or even a sign of life. I knew them very well, and was well aware that they were very unpredictable. My main worry was my carbine lying on the back seat: if there was anything going on in the area, it could instigate an investigation, even though I had an arms licence with me. This would mean detaining me, and I was thinking of the consequences for Sally in my possible absence.

Luckily this did not happen, and we crossed the border without any more trouble. It was then that I decided never to travel by car to Tanzania again.

Unexpected news awaited me at Nairobi. One of my Kikuyu workers, Patrick Munya, had been arrested, and had been in prison for the past three days:

Before I had left for Tanzania he had borrowed my Datsun light truck. He was a busy man; he grew corn and potatoes, and owned about ten pigs. I had no objection to him borrowing the truck, providing he took care of it. However, one morning he had hit a small girl on the main road: she had been in a hurry to get to school and had run in front of him. He had no time to stop, and she was killed.

Patrick was the most useful of my workmen, the only one in possession of a driving licence, and he would often carry out small chores for me, as well going on trips of hundreds of kilometres. The truck had also been held when he was arrested. I went to the police station with one of Patrick's cousins to find out exactly what the situation was, and the sergeant let us speak to Patrick, who was surprised by my visit; he was also very glad, as he knew for sure that I represented his only hope to get out of that awkward mess, and he begged me to pay his three hundred pounds' bail, as he did not have a single cent.

He was a good man, and was not the prison type. He told me that he was depressed, and felt like dying; indeed, from his appearance, it made me think that he would not survive a term in prison. I assured him that Sally and I would do everything we could to get him out of there, starting by paying his bail immediately. After the paper was signed, Patrick was released, the truck freed, and he resumed work that same morning.

The company car was, of course, insured. The insurance company provided a lawyer; Patrick's case was heard six months afterwards, and he was found not guilty.

About two weeks after this, I gave Josef Kiruri (Patrick's cousin) a lift so he could catch the *matatu* – a popular means of transport in Nairobi. *Matatus* are a sort of bus, and were exclusively used by the indigenous population, as they were very cheap. (However, although they were usually on time, they somehow always caused some sort of inconvenience.) I watched Josef rush towards a stationary *matatu* from my car. He jumped over a gutter, but suddenly fell to the ground, wincing in pain. I immediately rushed to his help, realising that he must have a serious problem with one of his tendons; he could now only move by hopping along on one leg. I supported him with his arm around my neck, and took him in the car to the nearby Nairobi hospital, where we joined a queue of patients one hundred metres long.

At dinnertime I told Sally about Josef's misfortune. We knew that he could not have touched food since at least seven o'clock in the morning, and sensed his desperation, as he would be waiting in this queue at the hospital after a hard day's work. His family would also be very worried about his absence. We looked into each other's eyes, and, almost in unison, we exclaimed: 'It is not right.' We then decided to go the hospital to give him food, drink and reassurance. In the refrigerator we found a half-chicken, superbly cooked by our chef, Rafael; we also brought ten roast potatoes, some bread and a bottle of beer. As well as satisfying his hunger and quenching his thirst, these gifts would significantly boost his morale.

At the hospital we found that his progress along the queue had not been very encouraging, and we guessed he would have to wait many hours before seeing the doctor. When he saw us he had a ponderous look on his face; clearly he was not sure of the purpose of our visit. After having told him that we came to see how things were going, we gave him the food, attracting the attention of others in the queue; I also reassured him about his monthly salary, which would be paid even if he was absent from work. When we left, a tear was running from his face – my two acts had been motivated purely by personal reasons; they had nothing to do with any terms of employment. I had won the esteem of the rest of my workers too; they were not used to such acts, and they now started to call me *Baba yetu* (our father).

It was during that year that Patrick and I nearly lost our lives.

I had managed to obtain a small work contract with an Italian road contractor, and my job was to install the lights to four or five buildings that were to house the workers. The job was at Kitale, more than three hundred kilometres from Nairobi, towards the Sudan border. I calculated that it would be necessary to make three trips to complete the job.

It was about two weeks after we had started the job, and I was about to make a second trip to Kitale with Patrick to take some more materials. In the afternoon I told Patrick to take me home, keep the truck through the night and come to get me at two o'clock the next morning. Sure enough, Patrick knocked on my door the next morning, so I said goodbye to Sally, and told her to expect me back in the late evening.

I drove the first forty kilometres on an asphalt road, and was in a good mood: I was glad to have left early, and was enjoying the fresh early-morning air. We arrived at a crossroads, and I noticed that a stationary bus was blocking our path. High on each of its rear sides were two illuminated red lights; I asked Patrick if he knew what they meant, and he told me that he thought they were simply to indicate that the bus was stationary. I slowed when passing the bus, and then gathered speed again; but I had not looked properly down the road, as my attention had been on the bus. In the middle of the road was a strange crescent-shaped instrument, over four metres long. Along all its length protruded sharp nails, each over twenty centimetres long, and only a few centimetres apart. We were already gaining speed, and in spite of my prompt reaction we were not able to avoid the obstacle, which shredded all four tyres.

I lowered the window to take a better look at the damage; but a second later a soldier appeared at the window, pointed a revolver at my head, and asked why I had not stopped. I told him that I had seen no reason for doing so; as far as I knew, the red lights were only a signal to proceed with caution. While I was talking, a number of soldiers had appeared from both sides of the road, all pointing rifles towards Patrick and myself. However, the commanding officer soon realised that we had nothing to do with the bandits that they expected to ambush. He told us we had been very lucky that we had not been killed; if we had touched the white strip on the road (which I could see was barely ten centimetres from the front tyre) they would have opened fire: they had orders not to take prisoners. But the African officer had recognised that this order was perhaps slightly rash, and decided to investigate first. I realised how lucky we had been, and immediately thought of my wife's reaction to the news that I had been killed by a score of rifle shots, having left her smiling on the doorstep only half an hour before. What an ironic situation it would have been!

Obviously we had to replace the tyres and tubes: one hundred pounds. With the help of a passing vehicle, I was able to reach a nearby petrol station, which could repair the damage. One of the nails had also punctured the exhaust pipe, which as a consequence was now very noisy, and we ran the risk of a police fine. Sure enough, after about another hundred kilometres we were stopped by an officer, who asked to see my driving licence. He returned it without comment, but said that the car was too noisy. I showed him the papers explaining the morning's events; but he told us that unless we paid him ten pounds he would impound the car. I was furious. In a low voice, Patrick calmly advised me to pay; 'Otherwise,' he said, 'we may have to return to Nairobi in some makeshift vehicle, and will have to contest the fine from there. In the meantime the electrical equipment from the open truck may be stolen, and we may not get the truck itself back for several months.' His argument made sense, and although I was upset, I had to surrender, I was in no position to oppose the police officer's arrogance. However, I told him he was lucky we were not in Nairobi, where I could report him. Then paid him the ten pounds. He barely smiled.

The last piece of road was not asphalt, and the rocky terrain made us lose an extra few hours. After nineteen and a half hours of chaos we finally arrived at our destination. It was nine-thirty.

Discouraged, I had lost all interest in the job and wanted to do only one thing: to leave as soon as possible. I made a quick inspection of the repairs with the help of a paraffin pressure-lamp, and after a small meal, went to bed at eleven o'clock, glad to know that I could depart again in the morning without any other fuss.

However, I had another surprise in Nairobi two days later. I had picked the car up after having the exhaust repaired, and on driving it for about one hundred metres one of the tyres went flat. Luckily this happened in front of a petrol station, so I removed the wheel and took it in to have it repaired. However, the man who was repairing it called me over and said that the tube was beyond repair, it had a tear ten centimetres long, and more patches than the dress of a harlequin. I was flabbergasted – I had bought and fitted a complete new set of tyres and tubes only a few days before! I then had all of the other wheels checked, including the spare wheel, and I could not believe my eyes. I had been swindled – all five wheels had been fitted with worn-out material. Exasperated, I went back to the garage to speak with the manager, where I found a very depressed Englishman enclosed in a small room. He listened to my story carefully, and said that similar things were occurring every day in the workshop. He added that he was alone, and powerless to do anything about it; he himself was looking forward to the end of his contract in two months, when he could leave the country. As a friend, he advised me not to take the matter further: it would be impossible to prove that the tyres had come from this garage. To make me feel better, he pointed out that I was not alone, and many scams are to do with things far more expensive than tyres. I knew that he was telling the truth, and bought a brand-new set of tyres and tubes.

The year 1974 in Kenya saw the start of the elephant extermination. There were rumours that some eastern nations were prepared to buy any quantity of ivory the market could provide; this was probably because there was a predicted scarcity, and there was a rush to stock up on it. At the beginning of the year, one kilogram of ivory was five pounds; after a few months it was over eighteen pounds. In the circumstances, most hunters (amateur or professional) decided to cash in on this lucrative pastime, and Vittorio and I decided to try our luck. So that April I suspended my company's activities explaining the reason for my absence and assuring the workers that their salaries would be paid as usual. I instructed them to return to work on the fourteenth day of my absence – if I was not there then, they could go home and simply return the next day. Naturally, this put them in a good mood.

Sally listened to my plans and made no objection; she thought that two large elephant tusks would bring good money in hard times and added that it would be fine to leave her at home alone.

The vehicle we were to use was the old off-road Volkswagen, which was the same sort of vehicle as the military jeep I had owned since the Dar-es-Salaam days, and was ideal for our needs. At Tarasaa I found Vittorio waiting for my arrival, and he was very pleased to see me.

Following some heavy rains, the Tana River had overflowed its banks, and the area was flooded, the water lapping the house. In the evening we sat on the veranda, in the light of a kerosene lamp and the company of millions of mosquitoes, listening to the frogs croaking in the background. We tried to repel the attacks of the insects with an aerosol spray based on lemon juice, and with this infernal smell we ensured about two hours of immunity from the insects. When this time elapsed the dear little beasts would again be on our naked shoulders and legs, and it was necessary to repeat the operation. Of course, it would have been easier to go to bed under a mosquito net.

The Giriama provided excellent assistance to hunters. They were savannah-dwellers and expert poachers, the original suppliers of ivory to the Arab merchants. They are still a primitive tribe, and most are pagans. The only tribe in Kenya that will eat everything, they will devour hippopotamus, elephant and crocodile, and their method for hunting the latter was unknown to me, until Vittorio told me of it:

They would firstly bind their legs with any sort of material to protect them from the reptile's bites (they would only hunt in places where the water was shallower than forty centimetres so they could see the larger crocodiles, and avoid them). In a group, they would then advance, forcing the reptiles into a corner. The idea was to get the smaller crocodiles to bite them on the legs; their movement would attract them, and it is well known that a crocodile will attack anything that moves; when they do bite, they are very tenacious, and reluctant to release their hold. The tribesman would then signal for his companions to intervene, and the reptile was killed with slashes of the machete.

Anyway, we employed two of the Giriamas to help us, and we started along a savannah path around six in the morning. These paths normally do not go anywhere; they usually go across the savannah for maybe twenty or thirty kilometres, and then stop abruptly – maybe they were made by people looking for firewood, or by hunters like us. When we came across a reasonably sized elephant print, the car was stopped and left a few hundred metres from the path. To be considered interesting, the imprint must have a diameter of at least forty centimetres.

There was a lot to learn from the Giriama trackers. We often encountered stains of liquid excrement that were larger then a metre across: the pachyderm was obviously suffering from diarrhoea, and one of the trackers explained that it had been wounded with a poisoned arrow and was now running to escape from the hunters. However, it would probably die within twenty-four hours. I found myself doubting that the poison – which is not a laxative – could cause diarrhoea. I imagined that it was perhaps due to its terror, as with a human who is extremely scared.

The arrows were effective but the bows were not very powerful. You had to aim at the elephant's belly, where the skin is thin and soft. The arrow had also to be fired at very close range, perhaps no more than a couple of metres. It is hard to penetrate the rough hide, but it does not have to go very deep at all to be deadly effective.

As I was marching behind one of the Giriamas, I had the opportunity of observing his moves closely. He guided us with considerable expertise, and would stop every now and then to examine the tracks that we encountered. When we got about fifty metres away from where he suspected elephants to be, he became more cautious pulling up his *futa* in case we had to run. (A *futa* a sort of ankle-long straight skirt, furled up firmly around the waist. It is widely used by men and women in many parts of Africa and Asia.) He had no hesitation to display his bottom; from that moment on he was changing his approach to the quarry. He was bending double, staying low, out of sight; and with his elongated neck stretching out he looked like a goose. Shuffling sideways his approach was similar to a crab's. I realised I was in the company of a hunting specialist. He now had the advantage of not having to turn round in case we had to retreat; the legs always remained apart, ready for an instantaneous escape in case of a pachyderm attack.

Sometime later I was escaping behind him after a charge, and I noticed that he kept grabbing handfuls of earth and throwing them into the air. The finer powder would then be taken by the wind, and from this he was able to work out which way to run to avoid the elephant tracking us. He was clearly an expert poacher: the manoeuvres that he knew were essential if you wanted to hunt elephants and stay alive. I have often heard reports of the Giriama touching the rear of elephants without being noticed!

However, after fourteen days, our hunt had been unsuccessful. We found no trail worth following; but it was consolation to have just participated in this fascinating sport. It was very physically demanding, as everything must be done on foot; it would have been much easier in the car, but it is not the same thing. There is a saying that elephant hunters completely lose interest in all other animals and I can confirm that it is true. The routine was always the same: if we did not encounter anything of interest, we would spend all morning marching in the same direction, looking for trails. In the afternoon we would continue hunting until we got back to the start point; the whole process was about a ten- or twelve-hour walk. We were equipped with only the basics: a two-litre flask of water, a tin of meat, some biscuits and our weapons.

Anyway, because of our lack of success, I decided to delay my return to Nairobi for another two days. On the morning of the last day we decided to use the car, but with no success. At six o'clock in the evening we were tired and discouraged, and had nothing to do but to return home, which was forty kilometres away. The sun was going down; there was about twenty minutes of light left. We were a few kilometres into the journey when we spotted some dung on the track. The Giriamas asked for the car to be stopped, as they wanted to examine the faeces. They got down from the vehicles, prodded the dung with their foot, and said that it was warm: it was worth looking for the beasts on foot. I told Vittorio that I was willing to give it one more try, but on the condition that we went no further than five hundred metres. One of the Giriamas promptly found the tracks, and after about three hundred metres we saw a group of four elephants, about forty metres away.

Two of them had beautiful well-above-average tusks, and they were not aware of our presence. One of the Giriamas told me which one to aim at, and I brought him down with a frontal shot. However, it had become too dark to think about removing the tusks, which would have required several hours of work. On the other hand, I was very reluctant to leave them there unguarded, as there was a chance that other poachers in the zone would have heard the rifle shot. One of the Giriamas told me that he could place a spell on them, and assured me that this would protect them until we returned in the morning. In the absence of a better suggestion, I reluctantly accepted his promise, and we abandoned the carcass for the night.

At five o'clock we were already on our way, but I doubted that we would still find the tusks attached to the elephant's head the next day. Amazingly, all we found was lions' traces, which appeared to have tried to eat the elephant without success. Perhaps they had been disturbed by our approach, and fled. The removal of the tusks took three hours.

The same evening, under the light of a paraffin lamp, with the mosquitoes trying to land on our backs, Vittorio and I reminisced about the years we had had in Africa, and discussed our hopes for the future. Mine, like most people's, were simple and clear: try to earn as much money as possible, while there was still time. Then buy a house on the coast and pass my last years in comfort, hopefully with a reliable pension from a European company. I believed these objectives were realistic and obtainable.

Vittorio had behaved in a happy-go-lucky way, like the locust of the tale. He was five years older than me, and did not have many hopes. In his mind he played with two of them, as old age disgusted him. He firstly hoped to get killed in a fight with a lion or two, and end his days like an ascetic holy man. I told him that he was doing nothing new: the old noblemen of Babylon also wanted to die this way. I also told him he should avoid this fate, as he would not have a proper burial: lions dislike leaving traces of their kills, and the acids in their stomach are perfectly capable of dissolving bone. This untraceable end seems to reduce the shine of the martyr's halo, and all that will be left is pity for a person who met a grisly end.

His other strange idea was to go from one village to another, preaching goodwill, adopting the appearance of a sage with a long white beard. To this I reminded him that old age is unpleasant under every garb, and he would not have been able to travel very far. But what would have been worse was travelling at three metres above the ground between the two humps of a camel: his arrival at a village would have been a very amusing scene, and I would not have minded being present at this event, which I am sure would apply to all the members of the village as well.

Before the return journey I took care to fill one end of the tusks with grass, to avoid staining the car with blood. As I said goodbye to my brother, I promised to let him have my off-road Volkswagen as a present when he came to Nairobi, earning an affectionate hug.

I sold the elephant tusks, a total weight of sixty-five kilograms, to an Indian shop for the price of one thousand, two hundred pounds. The value of the sale was equivalent to one quarter of the value of my apartment.

During the journey my thoughts were constantly of Sally; I was vaguely worried about my long absence. Although she was a capable and resolute woman, her precaution of sleeping with a loaded pistol on the bedside table was not sufficient to put my mind at rest. In addition to the iron bars, we had taken other security arrangements, but there was still a weak point: the main door. I have never understood why the great majority of doors of English houses were made with light wood, especially in the colonies. Even worse, some were fitted with panes of tinted or glazed glass, like our Nairobi apartment. In most cases these doors could be opened with a hard shove from the shoulder.

Sally and I tried to devise some experiments to make things difficult and dangerous for a potential intruder. All the inside doors were left open at night (in Dar-es-Salaam we had air-conditioning, so we could keep them closed), which made it possible for us to hear even the slightest noise from the other rooms. There was a small window above the larger ones – too small for even a small child to squeeze through – and we could leave these open to allow some more air to get around the house.

All the windows on the ground floor were fitted with iron gratings and curtains made of strong material. After sundown we would close all these curtains. Thus precaution deprived would-be intruders of gaining intimate knowledge of the interior of our house, and our movements around it. In the event of an intruder gaining access to the house, he would face a very angry master inside. Little did I know that it was to be sooner rather than later.

I arrived home at around two-thirty in the morning, and Sally was surprised and glad to see me. After a refreshing bath, I went straight to bed.

It must have been about half an hour later that Sally woke me, hitting me several times in my ribs with her elbow. She then told me that she had heard some strange noises coming from the girls' bedroom. Without switching the light on, I got up and went barefooted to investigate the noise, which I could now also hear. Sally followed me. When I entered the girls' room I could see what looked very much like a black arm protruding from the small window; the owner of the arm was obviously attempting to reach the handle of the lower windows, and his armpit was resting on the iron framework. One of the (single) beds was against the wall by the window, so I reckoned that if I stood on this I would be able to grab the wrist of the intruder with both hands, and then call the police. I was just about to grab it, when he suddenly withdrew the arm; maybe he had heard a noise when I was climbing onto the bed. We both remained there in silence for a few seconds, motionless, each uncertain of the other's presence. Eventually I thought that he had gone away, so I climbed down from the bed quietly, and moved slowly over to where the two parts of the curtain met. Then, I carefully moved one of the curtains to see if he was still there; however, during this manoeuvre I touched a bronze vase, which fell to the ground. Now that I had alerted him of my presence, I brusquely opened the curtain and saw that he was still grasping the iron bars of the windows. Upon coming face-to-face with me, he quickly jumped onto the sloping ground and ran away. It was obvious that he did not realise that even if he did open the window, he would not have been able to complete the operation because of the bars!

If an intrusion by other means was successful, then it could be far worse than a normal burglary, especially if the girls were by themselves. There were two more attempts to break in: surely not a coincidence.

A few months later I was in Malindi dealing with a large contract on one of the numerous hotels that was under construction – Mr Marini's Palm Tree Club. It was not an easy job due to the distance from Nairobi, and I had to leave two Kikuyu workers on the site until the work was complete; it also called for me to be absent from home once every two weeks to monitor the progress and transport materials. On each of these occasions I had to stop in Malindi for at least four days, sometimes even longer. Someone must have noted my regular absence from home; it was not difficult to follow my movements – all you had to do was to see if my truck was parked under the porch roof. I was convinced that the second intrusion attempt had been carried out in the same way as the first, therefore I think that the same people were involved.

There was another night when I had got back from Malindi at one-thirty in the morning. As usual, I had a bath and went to bed. However, my sleep lasted less than an hour: Sally tried to wake me with the usual dig in my ribs; but this time I did not wake, so in a loud voice she told me to look at the window. High up, hanging from the bars like a sausage in the winter months, was the figure of a man trying to get in. He had moved the curtains aside, and was again trying to open the larger window through the smaller one. The windows on this side of the house were considerably higher from the ground, but the obviously expert thief had managed it. The knave was now alarmed by Sally's voice and the sight of me moving menacingly towards the window, so he jumped onto the ground and ran down the slope. I then let go a pistol shot into the air to scare him, and saw him roll onto the ground out of fear, then get up again and disappear into the dark of the night.

A final attempt was actually made by our night watchman, who was incidentally a member of a tribe related to the Masai. I had engaged him to guard the premises at night (however, when he was sure that nobody was watching him, in the early morning hours, he would hide and sleep. I had caught him on more than one occasion, but was reluctant to discharge him, as I guessed that a new guardian would have behaved in exactly the same way – or maybe worse). I was away, and he had knocked insistently on our door at around three-thirty in the morning. Sally took the pistol and switched on the corridor light; she could see his silhouette through the glass. She walked up to the door and placed her forearm and the pistol against the glass, showing that she was ready to shoot. She then asked what he wanted in a rough voice, and he just mumbled incoherently; to this she interrupted and told him firmly in Swahili to be on his way; as she did this she waved the pistol, and he obeyed! It was never clear why he knocked on the house in the early hours of the morning, knowing full well that my wife was alone in the house.

When I returned Sally told me what had happened. I was furious. I went straight to the man and rained blows on him that he would remember for many years to come, telling him that should there be a next time, I would discharge him on the spot. From that day on, I had no more trouble from him.

An Italian professional hunter named Lolli lived next door to us in Westlands. We had known him since we lived in Dar-es-Salaam, and we were delighted to resume our friendship.

Linda was then sixteen, and had come back from London on a school vacation. Lolli had offered to take all three of us to the famous Masai Mara area, inhabited by the Masai tribe (this was before it became a reserve). He did not give me many details about the trip; he just briefly told me that he and an Italian businessman were in the process of setting up a luxury holiday resort, with about thirty state-of-the-art tents supposed to offer all the comforts of a house. They included two bedrooms, a bathroom with bathtub and shower, and a spacious, fully furnished living room. All were provided with robust zips, which ensured that the tourists were protected from insect stings and reptile bites.

Anyway, on this occasion Lolli wished to hunt, and he took along his large double-barrelled gun (similar to Tasan's rifle). He also had invited me to take my carbine, and although I was not really interested in hunting, I obliged. I did not know it yet, but that safari was to be the last time I took an active part in a hunting party. After having practised it for years, I finally understood the uselessness of killing animals for sport.

Our party was composed of six people. There was Lolli, an English friend of Lolli, Mr Jenkins and his wife, Sally, Linda and I.

Before descending to the flatlands below the Kikuyu-land plateau, Linda could admire the immense spectacle of the Rift Valley, which goes as far as the eye can see. We had a good vantage point, and from this angle we could see the full extent of the valley's development. There has been widespread suggestion – albeit not scientifically confirmed – that some time in the future this zone may divide completely, and split the continent in two.

When we arrived at Masai Mara late in the afternoon, we found the tourist camp empty. Lolli explained that they had just finished setting up the camp, and had not yet been able to find any clients, which, of course, was to our satisfaction.

Here we could easily walk round aimlessly from morning to evening, without a specific purpose or destination, satisfied by watching the wild beasts in the park. Linda was in ecstasy, and showed all the signs of enjoying her vacation enormously.

One day we met a herd of some twenty buffalo, about one hundred metres away from us. Lolli suggested I kill one and take the head home as a trophy, to which I answered that it was the last thing that I wished to have; I considered it ugly and out of place in an apartment. Jenkins intervened and said that he wished to have the head as a trophy, and asked to borrow my Magnum .375. I did not have any objections and handed over my rifle, which was already loaded and had five cartridges in the magazine. I assumed that as he was a friend of Lolli, he must be responsible; however, I soon realised that I had made a mistake: Jenkins started firing into the herd at random, one shot after another, and scared them away. He had managed to wound one of them slightly, which separated itself from the herd and ran away on its own. As our guide and professional hunter, and the person responsible for the behaviour of our party, Lolli now had to follow the tracks of the wounded beast and bring it down. He thought it would please Jenkins if he invited him along; but Jenkins had no intention of coming: he was terrified, so Lolli and the Masai got out of the car and went after the buffalo. I remained in the car with my gun, which I had taken back off Jenkins. However, it did not cross my mind that there now was only one round in the chamber: Jenkins had shot the other four in a few seconds. I knew Lolli and the Masai were perfectly capable, they were now about two hundred metres away, and out of sight.

At that moment something extraordinary happened to me: a very strong impulse told me to hurry and join the other two. I hesitated for a few seconds, jumped down from the car, and caught them up. We had walked a little way, when the Masai pointed out two motionless buffalo standing about forty metres away. We were not sure which one was wounded, as Jenkins had noted that the one he had shot was missing a tail (probably lost during an encounter with a lion or a hyena), but they were both facing us, rendering it impossible to identify our target. Lolli fired at random – an easy shot – and a buffalo let out a loud bellow and fell to the ground.

The other buffalo then turned round and ran, displaying his posterior, which we could now see was without a tail. Lolli should have brought that one down. Therefore, the hunt started again.

After about one kilometre, the Masai pointed out another two buffalo that, once more, were not standing far away, and again looking at us. Lolli was once more confronted with the dilemma of choosing which one to shoot. He brought down another of the beasts, which again emitted the usual bellow (buffalo always do that before dying). The other buffalo turned around again to show us he was the wounded one, so we started the hunt for the third time. However, this time we got the buffalo by himself, standing about thirty metres away. Lolli let off a shot, completely missing, and the bull charged at us, starting with his head down. Lolli was roughly ten metres in front of me. The beast stopped, obviously undecided as to which one of the two fiends he should attack first; this gave Lolli another quick opportunity to let off another hurried shot; but he missed again. It was then that the buffalo decided to attack Lolli, who had attracted the buffalo's attention by moving. Lolli had exhausted all of his ammunition, and was now walking backwards, keeping his eye on the advancing buffalo and shouting loudly to me: 'Shoot, shoot!' I aimed and pulled the trigger, but as I was trying to hurry the shot, I had forgotten to take off the safety first, and wasted about three seconds removing it. In the meantime Lolli had stumbled on some dry shrubs whilst retreating, falling over backwards, and the horns of the buffalo were now on him. So far they had only grazed him, and he had a light blood-red streak from the lower part of his stomach to the upper part of his thorax.

As I mentioned earlier, buffalo, like all animals of that species, do not trample on their adversaries when they are floored. However, this infuriated bovine had spread itself on the ground by Lolli's side, trying to gore its enemy with its horns. I rushed over and knelt by the beast's back, pointed my rifle into his anus, and fired my last cartridge – I hoped that my shot would make its way through his back, heart and head. He died instantly. Lolli, his face pallid and twisted, got up from the ground, and even forgot to thank me. The Masai did not feel compelled to intervene with his spear, as he was engaged as a guide only. We returned to the car, to everybody's relief, and Sally said she had been worried by the abnormal sequence of the five shots. She had recognised the first four as coming from the large calibre of Lolli's rifle; but then she had heard the slightly quieter fifth, which came from my Magnum.

The return journey to Nairobi was particularly uneventful. We arrived in the late afternoon and said goodbye to our friends Lolli and Jenkins. We were all satisfied with the pleasant conclusion to the adventure.

A few days later, I read some bad news in a newspaper concerning Mr Momberg, a Danish family friend, the manager of a coffee plantation in Thika, near Nairobi. We had met him in Lushoto, Tanzania, whilst visiting our daughters, who were studying at the same school as his son and daughter.

Whilst the family were asleep, they had heard some noises coming from outside. Momberg immediately realised what was happening, and called his son into his own bedroom. He then shut his daughter (who was of Linda's age) in a wardrobe, together with his alsatian; he hoped that the dog could provide a last line of defence for his daughter if the rest of them were massacred. Then Momberg prepared to face the bandits with his wife and son. The wife was armed with a foam fire extinguisher which she knew had a strong jet, and she placed herself behind the men. The son, a boy of eighteen, was disarmed, and stood by the side of his father, who had a heavy pickaxe handle. Momberg had been forcibly enlisted into the German Army, and was trained in close combat.

In the meantime, the criminals had managed to break down the main door, and had thrown themselves at one of the bedroom doors, the one where the ambush awaited. Momberg had left it unlocked, as they would have just broken it down anyway; as a result, the first of the bandits catapulted himself at the door, expecting it to be locked, and ran straight into Momberg's pickaxe handle; Momberg, instead of using at as a truncheon, thrust it through his breastbone, and he fell onto the floor, vomiting blood. The son quickly picked up his knife. In the meantime, Momberg's wife had covered the gang with white foam. (I could not suppress a funny thought upon hearing this part, and imagined it happening in a theatre, which would have been a comical scene.) The gang did not expect such a reception, and now started to retreat, pulling the lifeless corpse of their companion out by his feet. The Mombergs decided not to follow them out of the house into the dark, and waited by the door, pleased that none of their family had suffered any harm. A few days afterwards, they began to receive phone calls in Kikuyu, and although they could not understand them, it was fairly obvious that they were hurling insults and threats at them.

The English owner of the plantation lived with his family a few hundred metres from Momberg's house. After this attack on his manager, he told Momberg if he were attacked, he would switch on his alarm. Momberg would then have to rush to his help with a Masai guard who was armed with a spear.

One night, less than a week later, the siren awoke the Mombergs. Momberg dressed quickly and rushed towards his boss's house in his car, with the Masai in the back seat. They were driving along the track through the coffee trees when he heard a noise. Stupidly he stopped and put his head out of the window to listen out for the noise. A figure appeared out of the dark, armed with a machete. Momberg did not have time to move, and the weapon opened a deep wound in his head, although he was still conscious. With blood gushing down his face, he engaged a high gear and released the clutch too quickly, and the engine stalled. The Masai saw the situation worsening and grasped the opportunity to jump out of the car, and disappeared down the track. Momberg also got out of the car; but his escape was impossible, and a bunch of Africans attacked him with machetes. He sensed that he was about to be killed, and thought that the best thing he could do was take refuge under a nearby coffee plant, hoping to save his head from more machete blows. These plants are very low, a little higher than a metre and a half, with very dense foliage, and it would have been very difficult for the bandits to deliver any blows to the upper body. They then changed their tactics and bent down, trying to hit Momberg on his legs. Momberg was in great pain, and tried to run; but the assailants did not intend to show him any mercy, and struck him with more blows to his body, until he lost consciousness. The brigands, looking at his many wounds and immobile body, believed they had killed him, and left him there. Momberg regained consciousness after two hours and managed to stagger back to his house. His wife, who had no idea what happened, was shocked to see him covered with blood. Maybe the most serious blow was the first one to the head; it had dislodged a large portion of skin, which was now hanging down, nearly covering his eyes. Luckily, the blow had left the bone practically unscathed; but he had serious wounds all over his body, especially on his legs. He was taken to the Nairobi hospital, and his wife told us that he had to have one hundred and seventy stitches.

After this attack, Momberg finally understood that it was better to be armed with a pistol. However, he had chosen a miserable .22 calibre, which was highly inadequate to deal with such emergencies.

Every time Sally and I went to visit them on the plantation, I always sat in the back seat with the carbine, ready to shoot. We had heard rumours of incidents where bandits had attacked after placing a tree-trunk across the road.

The Momberg family remained in Kenya for a few more years. Eventually, the plantation was sold to an African, and Momberg lost his job. Like the majority of the European residents in East Africa at that time, he was confronted with the common dilemma: either remain in Kenya and abide by the unpleasant changes, or leave the country. He chose to move the family to South Africa, and it was with great regret that we lost contact with them.

In 1977 the Kenya works department called me – this was unexpected, as it had never happened before. They asked me to estimate the cost of installing a lightning conductor to a powder magazine near the north Kenyan border with Ethiopia and Somalia. I was very surprised that the job had been offered to me without the customary competitive bidding.

Fighting between Ethiopia and Somalia had been going for some time. In order to try and control the situation, the Kenyans had started to construct a road for military use in the border area. This area was deserted; most of the terrain consisted of large rock formations, and it was necessary to break these up with dynamite. The powder magazine, the only construction in the desert, was situated in an isolated spot. As it was in the open, there was a chance that it might attract a thunderbolt during one of the rare storms, and consequently explode. My task was to build an efficacious lightning conductor. (This was the first of three jobs offered to me by the Kenyan Government.)

In order to do an initial inspection of the area, I was assigned a small aeroplane, complete with pilot. After flying for six hours,

I was flown to the powder magazine, near to a four-hut village by the name of El Wak.

Two weeks later I had bought all of the necessary materials, and I informed the Government that I was ready to start the job. In view of the unsettled situation the on the northern frontier, I asked Duggie if he could lend me a rifle for self-defence, to which he readily agreed. A new Land Rover with a driver was placed at my disposal. I decided to take Stephen along with me: the most experienced of all my workers. When I was loading the car, I also thought to take a twenty-litre jerry can of water; but Stephen said that it was not necessary, and insisted that I leave it behind. I was a little reluctant, but I trusted his experience and left the can there.

The trip lasted seventeen hours, and took us through desolate regions baked by the hot sun, regions where there was not a drop of water, let alone any houses. Every now and then we would see ostriches, followed by flocks of their offspring. I did-not know how they could live in such areas. At other times we saw some isolated gerenu gazelle, who managed to nibble at the lower foliage of some small trees by standing on their hind legs and stretching their necks.

We were a few hundred kilometres from our destination when a woman suddenly appeared from nowhere; from her characteristics I guessed she was a Somali. She knelt down, and with her arms stretched upwards in a desperate gesture, she begged us to stop. I told the driver to brake, and she indicated towards her parched mouth: she was dying of thirst. However, as I had left the jerry can behind, we had to continue without helping her. I could not help telling Stephen that he should mind his own business and not give incorrect advice to other people.

At nine in the evening we encountered a roadblock with a small military detachment, which consisted of a pole across the road with two armed sentinels guarding it. They recognised the Land Rover as a government vehicle, and informed us that it was forbidden to travel in that zone at night. I tried to explain to him that there only fifty kilometres left to El Wak (less than one hour's travel); but he was very stubborn, and said that I could sleep in his tent. I would have preferred to sleep in the car, but realised that I probably would have offended him if I had not accepted his offer, so he took me to his tent, which was about one hundred metres away.

The dim light of the paraffin lamp was just sufficient to see that the tent contained two camp beds, and there was a soldier asleep in one of them. The officer kicked him lightly in the ribs and told him to get up. When he had gone out, I lay down on the bed, but could not get to sleep. The officer came back at two in the morning, and when he was in bed, he started to tell me about the situation in the neighbourhood. He said that it was a dangerous zone, full of ferocious Somali bandits who preferred to kill people rather than take them prisoner – it was not a good idea to surrender to them. I had been stopped because he had been ordered to prevent all motor vehicles travelling after sundown; the Somali bandits in the bush were capable of reading the desert – that is, they could tell that a vehicle was on the road by seeing the reflection of its headlights in the starry sky from thirty kilometres away. They would then hurry to the road to intercept it. Once they had killed the occupants, they would then empty the water from the radiator to quench their thirst – this was the only reason for their assault. The Kenyan military controlled the only known well for five hundred kilometres, and how the bandits survived without water was a mystery.

The officer explained that his soldiers came from all over Kenya. Some were born near the Great Lakes and were used to drinking a lot of water, and when in the desert they had to quench their thirst continuously. The Somalis were born and lived in regions where water was scarce, and did not have the same needs. They could survive for more than a week or two without drinking (this sounded incredible to me, but that is what the officer claimed).

He also told me that they were very hard to catch. When they were being followed by helicopters, they would rush to embrace the trunk of the nearest tree, and most of the time they would avoid the gaze of the helicopter's crew.

By now it was three o'clock. Before we went to sleep he told me he was a Christian, and intended to leave the army and become a preacher. However, he needed a beautiful bible, and asked me if I could get him one; I told him I was not sure – I was not part of the ecclesiastical circle. After this he finally let me sleep.

The next morning, I thanked the officer for his hospitality, drove on, and after about an hour arrived at El Wak. There I contacted the engineer, the only European staying in that place, and he showed me where I would be living for the next few days.

Later we went together to visit the powder magazine. With relief,

I had confirmation of my quick appraisal made during the first visit: the job presented no difficulty at all – it was mainly a question of manual labour. I told Stephen what he had to do, and I was free to look around. With great surprise, I discovered that behind the four huts of El Wak was a small river. However, I did not pay much attention to it as I was busy with work, and did not know where it started or how long it was. I had been told that I should be very careful if I went to investigate; there were many crocodiles in the river.

Not far from the powder magazine were two old dilapidated casemates and I learnt that I was standing in the zone between old Italian Somaliland and Kenya. The bullet-holes of machine-gun fire were still visible on the decrepit cement walls, and I immediately thought of the soldiers' absurd task of guarding the river. The terrain did not offer any cover, it was flat as far as the eye could see – very unfavourable for a prolonged offensive and counterattack. Moreover, they could have been easily surrounded, and the British troops would have had all the time in the world to wait for their surrender, which would not have taken long when hunger and thirst set in.

The District Commissioner was glad to hold a conversation with a European, and invited me to go with him to see the surroundings. He told me that the only accidents that occurred in El Wak always involved camels. People would fall from their back, be bitten, or even squashed when loading the animal. Accidents in motorcars were unknown in those places.

He told me that a few months ago he had managed to avoid being captured by a group of bandits. He was driving along the road when a group of armed Somalis signalled for him to stop. He then slowed down, giving the impression that he was obeying them, and when he got near accelerated suddenly, forcing the group to rush out of the way to avoid being run over. One of them took a shot at him; but it went through a window and out of the windscreen. Luckily, there were no other consequences.

He also mentioned the ongoing struggle between Somali and Ethiopian guerrillas. In that area, a narrow strip of Kenyan territory partially divides Somalia and Ethiopia (this zone was the Ogaden, believed to be rich with oil, and now belongs to Ethiopia). For a few weeks, thousands of Somali guerrillas crossed that narrow strip of land at El Wak, travelling in the direction of Ethiopia. The

Kenyan Government had ordered its troops not to be involved in the dispute. Not long afterwards, battles could be heard in the direction of Ethiopia, and went on for a few weeks. The Somalis were massacred, and the survivors retreated back across the strip to avoid being caught; if they were captured then they would be subjected to the most horrid tortures, including being skinned alive. However, some of them were freed and released, so they could tell their compatriots what would happen to them if they entered Ethiopian territory.

After completing the easy job at El Wak, I said goodbye to the Commissioner, thanking him for the warm welcome he had bestowed on me. We departed early in the morning, and got back to Nairobi without any trouble.

On Sunday morning I got into the habit of getting up at six in the morning and going to the Embakasi house for a few hours' exercise. I preferred to cycle along the old Mombasa road for a few kilometres; but it was part of the National Park, and for this reason it could present some potential danger from felines.

Once, I was pedalling energetically along, when a lioness ran across the road in front of me. She had not seen me, so she was not yet after me, but I rapidly calculated that I would encounter her face to face in a few seconds I stopped immediately and turned the bicycle around, ready to escape. The lioness had now seen me and stopped by the roadside, observing me from about seventy metres away, with great interest. We stood staring at each other for a few minutes, neither of us moving; I thought she was undecided whether to continue on her way or attack me; maybe she had not found a kill last night, and was hungry. I had just finished considering these questions, without finding an answer, when she decided to go on her way. However, I doubted that she had completely disappeared, and I was reluctant to go forwards. A few moments later, an African who was going in the same direction as me overtook me; but he stopped as soon as I warned him of the danger of the lioness. We were then both undecided whether to proceed, until suddenly we heard the yelling of monkeys from the dense wood a short distance away. The African said that she was now far away, and continued. I also agreed with him, and started pedalling again.

After a little while, I came across two Africans, who stopped me and asked if I could give them something to eat; they had been walking through the savannah for the past few days without food or drink. They were now completely exhausted, and were not sure if they could make it to Nairobi, still ten kilometres away; they also added that if I helped them, they would pay me with some gems, and one of then took a small sachet out of his sock which was indeed full of stones. Although I told them I could not help them straight away, they offered to choose a few gems for me. It was a very touching offer, and I decided to help them, so I told them to cut across a little grass patch and join the road leading to Nairobi. In the meantime I would go home to fetch my car and join them on that stretch of road; from there I could take them anywhere they wanted to go, and of course pay for the gems (red garnets of small value). So I found them on the road, took them to an African refreshment place, and we parted as good friends.

Regrettably, this adventure nearly cost me my life.

Stupidly, I thought of using my spare time to search for precious stones. In the newspapers recently there had been articles about the discovery of substantial deposits of rubies, which incidentally were also my favourite stones. I had even bought a book that explained how to identify the various precious stones; it even told you how to make certain of their authenticity by testing their hardness.

I had some work in Malindi, and I took this opportunity to go and ask Vittorio if he was interested in joining my hunt. I also decided to take Stephen along with me. However, I was annoyed at not finding Vittorio when I reached Malindi: he had gone to Tarasaa. I decided to make do without him, so I took Stephen and the same Giriama guide that had helped us to hunt the elephant. The guide, bless his soul, did not have the foggiest idea what a precious stone was, but he certainly liked travelling in the car all day, and suggested that we go to a faraway place called Goddana a Bio.

For the first ten kilometres the road was the same; it was the one that went into Somalia, and as I explained earlier, it was not asphalt. However, when it reached the village of Garsen, it joined an asphalt road, which eventually could have led to Garissa; but I am not sure of that. After twenty kilometres our guide told us to turn to the left, and we drove onto a dirt track. The terrain was very dry; grass was scarce, and the trees were sparse and small.

We crossed several tracks, which the guide said had been made by the Shell Oil Company during their years of searching for oil deposits. The ground had been drilled with no success; occasionally we encountered short lengths of tubes sticking out from the ground with their end closed. No oil was ever found in this area.

After driving for several hours, we punctured a tyre. This seemed very odd to me, as the ground was very soft and clean, and should not have presented any sort of trouble.

When we got to Goddana a Bio I realised that my trip had been useless. It was clear that I would never have found even a common stone in that place – had I needed one. The only things that represented the name on the map were a water-well and a pair of shepherds' houses (the well was important enough to be mentioned). While we were eating before going back, I realized how naïve and stupid I had been in going to look for precious stones in that manner. However, I take this as a positive lesson, which I have never forgotten.

While I was making these reflections, I saw the only person in one hundred kilometres since we left the main road. He looked to me like an Arab from Somalia and asked for a lift up to Garsen, and I consented. On the way back, I had a puncture after a few kilometres. This incident was much more serious than the first one, because I no longer had a spare wheel. I did the only thing I could do: I told Stephen to cut some dry grass with the intention of substituting this with the tube, hoping that it would last for a while before collapsing. However, when it was full of grass, I found it impossible to fit the tyre back onto the wheel rim, no matter how hard I tried; so I had to continue the voyage without one tyre. I had many kilometres to cover, and I was not sure the rim would stand the strain, as it was permanently in direct contact with the road. Unbelievably, after about another five or six kilometres I had a puncture in another tyre. I now had two wheels without tyres, and I thought that it was time to lighten the car, so I told Stephen to get out and continue on foot. I knew that this could mean that Stephen might die; but the guide was essential for me to find the way back. I tried to reassure Stephen that I would soon come back for him after I had repaired the tubes at Garsen; but he rightly objected to being left alone and unarmed in foreign terrain. I asked if he could find the way back, and he lied, telling me that he could. I felt reassured by Stephen's claim, and I made a mistake:

I told the guide and the other man (who also knew the area) to get out from the car, telling them that I would soon come back to collect them. They had no water or other equipment, but they agreed. So I carried on, and we soon arrived at a crossroads. I asked Stephen which route would lead us to the asphalt road. He hesitated for a few moments, and indicated to the right, but I had a strong feeling that he did not know the way. Nevertheless, I turned right.

After two hours of driving, the track seemed interminable: there was no trace of human presence. I started to worry, so I stopped the car and told Stephen to climb down. I knew it would be almost impossible to get him to tell me the truth; but I was willing to accept his answer, as it was better than my guess. I told him that we had driven for two hours from the crossroads, and the tank was half-empty. If he had told us the wrong route, then the petrol would run out after one hundred kilometres. We would then both have to walk back without water. I made him understand that we would then both die on that road. I talked to him in Swahili, in a calm, low tone of voice, but with a serious expression. This achieved the effect I was aiming at, and he promised not to tell any more lies. He then confessed that he did not have the faintest idea where we were, and I was glad that he had admitted this. Without getting angry, I turned the car around, and began to drive back to the well of Goddana a Bio. It was probable that our guides would cut across the savannah, and I guessed that we would not meet them again on the road.

I knew it would be a long way back to the crossroads, and I was not sure that we would come out of it alive. I ordered Stephen to watch for our tracks, and tell me when we reached the crossroads where we had taken a wrong turn. With relief, we arrived at the crossroads, and I turned left to return to the well. You could not imagine my pleasure in meeting our guides, who had indeed decided to continue the journey on foot, following the tracks. I invited them to sit in the back, and asked Stephen to sit on the front wing; this was the side with the tyre, and would hopefully relieve the other side of some weight.

After a curve some thirty kilometres on, we encountered a pack of wild dogs in superb physical condition. They were right in the middle of the track, and Stephen showed signs of panicking and was about to get down. I told him stay put, and watched the beasts with my rifle ready in case they attacked. As I had expected, they did not consider Stephen edible, and although they stared at him, they did nothing.

I was worried about the state of the wheel rims and stopped to check them frequently. After a substantial distance I discovered that they were in a lot better condition than I expected, and I was convinced that the ground would not damage them too much. This allowed me to increase our speed a little.

At about nine o'clock we joined the asphalt road. The village of Garsen was now only twenty kilometres away; but this would be a difficult stretch, as the rims probably would not stand the hard road. As expected, they buckled down to the hardest part of the rim; but this resisted, keeping some sort of shape, and we managed to reach Garsen. Here I refuelled the car, but could not buy new wheels or tubes. So we revitalised ourselves with several bottles of orange juice, said goodbye and thank you to our guides, and set of for Tarasaa, ten kilometres away. Luckily this was another sandy track and did not worsen the state of the rims. When we reached the final crossroads, we were only two kilometres from Vittorio's house. This section of track had obviously never had any maintenance and was extremely dusty; the harder base was covered with more than thirty centimetres of fine dust. With only two tyres, the car was hardly able to move, and I had to force the engine forward. We had got about halfway when the car got stuck and refused to go any further. I did not want to end up with a pile of scrap under my feet, so we decided to carry on by foot. Stephen brought the toolbox in case some passing thief should pinch it, and I took the rifle. By now it was dark, and I considered this piece of road to be very dangerous because of the high number of lions in the area.

When I knocked on Vittorio's door it was one-thirty in the morning. Vittorio told me that at first light he was going to tell the police to start searching.

Later that morning the two wheel rims were repaired in Vittorio's workshop by electric welding. The Renault 5 and its small engine had been the true hero of this unfortunate adventure. Indomitable all along the rough course, the engine did not give the faintest sign of yielding. After the third puncture, and the almost fatal decision to leave the guides, I had realised that our lives were in danger. We were lost in the desert, and it would have been impossible to undertake the return journey on foot, especially without water. This made me think of another time, when Sally and I were very young. We had seriously considered using our six months' leave to cross the Sahara by car, via Uganda, Sudan, Algeria and then eventually through to Spain. Had we had attempted this, I am sure you can guess how it would have ended.

On Monday I was able to return to Nairobi, briefly stopping in Mombasa to replace the damaged wheel rims.

Chapter 8

The year 1978 was a decisive one in many respects. My company was doing well, so much so as to make us consider staying in Kenya permanently. At the beginning of that year I had managed to enter the circle repairing heavy machinery on coffee plantations, and I was regularly called for jobs – not very big ones, but nevertheless quite lucrative. Moreover, I had become the associate of a firm operating in the field of electric motor rewinding, which was perfect for my area of expertise. These last two activities were giving me good financial returns.

The Government had installed a policy that more or less ensured that coffee plantations were sold to African investors. The new owners had little experience, and as a result the machinery was seriously neglected; indeed, after the mass exodus of skilled Europeans following Independence, most machinery was now in need of a thorough overhaul, which, of course, was to my advantage.

However, there was also a disadvantage, and black clouds were on the horizon. My materials had been stolen on several jobs in Malindi, and my house had been burgled at Embakasi. When an attempt was made to steal one of my vans at Embakasi, it was only thwarted by the engine intelligently stalling: something that had never happened before, and never did again. The attitude of the indigenous population towards the Europeans was changing for the worse. It was easy to get involved in situations where a simple difference of opinion became a misunderstanding, and would come very close to a clamorous brawl.

It was quite usual for large British construction companies who had won substantial contracts to subcontract part of their work to a smaller firm, which would then share part of their contract with minor subcontractors. These minor subcontractors would then employ a third class of subcontractor, mostly electrical and hydraulic specialists.

The second class of subcontractor was composed almost entirely of Indians. They had the bad habit of keeping the payment for the third class of subcontractor, which included me. There is a saying in Italy for someone who pretends not to understand: 'He is playing the Indian.' This behaviour complicated and confused my already serious enough affairs, and I was getting fed up of living there.

I had just got back home one day at eight-thirty in the evening. It had been a particularly heavy day, and now somebody was knocking on the door. I opened it to find the notoriously arrogant African servant of an English neighbour who lived in our apartment block. She told me that our gardener – her next-door neighbour in the servants' quarters – had not answered her calls since nine o'clock in the morning, and suggested that I go and investigate. I found the gardener's room door partly open (indicating someone had been in and out), and went in without hesitation. He was lying dead on the floor near the bed, and I immediately realised that he died during sexual intercourse, almost surely in the arms of the girl. On the cement floor were the abundant traces of the last moments of his life. I then committed the mistake of phoning the police. The person who answered realised that I was a European, and said that I should stay at home – he would be arriving shortly. I explained that I was not the first person to discover the dead man; therefore it would be more beneficial to question the girl, and I gave him her name. It was clear that I had been tricked by the woman, who had shrewdly avoided reporting the matter that morning. She had waited for twelve hours until I got home, and then passed me the hot potato, leaving me to deal with the police. The only way for me to avoid thorny questioning was to disappear with Sally; if I did not, then I would questioned as if I was a suspect, and I did not like that idea at all. I told Sally to telephone our friends Aldo and Pina and tell them we would go to their house for dinner, and stay until midnight. The next day the body of the gardener was removed, and the police did not ask to see me.

In the meantime, criminal activity in Nairobi was increasing, particularly against tourists. President Moi gave orders to the police not to capture any more criminals in the town, but kill them on the spot. Sometimes these street executions could be witnessed by the passer-by. The criminal would desperately try to escape by running along the road, knowing that if he were caught he would be killed. However, escape was very difficult. It is a custom of the local Africans in Nairobi to indicate criminals by shouting: '*Huyu, huyu, kamata!*' (it's him, it's him, catch him!). Sometimes the scared bandit would then give up all hope of escape and appeal for the officer's mercy. However, the officer would then promptly refuse and a pistol shot would follow, usually to the front of the body.

Robbers usually became more active towards the end of the month, when they knew that people would have their pockets full of their monthly salary. If the victim had no money, he would get a good hiding anyway, and some friendly advice to have money in his pockets next time – if he wanted to avoid another thrashing. At times the level of crime became comical.

Patrick once told me the story of the owner of a small patch of land near to his. It was dark, and he was going to work along an old, small track. At the bottom of the valley he was forced to stop because a tree-trunk was blocking the road. A group of bandits then appeared, and asked him where he kept his money. When they were certain that he did not have a cent with him, they thrashed him to near unconsciousness and then let him go. There was a Christian mission up ahead, and he decided to go and find the doctor, as he did not think he could continue the trip.

A couple of hours later his wounds were stitched, so he decided to return home. When he reached the valley he found the same tree-trunk as before, and the same bandits. He found it impossible to convince them that he was the same person, so eventually they just asked him if he had gone to get the money anyway, and at his negative reply gave him another thrashing, and then let him go. When he told me this story, Patrick seemed very amused, as if it was the joke of the century; I have to admit I also saw the funny side of it all.

At the end of June, after the elephant slaughter, the Government announced a ban on the hunting of all animals. At the same time, all firearms had to be handed over to the police, except members of gun clubs (luckily this included Sally, who was able to keep her pistol). We believed we had the right to carry them for self-defence – we had discussed the matter before – and decided that if there were a total ban, we would leave the territory.

Shortly before renouncing my weapons, I was in Tarasaa with Vittorio, discussing the decree for the umpteenth time. Having nothing else to do, Vittorio decided that we should go hunting ducks.

It was in the late afternoon, about six o'clock, when the first evening shadows began to appear. We were a couple of kilometres from the house, with our legs immersed thirty centimetres deep in a marshy swamp. The lake had been formed by the recent rains and had a diameter of about five hundred metres. Hunting ducks was the last thing I wished to do that day. What was more, the ducks would have just flown from a lake in Siberia, and I knew from experience that the meat would be a tough as a vulture's. I certainly had no desire to test it with my teeth. Vittorio was attempting to get near them; but the shrewd ducks kept just out of range, always watching. It was clear that they knew about the shotguns of all continents. It was now too late to continue, and at that moment I was struck with a very strong premonition, like with the buffalo at Masai Mara and the hippo on the Kilombero River. I knew that from the way they hit me they were not to be taken lightly. In this case, it told me it was time to leave Africa, and in a flash exposed the negative and dangerous sides of my life in this continent, leaving me to work out the rest.

The premonition had taken advantage of the depressing moment when I was immersed in the marshy swamp. It suggested that if I stayed in Africa my life would come to an end, although it obviously did not specify exactly what would happen. When we arrived home, I abruptly announced to Vittorio that I would leave Kenya and return to Europe within two years.

In the meantime, Lucy had married Richard Varian and eventually had two beautiful girls, Emily and Jennifer, and Linda married Barry Unwin and had two lovely boys, Thomas and Kieren. So with them both settled, we could not want for more.

Those two years were fairly uneventful, and in the April of 1980, Sally was ready to return to Europe. We were separating for only the second time in over thirty years. Lucy and Linda met her at London Airport. They could hardly believe that we had made the decision to return permanently; now their mother could be with them at all times.

They would have to wait another four months for my return; I had to complete some work, and close a pending case against those who had failed to pay for my services. Moreover, in the last month I had dedicated myself to trying to find employment for my workers. All of them had expressed a desire to work for a European company, and four of them (including Patrick) did not have any trouble: I got an associate company to employ them. Stephen returned to Tanzania, whilst Mutua, the Mocamba, went to work for an Indian electrical contractor whom I knew from way back in Dar-es-Salaam.

In the last days before my departure, with all my ex-workers settled in new jobs, I donated my Datsun truck to Patrick (I had previously agreed this with Sally). When I told him, he could not believe his ears. I told him to take good care of it: it would be very useful for his farming job. Until I found the necessary documents to transfer the vehicle to his name, Patrick was terrified that I would change my mind: he knew that I could easily sell it for fifteen hundred pounds sterling, and that was in 1980.

Kenyan law decreed that at the end of their contract, workers should receive half a month's salary for every year of work completed with the firm. I added two hundred pounds sterling to this amount. Some of them had tears in their eyes when they were saying goodbye to me. The most moving goodbye was from my cook, an old man whose son was ill with tuberculosis He had a sad but good face, showing all of the hardness of life, and was too old to have any hope of finding another job. I gave him special treatment, allowing him to buy a small herd of cows: this had always been his greatest desire, and his last hope to end his life happily. He said goodbye to me with many tears in his eyes: I always thought that Africans did not know how to cry. As a sign of gratitude, he promised me that he would name the best cow of the herd Lamberto. Now I can sleep in peace, knowing that somewhere on the banks of Lake Victoria there is a cow that bears my name.

Vittorio was not present at my departure, so I sent him my goodbyes by post, wishing him the best for the rest of his stay. Patrick took me to Nairobi Airport, proudly driving his new Datsun truck. Patrick and my cook, Rafael, did everything they could to make my last few days in Kenya comfortable and happy for me.

It is impossible to imagine the feeling in my heart when I flew over my Africa for the presumed last time.

However, in June 1984, Vittorio died in an aircraft accident. The pilot was a young Indian with only one hundred hours of flying experience, and he had made the error of being trapped in a heavy thunderstorm. One of the wings of the small aircraft broke and his body, together with that of the German Consul, was thrown out. It appears that the pilot then directed the aircraft towards a small river in an attempt to land, but he was killed, together with the remaining five passengers. Vittorio's body was eventually found completely naked; he had been robbed of all of his clothing and money, the same fate that our father endured fifty-seven years before.

Due to difficult circumstances, I could not be present at his funeral. However, after his death I did go back to Kenya one more time. My former Kikuyu workers were waiting for me; they did not want to miss the opportunity to see me again, and had improvised a special feast in my honour. With pride, Patrick showed me his truck and, as he had promised, it was still in the same immaculate condition as I had left it.

At the airport – this time my final goodbye to Kenya – I had the pleasure of having all my ex-workers there. They had come to shake hands with me, and say for the last time: '*Kwenda salama sana baba yetu*' (Go on your way happy and safely, our father).

Goodbye Africa – I miss you, you are always in my heart.